The
Successful
Landlord

The
Successful
Landlord

How to Make Money Without
Making Yourself Nuts

Kenneth M. Roth

₳MACOM

American Management Association

New York • Atlanta • Brussels • Chicago • Mexico City • San Francisco
Shanghai • Tokyo • Toronto • Washington, D.C.

Special discounts on bulk quantities of AMACOM books are available to corporations, professional associations, and other organizations. For details, contact Special Sales Department, AMACOM, a division of American Management Association, 1601 Broadway, New York, NY 10019.
Tel.: 212-903-8316   Fax: 212-903-8083
Web site: www.amacombooks.org

This publication is designed to provide accurate and authoritative information in regard to the subject matter covered. It is sold with the understanding that the publisher is not engaged in rendering legal, accounting, or other professional service. If legal advice or other expert assistance is required, the services of a competent professional person should be sought.

Library of Congress Cataloging-in-Publication Data

Roth, Kenneth M.
    The successful landlord / Kenneth M. Roth.
        p.   cm.
    Includes index.
    ISBN 0-8144-7228-1
    1. Real estate management.   2. Real estate investment.   3. Rental housing—Management.   4. Landlord and tenant.   I. Title.

HD1394.R68   2004
333.5'068—dc22

                                            2003020909

Printing number
10   9   8   7   6   5   4   3   2   1

*To my wife, Nora, who gave me the confidence
(as well as the snacks) to finish this book.*

Contents

Preface. How to Use This Book and Other Required Business ix

PART ONE

Chapter 1. Attitude and Leadership 3

Chapter 2. Valuing Your Property: "You Want How Much a Month?" 11

Chapter 3. Terms and Conditions: "Why Can't I Keep an
Aardvark in the Apartment?" 27

Chapter 4. Prelude to the Lease: Checking the Prospective
Tenant (Legally) 57

PART TWO

Chapter 5. The Lease: "Oh, No, More Documents to Sign" 85

Chapter 6. The Lease Continues 113

Chapter 7. The Tenants Are Moving in Next Week:
What Have I Done (and What Do I Do Now)? 153

Chapter 8. "Honey, the Rent Check Didn't Arrive":
Problems with Tenants 165

Chapter 9. End of the Tenancy: "Do I Have to Return the Security?" 191

PART THREE

Chapter 10. "Honey, It's the Accountant":
Taxes and Other Legal Considerations 205

Chapter 11. The Importance of Insurance "My Neighbor's Daughter Tripped on My Carpet (and She's a Ballerina)" 219

Chapter 12. Some Final Observations 233

Appendix A. Test Your Skills 245

Appendix B. Residential Lease Agreement 255

Appendix C. Model Letters and Forms 267

  Action of Lease Application Based on Credit and Background Check 267

  Lease Cover Letter 268

  Authorization to Release Records 269

  Initial Notification Letter (Security Deposit) 269

  Late Notice 270

  Lease Application Form 271

  Notice of Inspection 274

  Notice of Previous Entry 274

  Returned Check 275

  Security Deposit Letter 275

  Sample Inventory 276

  Tenant Warning Notice 277

  Welcome Letter 278

Index 279

Preface
How to Use This Book and Other Required Business

Last year, my wife and I bought a property in Scotland. It is a wonderful condominium apartment in downtown Glasgow, with beautiful views and convenient to just about everything, including the rest of Europe. The problem is that we don't get to Scotland very often. We have no doubt that as an investment, the apartment will appreciate in value over the next few years, but keeping it empty while paying the mortgage and other maintenance fees in pounds sterling is not good business and was becoming quite expensive. To resolve the problem, we leased the apartment. The rental income pays the mortgage and associated fees and generates a tidy profit for us. In this book, I will show you how you too can become a successful landlord while investing for the future.

If you've purchased this book, perhaps you have an empty apartment that you wish to rent, a guesthouse, or even a spare bedroom. Maybe you purchased a condominium in Miami or Colorado as an investment, and while you await its appreciation in value, you want to rent it to offset the taxes and other maintenance payments. Maybe you invested in a "fixer-upper" that you intend to repair and rent for added income. Possibly, you are in the military or work for a large corporation and you need to rent your house while you are away on active duty or at your corporate headquarters in another state.

You don't have to be a real estate magnate to lease property. Everyone who owns property may potentially lease it. In fact, when you lease your property, you are engaging in one of the world's oldest professions. No, not that profession, but the profession of being a landlord. Let's explore a bit of history to illustrate the point.

History of Landlording

Before the Industrial Revolution created wealth based on factories making products for mass consumption, wealth was measured in terms of land. Even today, according to *Business Life* magazine, the wealthiest man in Great Britain is Gerald Grosvenor, the Duke of Westminster (*Business Life* magazine, April 2003). According to *Business Life,* the Duke owns 129,300 prime acres of British soil, including a sizable chunk of what is today central London. The Duke's ancestors came into this rather tidy package in 1677 through marriage. *Business Life* estimates the Duke's land to be worth around 11.5 billion pounds sterling, which is approximately 19 billion U.S. dollars. What does the Duke do with his land? Well, in part, he develops it and then leases it.

The history of *landlording,* as it is sometimes referred to, is quite colorful. It is a tale of kings and queens, knights in armor, and lords and ladies—the stuff of old movies, actually. The king was technically the owner of all the land in the kingdom. In this capacity, he would issue grants to those who supported him (in those days, usually members of his family), much the same as the U.S. President today gives Cabinet positions or ambassadorships to those who supported his election. But back in the old days, these grants of land came with titles that were and still are passed down from generation to generation. Along with the Duke of Westminster, the Dukes of York (a name that made it to the United States) and Nottingham are familiar examples. The Sheriff of Nottingham, the mythical Robin Hood's archenemy, worked for the Duke of Nottingham, whose ancestor, the first Nottingham, had originally received the land grant for that area.

The owner of a grant allowed the local denizens to live on the land and protected them in return for their farming the land. Later on, these "lords of the manor," as they were referred to, began to demand taxes from the residents, who were known as the *tenants.*

These "land lords" also required the younger male family members to serve in their armies as consideration for allowing their families to remain on the land. Sometimes, these lords became so powerful that they challenged the authority of the king. Other times, the landlords were so cruel and oppressive that the tenants revolted. William Tell (who, according to legend, shot an apple off his son's head) is an example of such a hero.

Today, similarly, when you lease your property, you are not merely lending your spare bedroom to a boarder for a fee, but you are carrying on a profession that is rooted in history. Over the centuries the art of being a landlord has continued to develop, not only in terms of the law, but also as the business of leasing property. As the title of this book indicates, this is about being a successful landlord.

In the ensuing chapters, we discuss such specific items as the law, taxes, and insurance, as well as some more ephemeral or intangible topics such as the psychology or attitude the successful landlord should maintain. Indeed, it is often those intangibles that separate the successful landlord from one who is constantly frustrated with "bad tenants." Of course, there will always be a bad tenant at some point in your landlording career, and we explore various strategies to recognize and avoid them (although this is not always possible) and how to deal with the situation, should it arise. But one of the main themes I treat in this book is that being a successful landlord is as much an art as it is governed by statutes and regulations. For example, it requires of the landlord certain leadership qualities. We shall see that if, as the landlord, you do not exhibit leadership qualities, you will be subservient to your tenants, and that is not a healthy and ultimately successful situation for either the landlord or the tenant.

"But Ken," you say, "all I want to do is rent my upstairs bedroom. This sounds like the *Art of War for Landlords,* and I have to become a cross between General Patton and Sun Tzu." Fair enough; you don't have to be General Patton, but being a successful landlord is more than putting an ad in the local newspaper and collecting the rent each month. There are certain guidelines and considerations that every landlord should follow in renting his or her property, up to and including large rental complexes. This book concentrates on the landlord who is renting on a smaller scale, such as a second home or condominium, an investment property, and, yes, the upstairs bedroom as well.

Part One

In considering how to approach the subject, I decided to divide the book into the following areas. First, we consider the actual decision to rent. Why should you rent your property, and what should be your rental price? How long should the term of the lease be? Should it be one year or perhaps several? Will you allow pets? Will you rent to families with children? How many people will you allow to occupy your property? How many guests will you allow the tenants to have at a given time? Further, will you lease your property furnished or unfurnished, and how much of a security deposit will you require?

You, the landlord, must consider all of these issues before you begin your search for a tenant, and we discuss the ramifications of these decisions in this book. Once you have made these decisions, the next area of exploration is the search for the tenant and what to do when someone expresses interest in leasing your property. Should you take the first prospect? How do you conduct an interview, and what about a credit check? Don't worry—it is not that complicated if you know what to do.

Part Two

Okay—you found a good prospect to rent your property, but what sort of agreement do you use? How do you obtain a lease agreement, and what should it contain? Do you need an attorney? You may find the answers to these questions a bit surprising, but please don't skip to the section on leases right away. Take it in stages. Let us assume you do have a signed lease. What should you do before the tenant moves in?

The great day has come. The tenant has arrived and has successfully moved in. Better still, the rent is being paid on time each month. The world is a wonderful place, and there is joy throughout your realm. But then, tranquility ends, the universal equilibrium is disrupted, the rent is late. What do you do now? The fact is that landlord-tenant disputes are common, so common that in many judicial districts there are landlord-tenant courts to address them. However, not every dispute requires a Perry Mason. Sometimes a little common sense (the proper attitude and leadership qualities) goes a long way in resolving a dispute, while other times you should be prepared for the worst, even if you follow every guideline in this or any other book on the market. But if you do follow the precepts set forth in this book, the odds that you will have to go to court should be greatly reduced.

On occasion, nothing goes wrong during the tenancy, but problems arise after the tenant moves out. Very often, the tenant is wonderful and pays on time for two years, but when he or she moves out, your property is left in terrible condition. "Ah," you say, "not to worry; I have the security deposit." But what does the law really have to say about security deposits? When can you withhold this money and when must you give it back, regardless of whether or not you personally think the tenant deserves to have it returned? Once again, how this phase of the relationship between you as the landlord and your tenant gets resolved often depends on the attitude of the landlord, and we explore this topic in some detail. Withholding security is an extremely misunderstood area of the law and is often the needless cause of disputes in what should have otherwise been a problem-free relationship.

Part Three

There are other matters that we need to be concerned with, and those are considered in the final portion of the book. Taxes are an important issue. There are various tax consequences of the rental transaction, depending on your individual economic situation. There are also certain legal ramifications. For example, should you incorporate before you become a landlord? What are the benefits of incorporation? Are there any detriments, and what about the tax consequences of incorporation? Insurance is another area that requires discussion and is often overlooked by the novice landlord. There are various types of insurance that should be required by both the landlord and the tenant. We will look very carefully at this important part of the landlord-tenant transaction.

"Wow, and all I wanted to do was rent my upstairs bedroom." Unfortunately, we live in a complicated world. As we have already seen, the landlord-tenant laws have taken centuries to develop and encompass every stage of the transaction. However, once the various components are broken down and individually analyzed, you should have a profitable and enjoyable career as a landlord.

In our brief historical synopsis, we have seen that the acquisition of real estate has been the symbol of wealth, power, and success since time immemorial. Even animals are territorial. They instinctively value and protect their portion of the land. In the modern world, the leasing of real estate for income purposes is one of the highest and best uses of real property, and so leasing your property is something you should always be prepared to do.

One final note before we get started. The principles and ideas expressed in this book are meant to be general in nature, so that they should apply anywhere property may be lawfully leased, at least in areas that are historically referred to as "Western civilization." It is my observation and opinion, based on my travels and research in the United States, South America, and Europe, that the essential elements of the real estate transaction are very similar. This should not be surprising, as many legal systems have a common derivation, from either British common law or the Code Napoleon (the French legal system), as we shall discuss shortly. There are going to be some technical legal differences in the way the various legal systems operate, both within the fifty United States as well as other nations around the world.

There are also going to be differences in the customs of the many nationalities who interact in the global economy, which one has to be sensitive to as well. For example, the laws of Louisiana are different from the laws of New York, since Louisiana law is based on the Code Napoleon, whereas the rest of the United States is based on British common law. Does that mean that if you live in New York, you can't own property and lease it in Louisiana? Of course it doesn't. Does it mean you may have to do some research into Louisiana landlord-tenant law? Sure it does, but once you read this book, you should know how to conduct that research without too much effort.

You should be able to appreciate the differences in the various laws as they apply to leasing property. What happens if you own property overseas? The landlord-tenant laws are somewhat different in England from those in Scotland, although both belong to the United Kingdom, and both are different from the laws of France.

But whether you own a flat in London or a guesthouse in back of your home in Lubbock, Texas, the basic concepts of being a landlord are arguably universal. This is understandable because many of the world's legal systems date back to the Babylonian king Hammurabi, who drafted what is commonly recognized as the first written statutory civil law code for everyday governing use. Also, different cultures have different customs and understandings. Numerous books have been written on the differences in conducting business with the Japanese because their culture and history are so different from ours. But that is form over substance. In dealing with different nationalities, you may need to alter your approach somewhat to accommodate the cultural sensitivities of those other nationalities, but the basic goals of your transaction are still the same. As a landlord, your goal is to obtain a tenant who pays his or her rent on time and, frankly, gives you a minimum of aggravation. That objective doesn't change, and the basic methodology of achieving it doesn't change, either.

I'm including this information because I want you to appreciate and have an understanding of the historical significance of what you are going to undertake. I also want you to understand that this is a serious business that requires your patience and dedication if you want to be successful. Many landlords who own one or two properties, as opposed to a rental complex, feel that they can take shortcuts. "Give me a quick lease agreement and get on with it; I can't be annoyed with all that legal nonsense," they say. I don't subscribe to that, and neither should you. It took centuries to get to where we are today in landlord-tenant law. There are no shortcuts. However, if you do it right, it is exciting, fun, and profitable. Increased income is a good thing, and being a successful landlord will increase your income.

To help you understand the ideas I am putting forth, I have drawn examples from my more than twenty years in the real estate and legal business, as well as being a landlord myself. These examples are a compilation of our experiences, and if you think you recognize yourself in an example, or, to paraphrase a popular song, "you're so vain, I bet you think this example is about you," it's not so. While many of the book's examples are based on true episodes, they have been altered or modified to meet the specific teaching points illustrated, and most brokers and attorneys have had similar experiences in their own careers. Any actual similarity or resemblance to persons living or dead is purely coincidental, and the names used are all fictitious.

So how do you use this book? I suggest you read it once in its entirety and then return and read it again, chapter by chapter, as necessary until each concept is understood. Refer to the lease or the forms as required to help in understanding the points. In addition, there are many references to state law. Although I am admitted to the practice of law in several states, including Florida and New York, and the District of Columbia, there are fifty states, the District of Columbia, and Puerto Rico to deal with, and each has its own variations of the law. Therefore, it is going to be necessary for you to supplement your education with private research. However, with the Internet, it is not too hard. If you can't do it, ask any ten-year-old, who probably knows more about computers and the Internet than most so-called experts. You can also research the old-fashioned way, at the library or courthouse.

Now, let's discuss forms. Don't rely on forms. Rely on your knowledge of what it takes to be a successful landlord. Rely on your conceptual knowledge and application of common sense and, at least, a working understanding of the landlord-tenant laws. This does not mean that you must go to law school. To be sure, there may come a time when you are forced to consult an attorney. If that unfortunate situation should arise, I want you to be able to have an intelligent conversation about whatever your landlord-tenant situation is. I hope that, after reading this book, the necessity of consulting with an attorney will be minimal, if at all.

There is an old attorney joke that goes something like this. A client walks into a lawyer's office and says, "I'm looking for an attorney who's had both arms amputated." Somewhat astonished, the lawyer replies, "Why would you want an attorney with no arms?" The client replies, "Because I'm sick and tired of hearing you guys answer questions with 'on the one hand it's this way and on the other hand it's that way.'" Unfortunately, that is how the law is. There are very few clear-cut answers. Each case is fact sensitive and specific. Therefore, the information and forms provided in this book are of a general nature, and each case must be looked at based on its individual facts. However, this book provides you with sufficient information and examples to help you solve your landlord-tenant problems or gives you sufficient guidance to look for the answers on your own. When you can accomplish this, you are a true professional landlord.

To help you reason out the legal as well as the practical aspects of becoming a successful landlord, I have interspersed various multiple-choice questions based on some common scenarios that you may encounter in your career. Take the tests and don't cheat. The answers are found immediately after the questions and are analyzed. Don't take them too seriously. They are there to help. So have fun, and best of luck.

Acknowledgments

Before getting started, I would like to express my thanks to my wife, Nora, who has been with me for twenty-three years. We have played, fought, and worked together in real estate, and she encouraged and helped me to write this book. She is the heart, soul, and salesperson of our company and has made working in real estate fun as well as profitable. She is also a first-rate landlord.

Ken Roth

PART ONE

CHAPTER 1

Attitude and Leadership

Before we enter into the fine points of leasing property, I want to discuss two crucial concepts that you need to master to become a successful landlord. These are *attitude* and *leadership*.

There are just so many ways to write a lease, or maintain a security deposit, or evict a tenant. Forms, procedures, and law govern the various technical stages of the leasing process, and once you understand what to do and how to do it, that's pretty much it. But how you conduct yourself in the landlord-tenant transaction is entirely up to you.

Attitude

Your attitude, your behavior, your personality, and your reactions are all yours to control. There is no statute or form that tells you how to act with regard to your tenant. But how you conduct yourself in dealing with your tenant often determines whether or not you have a successful business relationship, and ultimately, that is what we are concerned with here. That is the "art" of being a successful landlord and the whole point of leasing a property. Nobody legitimately transacts business with the intent to fail.

Leadership

When you enter into a landlord-tenant relationship through a lease agreement, you become a party to what is known as a *bilateral* or two-party agreement. However, unlike in other two-party contracts, in the landlord-tenant situation, the parties are not really equal as a matter of law. When the tenant signs the lease, he or she acquires what is known as a *leasehold interest* in the leased property, *your* property.

What Is Leasehold Interest?

You as the landlord still retain ownership rights, which is the superior legal interest. More simply stated, from a legal standpoint, the tenant may have the temporary right to occupy the property, but you still own it, and that's more important. That being the case, you had better be the dominant party, and you need to make that clear to your tenant. "Yes, tenant, you are going to live in my house (or condominium, or igloo, for that matter), but it is still mine, and you will respect me, my property, and the terms of our agreement while you are there." If you exhibit this attitude up front, you will save yourself a lot of aggravation down the road.

The Adversarial Nature of the Agreement

The other point to remember is that the formation of a bilateral agreement is inherently adversarial in nature. Having said this, it does not imply that every tenant should be treated as a treacherous opponent who is out to get you. Tennis, poker, and even golf are inherently adversarial. That is the nature of competitive sports and games. Although you try to best your opponent, it does not mean he or she is a bad person.

Similarly, in business, it is perfectly normal for the parties to a potential agreement to try to negotiate to their best advantage and incorporate those advantages into the contract, in this case the lease agreement. But contracts are written by humans, and since humans, lawyers included, are fallible, the words they craft into a contract can never be perfect. As a consequence, any contract can be subject to interpretation, even if the interpretation is inane. Tenants are no different. If there is an opportunity to gain an advantage, they generally will make the attempt unless you establish early on that you as a landlord will not be trifled with. The weakest argument can win a dispute if you can convince someone of its viability.

The trick in negotiating with a potential tenant is to establish by force of personality a no-nonsense parameter with regard to your lease agreement. If you do this, your attitude is that of a leader and you are exhibiting the quality of leadership. Your tenant will be happy because he or she will know the boundaries, and a contented tenant makes for a happy landlord.

Killing Them—or Yourself—with Kindness

Several years ago, Nora, my wife and partner in our real estate business, leased a house on behalf of a landlord. The landlord, a nice, even-tempered, somewhat shy fellow, was determined to bend over backward to please his tenant. "I'll kill him with kindness" was his favorite expression. In the months that followed, the tenant literally tortured the poor landlord with endless demands. Nothing was good enough, and a statement that the landlord was in breach of the lease followed every demand. A call from the tenant's attorney was also threatened if the landlord did not meet the demands. Finally, in desperation, the landlord contacted us and advised us of the situation. "I tried to please him, but nothing is good enough," he pleaded.

So much for the theory of killing the tenant with kindness. We wrote a letter to the tenant advising him that we would now be acting on behalf of the landlord and that all requests were to come through our office. The landlord was instructed not to communicate with the tenant under any circumstances. Shortly thereafter, the call came. It was the tenant demanding that the inside of the house be painted.

We pointed out that the lease specifically called for the house to be painted at the onset of the lease in a color chosen by the tenant, and this had been done. There was no further obligation to repaint during the period of the lease. "But I don't like the color, and the lease says the house was to be painted in the color of my choice; you're breaching the lease; you'll hear from my lawyer." We pointed out that the lease clearly stated that the tenant got his paint job prior to moving in, and in the color of his choice. There was no reasonable interpretation of the clause of the lease that could be construed to allow the tenant to change his mind each time he wanted the interior painted a new color. We stated that under no circumstances would the landlord repaint, and if the tenant wished to challenge us on this point, we could recommend several good real estate attorneys for him to consult if his own lawyer was busy. We also asked for the name and phone number of the tenant's attorney (which, not surprisingly, was never provided to us). That ended the conversation.

The tenant made several more attempts to contact the landlord, but each time he was summarily referred back to us. We never spoke to the tenant again until the end of the lease, which was renewed (without a new paint job) for another two years and without further incident.

The point of the story is that without any harsh words, we quickly established that we were going to be the dominant party in this transaction—no yelling, no debating, but a firm, professional attitude that said, "We are in control, there is a lease, you will follow it, and no amount of threats or ranting about alleged breaches and contacting attorneys is going to lend credence to an obviously spurious interpretation." Being a leader doesn't mean you have to yell and bully, but it does mean you have to be firm and let those whom you want as followers know where you stand and what they can expect from you. Those are also qualities of leadership.

I once served under a Marine colonel who had tried to trade in his tough guy persona for a "kinder, gentler" one. It didn't last long. I met him for lunch one afternoon after he had punished a young officer for preparing some obviously sloppy work. "What happened to the new nicer version, Colonel?" I asked. He replied, somewhat sadly, "Ken, people tend to mistake kindness for weakness, and I won't make that mistake again."

It may be a sad commentary on human nature, and you may not agree with it, but let me suggest that the time to challenge this theory is distinctly not when you are about to lease your property to a total stranger—actually, not even if you are renting it to your sister-in-law. It doesn't matter; business is business. In most cases, your tenant will follow your example. If you are professional and you conduct your affairs by the book, or lease, as the case may be, the odds that your tenants will respect both you and your property are greatly enhanced.

Remember, if you try to be a "buddy" to your tenant rather than a landlord, you may find yourself in a position where you have to tell your buddy "no" to some request. Perhaps he or she wants a renovation (not required in the lease) that you are not willing to perform, or, worse, your "buddy" wants to pay the rent "a bit late" this month. By establishing your professional parameters up front, you ensure that the tenant understands that complying with the lease must be paramount on his or her list of priorities and that he or she cannot count on your "friendship" to extract favors. In turn, you, the landlord, are not put in any uncomfortable position if you have to make a business decision denying your tenant's request.

Professional, Not Tyrannical

Having said this, however, let me quickly caution that being firm and professional and establishing the upper hand is not an excuse for you, as landlord, to become a totalitarian dictator. There will be legitimate requests from the tenant for repairs or other problems that may arise during the tenancy, and you should be prepared to deal with them promptly and efficiently in accordance with the lease agreement. For example, if you are required to make a repair, make sure the repair gets done quickly. We have a detailed discussion on the respective responsibilities of the landlord and the tenant in Chapter 5, on leases.

For now, the point is that while it's important to be the leader, once this is achieved, you should not abuse that position or you will lose your advantage. The key is to be firm but fair. That's the lesson on leadership. You don't have to be Captain Kirk to be a successful landlord, but you do need to be aware of your position in the transaction, that of a landlord and property owner.

Now it's time to get down to specifics. The first thing we need to discuss before you go out and find a tenant is how much you are going to charge for rent. What is the rental value of your property? Chapter 2 treats this subject.

Valuing Your Property

"You Want How Much a Month?"

Armed with your new leadership skills, you now go in search of a tenant. But wait, not so fast! We need to discuss a few things, like how much money you are going to ask for rent. What is your property worth on the rental market? Making this determination is going to require research and objectivity on your part. The first thing you need to do is take a few moments to evaluate your property. We'll use a condominium apartment as an example, although the methodology works for any type of property anywhere in the world.

Deciding on the Rent

Let us suppose that you (and your significant other, as applicable) purchased a condominium in Miami, but your primary residence is a house in New York City, where your business is located. Your plan was to spend a few months of the year in Miami (preferably during the winter), but your business would not allow it, and now you have to decide what to do with the property. The condo has a mortgage as well as monthly assessments, known as *maintenance.* For our purposes, suppose the mortgage is $1,000 per month. In addition, the maintenance is $450 per month, and the property tax is $4,080 per year. The board of directors has announced a $4,800 per year special assessment for the next three years, to be paid monthly in equal installments of $400. (Don't panic if you are mathematically challenged. The math doesn't get more complicated than this.) The building is two blocks from the beach. The apartment (or "unit," as it is referred to in the real estate trade) has carpeting in the bedrooms, marble in the bathrooms, and tile floors everywhere else. The unit is approximately 1,200 square feet, has a view of the ocean—but is not "direct ocean front"—and is on the eighth floor. There are two bedrooms and two baths. The master bedroom is painted light blue. The second bedroom, which was going to be for "little Joanie," is pink with a border of angels handpainted by your brother-in-law, the artist, who came all the way from California (and spent more time in the unit than you did) to help with the decorating. The rest of the unit is a light green. The bathrooms are magenta. The furniture is a combination of purchases that you made on your initial trip to Miami and gifts from family members, as well as extra "stuff" you shipped from New York. Okay, how much should you rent it for?

You might start by figuring out that you need at least $1,000 per month to cover the mortgage and $450 per month to pay the maintenance fee. The taxes are $4,080 per year, which is $340 per month, and the special assessment is an additional $400 per month. This is a total of $2,190 per month that you need to cover expenses. But suppose you also want a profit of, say, $1,000 per month. Rounded off, you should rent it for $3,200 per month. Besides, your Uncle Ralph owns a condominium, and he rents his for $3,500 per month, so you are coming in below market. That doesn't figure in the added cost of a vacation, now that you can't use the condo. You could be right by using this method, but it would be pure luck. I imagine that if you were to close this book now and proceed with the rental based on your analysis, you would be doomed to failure.

I have stated that there is a universal methodology for the valuation of a rental property, and following this methodology should give you the true market value of your property such that if you advertise it at that price, it will rent. Based on the scenario presented above, you don't have enough information to make any kind of realistic determination. I also stated at the onset that you would have to be objective and do some research. But before we talk about objectivity, let's discuss commitment.

Commitment

Commitment is important in any endeavor. If you are not committed to the task, in all likelihood, you will fail. So the first question is, how committed are you to renting this property? If your attitude is one of "I don't really care if it rents or not," you don't need a book about being a landlord. Call a local real estate agent, tell him or her what rental income you want for the property, and let the agent handle it. In all probability, it won't rent, but that doesn't matter, as you don't care. However, if you are truly serious about leasing your property and becoming a landlord, which should be the assumption if you purchased this book, it is going to take commitment and some hard objective choices. With that preface in mind, let's proceed with our discussion on objectivity, and then we shall see how commitment and objectivity come together.

Objectivity

When I say that you must be objective, I mean that you have to remove all sentimentality from the equation. The first thing you need to do is physically evaluate the property. If you have to travel to Miami or wherever to do it, make the trip. After all, you traveled to that location at least once to make the purchase. That's commitment. Then walk through the property and be mercilessly objective.

Decoration

Let's start with the decoration. Decoration involves taste, and taste is subjective. Pink walls with little angels may be just darling for some, but not if your tenant is a professional football player. What you want is the broadest pool of prospective applicants, or "prospects," so you aim for neutral colors. Nobody objects to white walls. Your brother-in-law will scream, but he isn't renting the unit. Soothe his feelings as best you can, but unless he is going to rent the place, paint it white.

When any of our clients are resistant to the concept of redecorating, they usually say something like, "We'll just leave it the way it is, and if the tenant wants, he can change it." This never works! A prospect comes to see a unit and envisions himself or herself living in the property according to his or her individual taste, not seeing beyond the current decoration. It is a fallacy to believe those who say they don't care about decoration; they just want to see if the property is suitable. They are kidding themselves and wasting your time. People, including professionals, are affected by decoration. That's why "model apartments" in large rental complexes are decorated in the style the developer or leasing agency thinks will appeal to the majority of prospects visiting the property.

A unit in South Beach, Florida, or the SoHo district of New York will be decorated differently from a cabin in the Colorado Rockies, a town house in London, or a split-level house in suburban Los Angeles. Unless you intend to spend, or have already spent, countless dollars on a professional decorator and literally can't change the style, white walls (or at least off-white) are the way to go. Next, look at the furniture.

Furniture, like wall coloring, is subjective. Some people like modern, some traditional, others antique. In our example, there seems to be a little of everything. A polite word in the decorating game is "eclectic." My wife and I once had a professional decorator for a client, and we invited her to our apartment to write a contract for the sale of her house. "My, what a darling apartment," she said, without much emotion, "and the furniture is so, um, eclectic." To paraphrase the old saying, "If you can't say anything nice about one's taste, don't say anything, or say it's eclectic." The truth is that she was right. We had furniture in that apartment that was bought specifically for the apartment, but other pieces were from previous apartments, and, yes, "stuff" from our parents' homes as well. To us it was tastefully decorated. Of course, there were the memories, all those memories: our first couch, pictures all over the place of Nora and me and our respective families dating back to our childhood. Pure clutter!

There is no room for sentimentality. The prospective tenants have not been a part of your life experience and therefore won't identify with it. They won't see all the charm that you do. To them you have an eclectically decorated apartment filled with junk, and they will move on to the next prospect. The same rules apply if you bought a fixer-upper or "handyman's special" that you are going to repair and lease for rental income. Don't overimprove the property; keep it neutral. A friend of mine in Scotland refers to this as "doing the cheap and cheerful."

Furnished vs. Unfurnished

One of the first things you need to decide is whether you are going to lease the unit furnished or unfurnished. The rule of thumb is that most tenants who are going to rent for a year or more will have their own furniture and won't want yours. So if you are looking for a long-term tenant, it is wiser to lease unfurnished. The property will show better, and it will be easier for the prospects to imagine the unit with their own furnishings and memorabilia. The one exception is the extra bedroom and bath in the back of the house or upstairs portion of the property. That should always be rented furnished, regardless of the lease term, because more than likely, anybody renting a room and a bath won't be bringing furniture. If you are going to rent seasonally, it is safe to assume that the tenant will not be bringing his or her own furniture and will want the property furnished. This is where merciless objectivity comes in. The command here is "remove clutter." First, get rid of the photos. Aside from the fact that they may be viewed as clutter, they can also be a distraction.

We represented a young, newlywed couple whose apartment was full of their wedding pictures. Everybody who came to the unit remarked how nice the bride looked in the pictures or what a handsome couple they made, and many of the couples began to reminisce about their own weddings. Several of the single male prospects thought they recognized the girl, while one thought he might have actually dated her (which, if true, was potentially more information than we needed or wanted to know). It was a real pain, because the prospects were concentrating on the pictures and not on the unit. Those pictures became the main focus instead of the property. Finally, we told the clients to remove the pictures. They were hurt, but business is business. Basically, they had to choose whether they wanted the apartment to be a monument and tribute to their everlasting love or wanted to have it rented sometime before their twentieth anniversary. We assured them that the cast and crew of *The Love Boat* were not in the market for the apartment. Reluctantly, but wisely, they chose to get the apartment rented, and we accomplished it shortly thereafter, *sans* the distractions.

Let's assume that you have elected to remove the furniture and you have painted the walls white (over the irate objections of your brother-in-law). You now need to consider the floors as the next phase of your survey. (Don't worry, I won't abandon the short-term renters, and we shall consider the furnished unit, also).

Flooring

Flooring presents a different problem. Freshening up an apartment with a few coats of paint is fairly simple and inexpensive, but changing a floor is an entirely different matter. In our example, the subject apartment has marble in the bathrooms, tile in the living and dining areas, and carpet in the bedrooms. Let's start with the carpet, because, frankly, that is the easiest to deal with. Here's where merciless objectivity rears its head once again. Look at the carpets. Hopefully, your brother-in-law's decorating skills were limited to the walls, and the carpeting is neutral beige. If they are black or red or some outlandish combination of colors, it may pay to replace the carpets with a decent but not overly expensive beige carpet. It is neutral in terms of subjective taste and doesn't show the dirt too badly. For you high rollers, if you have a high-end luxury property, you can't go too cheap on the floors. Berber carpeting is usually a safe bet in those cases. Remember, be objective. Is the carpet really clean, or did you just go over it with some carpet freshener? Does it have stains? Does it still show markings from your furniture or from the previous occupants? Be honest! Should you replace that carpet? Only you and your business conscience can make that final determination.

With regard to tile and marble, one can only hope that they are fairly neutral in color, because it is far more expensive to replace marble or tile. We had one case where the entire apartment floor was done in bright terra-cotta tile. It was fine as long as your furnishings had a Mexican motif, but it very much narrowed the field of applicants for rental, because most people did not share the specific taste of the owner. I'm not suggesting that you pull up the floors just because they are not beige. For now, understand conceptually how subjective taste factors into the ability to rent a property.

This isn't a book on decorating, but in order to become a landlord, you have to secure a tenant. To do that, you need to take certain preparatory steps that will help you rent the unit at the highest possible value, whatever that figure will ultimately be. Proper preparation of the unit will translate into maximizing your potential income, as we shall now see.

You've read the book and were brutally honest with yourself. You repainted the apartment white and put new beige carpeting in the bedrooms. Fortunately, the tile was white to begin with, and the marble in the bathrooms was actually neutral beige. Did you remember to clean the appliances in the kitchen and make sure they were in proper working order? What about the lights; are they all in good operating condition? Excellent work! The place is ready to show. This is where the research comes in.

Research

Get a couple of local newspapers with real estate sections. Check the rental listings and see what is available in your building in apartments *similar* to yours. What constitutes similar? Try to find a two-bedroom, two-bath unit facing the ocean and the city in your line. Start there. If you can't find a unit in the same line as yours, see if any others in the building are for rent with the same approximate square footage as your unit. The newspaper may not give you all the information you need, and you might have to make a phone call.

Do it! Most landlords or their agents will share information with you such as what the last rental price was and how long the unit has been on the market at the current asking price. Talk to the building managers; they are usually a font of information. If you don't find a comparable unit in your building, try the one nearest to your location. Obviously, if the next building is oceanfront or overlooking a golf course, that will be a factor. Many real estate agents will provide you with a list of the "comps" for your building free of charge. However, knowing what landlords are asking for rent and what actual tenants are paying for rent are two very different things. Ultimately, you want to know the price that tenants are actually paying to live in your building. But then, why not just hire a real estate or rental agent and let the agent figure it out? If you want to be a landlord, you can call professionals, but you still need to know how to value a property even if you employ a broker. Let's see why.

Certainly, a good agent will show you the "comps" and make a suggestion about the price you should ask, but most won't insist or turn you away if you disagree. If you name some outlandish figure, many brokers will take the listing in the hopes that ultimately you will come to your senses. That's a waste of time. Each month the unit stays empty is a month you lose income and pay mortgage, assessments, and taxes out of your own pocket. Also, many brokers will simply look at the listings in the building or neighborhood and list property at the same price as a similar unit without checking to see how many units actually rented at those prices. It's your property, and regardless of whether you use a leasing agent or do it yourself, you should be involved with your property, much the same way as you would be involved with your doctor, lawyer, or accountant. It's part of your job as a landlord.

Let's say you've done your research and the results are as follows:

1. There are 150 units in the building.

2. Of the 150 units, 50 are for rent.

3. Of the 50 for rent, 20 are two-bedroom, two-bath units of similar square footage.

4. Fifteen of the two bedrooms are on higher floors.

5. Eight are furnished.

6. Of the 150 units, 25 are currently rented for one year or more.

7. Of the twenty-five currently rented, ten are two-bedroom, two-bath units similar to yours.

8. Of the ten rented, six are on higher floors.

9. A tenth-floor unit in your line has just rented for $1,500 per month for a year, unfurnished.

10. A fourth-floor unit in your line rented last month for $750 per month for a year, unfurnished.

11. A twenty-fifth-floor unit in your line (the penthouse) has just rented for $2,000 per month for a year, unfurnished.

12. A fifteenth-floor unit rented five months ago for six months (winter) for $2,800 per month, furnished.

13. A nineteenth-floor unit in your line rented two years ago on a three-year lease, and the current rent is $3,000 per month.

Do you have enough information? I think so. I'm using a fairly upscale condominium, but whether you are talking about $3,000 or $300 per month, the analysis is still the same. What does a similar property in your neighborhood rent for? That is what you are looking for. Now let's analyze our findings a bit further.

As you can see, we have a lot of information. Some of it is extraneous, or at least of limited value. Essential is the fact that there are twenty-five apartments currently rented, of which ten units are similar to yours. That is good news, because it shows that there is a market for your style unit in your building. The bad news is that there are also twenty units currently for rent that are similar to yours, which means you have some competition. We also know that fifteen of the units are on higher floors, and, traditionally, the higher floors bring slightly higher prices because of better views. If your unit shows better than the tenth-floor unit just rented, the fact that it is two floors lower should not affect the price significantly. Since your unit is neutrally decorated and clean, you are very competitive. Remember those dreadful aptitude tests you got in school? Let's try a multiple-choice question based on the above-stated scenario to see if you have the concept.

Question: What is the rental price you should ask, based on the facts presented above? a. $2,800 per month; b. $1,400 per month; c. $1,500 per month; d. $3,236 per month; e. none of the above

If you chose *c*, you are correct. Choice *a* is clearly incorrect. A fifteenth-floor furnished unit, leased seasonally, will command more money than an eighth-floor unfurnished long-term lease. Tenants who rent for the season pay a premium for the fact that the landlord is leasing a unit with furniture (and, in most cases, all the extras, including linens and dishes) for a short time only. The units get more wear and tear, and the landlord has additional clean-up expenses each time the tenant moves out. These are incorporated in the rent. Also, a seasonal unit is not a "comp." We are looking at long-term unfurnished units. If you chose *b*, that is a trick answer; $1,400 is the figure that you should ultimately settle on based on an asking price of $1,500 per month and allowing the tenant to negotiate $100 because you are two floors lower than the closest "comp." Choice *c* is of course the correct answer because the closest "comp" is the tenth-floor unit in your line, which was just leased at $1,500. You are certainly well within your rights to ask the same amount for a unit that is significantly similar to yours. Choice *d* is incorrect because there is no basis for it. At the outset of the chapter, we assumed that you would need about $2,190 to cover expenses, plus $1,000 per month profit, but that is not possible.

Don't ask for $3,200 per month and hope some dummy walks in, falls in love with the place, and rents it. It just doesn't happen that way. For one thing, most tenants have done the same homework I have recommended that you do, and they know the market. Even if they haven't done the research, just by virtue of the fact that they've seen several apartments, they have a pretty good picture of what is going on. I'm not saying it never happens; it does once in a while, but it's like playing a slot machine. What are the odds that your machine will be the one that pays the jackpot, and how many quarters are you willing to sacrifice to find out? Any real gambler will tell you that slots are the worst odds in the casino.

The next argument prospective landlords have is "I won't rent it until I get my price—I need to make my expenses." I can't tell you how much I disagree with that type of thinking. There is a concept in business known as the "present value of money." It means, roughly, that a dollar earned today is worth more than waiting twelve months to get, say, $2. Or more simply put, "a bird in the hand is worth two in the bush." Basically, if you can get $1,400 today, it makes much more sense to lease the unit and reduce your carrying costs than to leave it empty in the hope that it will rent in the future while you are paying the full monthly load.

People who argue that they must make their expenses are often rich enough that they don't need to. Don't fall for that argument. A related and equally fallacious suggestion is, "Let's price it high, and if the prospect wants it, we can always negotiate." Not true. You have to get the prospect to see your unit before you can negotiate. Most prospects are intimidated by high prices or are afraid to make offers that they feel are so far away from the asking price as to insult the owner, so they bypass the property. Either that or they feel the owner is so greedy that they don't want to deal with such a person. Whatever the reason, listing high and waiting for someone to fall in love with your apartment is unrealistic and a strategy that almost always fails.

This rental example may seem scary; even without profit, you would be in the negative. While the scenario I presented does happen, especially with expensive properties where the market is flooded (too many properties, not enough tenants), the scenario presented is what is known as a "straw man" argument. It is set up so that I can present all the different arguments that prospective landlords make in the valuation process. In a good market, you should be able to make your expenses and a profit as well. The purchase of income-producing property is another topic for another book.

Be Neat

As promised, here is a thought concerning furnished property. If you choose to rent furnished, the property must be scrupulously clean and organized. If you are living in the property while you are attempting to lease it, you can't leave beer cans and towels lying around. It must be a showplace, uncluttered and impeccable. Not only is this important in securing a tenant, but it sends a message to that tenant that you are neat and organized and you expect him or her to be neat as well. It sends the right message. If you show no respect for your property and you are the owner, why should a mere tenant show any respect at all? Remember that the tenant has the lesser interest. One landlord we know has a property that she rents seasonally for income purposes. No matter what the market, good or bad, her property always leases. Aside from the fact that it is priced correctly, she is scrupulously clean and organized. If you open a cupboard (and most prospects do), the contents are lined up in rows, according to size. The same is true for the refrigerator. Every towel, every sheet, every knickknack is in place. It's hard to believe, but it works.

The Four Ps

Doing it right is usually harder up front and easier in the long run. When you think about it, most of this is common sense, and it becomes second nature, just like any other process you repeat over and over. As I said before and will continue to stress, this is business. In marketing you learn the "four Ps" of a product: price, packaging, position, and promotion. Your property is your product.

Price

Price is the most important, because you can have the nicest packaging, but if it is too expensive, nobody will buy it. If it's too cheap, it will be perceived as being undesirable, and you certainly won't be maximizing the profit on your investment.

Packaging

The next is packaging. Once price is established, you need an attractive package to be competitive. That is why I stress having the unit properly decorated and in "show condition." Neatness counts.

Position

Position relates to where you place your product in the market. Since property "is where it is," your position is pretty much established. You can't move your product around the supermarket or department store looking for an optimum location, like a bottle of wine or blue jeans. Thus, if your unit is in the city, you can't move it to the beach or the mountains. Because your position is fixed, you must put added emphasis on price and packaging, which is why we place so much emphasis on them. It is the reason you must be mercilessly objective. That is also why it doesn't matter one iota what price Uncle Ralph (remember him?) rented his unit for, unless it could be considered a "comp" to yours. His position may be very different from yours, even if it is the same size unit. If it is oceanfront, near skiing, or by a golf course, that relative position changes the valuation.

Promotion

Promotion is the final "P." I'm not so much concerned with this area, since there are only a few accepted ways of marketing a rental property. Place an ad in the local newspaper; put a sign up on the bulletin board at your local university, house of worship, or even military base if there is one in the area; and, of course, list with a broker.

Lease Agreement

So there you have it—you have prepared your unit and priced it correctly, and now you have chosen to place an ad in the local newspaper as your method of marketing. Are you ready? Well, almost. Before you go hunting, you need a gun, and the gun has to be loaded. In this case, your gun is your lease agreement, and your ammunition is the contents of the lease. What should your agreement state? Yes, we have reached what you have been waiting for, what you probably bought this book for, a consideration of that document that, aside from the Magna Carta and the Declaration of Independence, is the most famous document in the free world, the lease. The next three chapters are dedicated to the lease agreement, the very essence of the landlord-tenant relationship.

CHAPTER 3

Terms and Conditions

"Why Can't I Keep an Aardvark in the Apartment?"

The Lease

The great moment has arrived! We are going to discuss the lease agreement. The lease is the basic contract between you and your tenant. It describes in detail the ground rules for the rental of your property. Legally (and I'm sure some lawyers would take issue with this statement), all a lease really needs to state is the names of the parties, the location of the property leased, the amount of the rent, when and where it must be paid, and the term of the lease. That's it—one paragraph, and you are in business.

The fact is that state statutes generally cover the rest of the major responsibilities of the landlord and tenant. Yet most leases, including the sample lease provided in this work (Appendix B), are considerably longer and cover a wide range of topics. There are various reasons for this, aside from the joke that lawyers make things more complicated because they need to make a living. Statutes are fairly general in nature, and you want the specific details of your relationship with the tenant itemized. While a state statute may generally indicate what the landlord's responsibilities are with regard to providing essential services such as proper heating, or how security deposits are to be held by the landlord and later disbursed at the end of the lease term, they don't cover the more specific details. Examples such as who is responsible for watering the lawn or whether pets are allowed, or even how many people you are going to allow as guests in the leased property, are not covered in statutes. These are stipulated in the lease agreement.

In this chapter we consider some of these issues. You as the landlord need to be aware of them before you advertise for a tenant, because the time to consider these details is not during the showing of the property or during the lease negotiation, and certainly not after the lease is signed. The more details you work out ahead of time, the less controversy you are likely to have during the term of the lease. In Chapter 1, we discussed one of the qualities of leadership as being able to let your followers, in this case the tenants, know what to expect from you. In addition, we examined as part of the "Four Ps" the concepts of promotion and packaging. In the present chapter, we decide what specifics to place in the lease and relate those specifics to both leadership qualities and marketing concepts.

Monthly Price

The first thing we need to do is set up our working scenario. In the last chapter, we looked at a condominium situation. In this chapter, let's use a house as an example. Remember that the concepts put forth in this book relate to all types of residential income property, so we are not restricted to one example. What are our parameters? The house is a three-bedroom, three-and-one-half-bath, two-story brick home in a suburban neighborhood in a northern-tier state, which has a harsh winter.

The home has a fenced-in backyard as well as a front lawn, both with trees, grass, and landscaping, an outdoor above-ground swimming pool (heated), a swing set, and a trampoline. The house has a two-car garage. The floors are newly carpeted, and the kitchen has a three-year-old linoleum floor. The kitchen appliances are five years old and in working order. There is a finished basement, which serves as a recreation room and has a five-year-old pool table, which you will be leaving. The walls were freshly painted (white), and the downstairs den has a faux wood finish on the walls and tile floors. The house is ten years old. Although the community isn't gated, there is a neighborhood association and a clubhouse with a gymnasium, tennis courts, and a basketball court. Nearby, there is a state park that, depending on the season, allows hunting and fishing in its lakes (with the proper licenses). In the winter the lakes freeze and ice-skating is permitted. There is a ski area about one hour away.

You have checked the "comps" for rentals of similar property in your neighborhood and discovered that you can rent your home for $1,500 per month, unfurnished. The military installation a few miles down the road provides a constant supply of potential tenants, and the market is brisk. You elect to place an ad with the base military housing office as your method of advertising the property. During the term of the lease, you will be living in your condo in South Florida, where it is sunny and warm. No more ice fishing for you.

The Security Deposit

Before you place your ad at the base housing office, what factors should you consider? The first and most obvious issue is the amount of rent that the market in that area will bear. You've established $1,500 per month as a fair market price. But what about the security deposit? We have an in-depth discussion of the security deposit in Chapter 9, but for now, our focus will be on how much security we are going to require. What do we know about the house? It has a swimming pool, which needs care both in the summer, when it is in use, and in the winter, when it is shut down and covered to make sure pipes or connections don't freeze. The front and backyards require maintenance as well. Generally, apartment leases usually require the equivalent of the first month's rent payment, the last month's rent, and a security deposit of one month. In this case, we are dealing with a fairly complex house arrangement, so it would not be unwise or out of place to require two months of security deposit.

So now we have established two criteria: the rental amount and the security deposit. You also are going to want those monies paid on signing of the lease. This means that your tenant must have $6,000 in available funds to sign the lease. You can pretty much anticipate a request by the tenant to pay half on signing and half prior to moving in. That is a reasonable request provided that you specify which half is being paid, the security or the advance rent. It's not just money. The different categories have different legal significance. I would recommend designating the initial payment as security and the first and last months' rent to be paid prior to move-in. The reason for this is tactical as well as legal. All tenants (or at least the vast majority) firmly believe that security is a necessary evil created by lawyers and that they are never going to damage your property. They are paying you the security only because it is an accepted norm in the industry and you are insisting on it.

On the other hand, rent is something that must be paid. It is the essential element of the contract, and nobody expects not to pay rent. Therefore, at move-in, the tenant is less likely to ask for more time to pay the second half of the monies if it is designated as rent rather than security deposits. "Mr. Landlord, I'm still waiting for my last landlord to refund my security deposit. Tell you what, since I already paid your first and last months' rent, why don't I just move in and I'll get you the security in a few weeks? After all, I paid the rent, and I'm entitled to move in." Nice try, but it doesn't work. Both the rent and the security deposit are elements of the contract, which the tenant must perform. However, it saves you having to debate this issue if you designate the initial payment as security. The argument "Look, Mr. Landlord, since I already paid you two months' security, why don't I just move in and pay you the rent when I get my security deposit back from my last landlord?" sounds a lot less convincing. So, your lease is going to specify that on its signing, the two months' security will be paid. The lease will further stipulate that not less than forty-eight hours prior to move-in you will be paid the first and last months' rent, either by cashier's check or in cash. In this way, you will not find yourself in the position of holding a check that takes two weeks to clear and bounces while the tenant is living on your property.

Tenants Who Don't Pay

Be well advised that even the wealthiest clients bounce checks. If the tenant is already living on your property, there is not much you can do unless you want to fight from day one. Therefore, it is much better if the keys are turned over on the date specified in the lease as the move-in date, assuming all payments have been made and funds cleared. If the tenant doesn't want to pay the additional funds two days before move-in, you obviously have another problem, which is noncompliance with the lease agreement, and we address that issue later on. For now, let's assume everything is going well.

Lease Term and Increases

The lease term states how long this lease is going to be in effect—one year or perhaps longer. Let us say you will accept a three-year lease. Will you want an increase in rent each year? There are a few points we need to consider. First, it is perfectly logical to accept yearly increases in multiple-year leases, at least from the landlord's point of view. After all, the cost of living goes up each year, which means your expenses go up; why shouldn't that be reflected in your rental income? Cost-of-living increases are usually based on the consumer price index, which fundamentally involves complex and unfathomable calculations based on how much it costs the average shopper to fill an average-size shopping cart at the average supermarket with such staples as milk, potatoes, and bread.

From the tenant's point of view, he or she is signing a three-year lease to lock in a rent and doesn't want to pay any increases. Most residential multiterm leases incorporate some form of cost-of-living increase. However, as you do not have the power of a lease management company that is in charge of 1,000 units in an urban center behind you, you must consider this point very carefully. Being a landlord is an exhibition of your entrepreneurial spirit. This country was founded on that spirit, and it is laudable. The problem arises when your spirit gets in the way of common sense.

We recently represented both the landlord and the tenant in a dispute (this is legal, according to Florida real estate law, as long as you disclose the dual relationship to both parties). The tenant wanted a three-year lease with a fixed rent for the term and a clause in the lease that allowed him to cancel the agreement with a 30-day notice to the landlord, which is also referred to as an "out clause." The landlord countered with a 10 percent cost-of-living increase each year and no out clause. Negotiations ensued, and the landlord finally agreed to lease the unit with a 5 percent increase each year in the rent amount and a 60-day out clause after the first year. By the time this offer was finally communicated to the tenant, he had cooled on the unit and decided to remain where he was. The rental market in South Florida was soft at that time, and the unit remained vacant for several more months.

The lesson learned here is the old adage of keeping it simple. When you have one or two units that you are renting to supplement your income and make use of your unoccupied property, getting too clever may be counterproductive.

Actually, 5 percent is not outrageous. Simply translate it into a dollar amount in the lease agreement. Cost-of-living increases are official sounding, but you are better off stating your terms simply and directly and avoiding showing how economically savvy you are. Ultimately, the idea is to lease your property. A soft real estate market, where there is a lot of property available and not too many prospective tenants, is not a time to engage in complicated negotiations and lease agreements. Conversely, in a strong market, the sky can be the limit. Once again, objectivity plays a large factor here. You have to recognize the market forces and work with them to keep the income stream going.

So far, having considered the current real estate rental market in your area, you have decided that you would rather get a tenant in quickly (remember the present value of money) by offering to give a two-year fixed-term lease with no fancy increases. Besides, there are several houses in the area for lease, and the economy appears to be slowing down. There are also rumors of the military installation's closing in a few years due to budget cuts, so a two-year lease would not be intimidating. Besides, winter is approaching and you want to get to Florida.

Occupancy and Use of the Leased Property

Number of Tenants

What else do you think you should consider? After all, you have the price, the term of the lease, and the security deposit. That pretty much covers it, right? What about the number of people who can stay in the house? Can you restrict that? Of course you can. Enforcing it may be a different story, but for now, let's remain with what you may consider legally.

Let's say that John and Mary rent your house. John and Mary have a child, Markie. They move in and subsequently invite their friends Paul and Paula to live with them. Paul and Paula invite Phil and Phyllis and their two children, who pay rent to Paul and Paula. Obviously, there are a myriad of legal and ethical problems involved here, but setting those aside for the moment, imagine the wear and tear on the house. You leased your house as a residential property, not a hotel. So you will want a statement in the lease indicating that the tenants shall use the premises only for "residential purposes" and specify the number of people who will occupy the house, in this case two adults and one child.

Guests

You may also indicate that guests may not remain on the premises for more than a two-week period without the express consent of the landlord. If Mom wants to stay for the summer, you shouldn't object, but you should also know about it.

Subletting

You will also want a statement forbidding the subletting of the house without the express consent of the landlord.

If the prospective tenant says something like: "But we are paying rent, we can do what we want. As long as we pay on time, you, Mr. Landlord, have no right to tell us what to do." This may be a red flag that indicates that you need to move on to the next prospect, because this tenant is beginning to sound like trouble.

You should try to exert your leadership qualities over the tenant and impress on him or her that your ownership interest allows you to retain certain controls over your property. If you cannot make the prospective tenant grasp the concept that leasehold is not a free-for-all, again, you may be well advised to pass on this deal and wait for the next one, the present value of money notwithstanding. I have seen cases where it would have been better to let the property remain vacant than to lease to a bad tenant. It is really an issue of whether the present value of money exceeds the present value of aggravation. But for now, know that the learning point is that you can and should restrict the number of occupants allowed to live on the property.

Use of the Property

We touched on this with the example of Paul and Paula, above, but let's expand on this point. Standard lease agreements often restrict use of the premises for any kind of business purpose or profession. This is a pretty broad restriction and requires some consideration. For example, if you were to lease your house to a writer, that is his profession. Is it reasonable to make him open an office to write his books if your study is adequate to the task? Obviously not, and it might cost you a good tenant if you remained firm on this point. What about a criminal attorney who wants to see his clients at home because it is more convenient than traveling to his office downtown? Can you restrict the attorney from bringing accused criminals to your home? Isn't a person considered innocent until proven guilty? Let's take it a step further. What do you think about someone running a flea market out of your garage? Local zoning ordinances might take care of that situation, but the authorities usually take action only if they are alerted by a complaint from the neighbors. By that time, you as the owner may inherit some type of liability as the owner of the property.

There are numerous cases where the tenants open a baby-sitting service or day-care provider (as it is now called) operation out of their home. What if a baby is injured in your house and you are sued as the owner of the property? Will your insurance cover it? Probably not, since baby-sitting services are commercial enterprises and are generally considered as being outside the scope of your residential landlord renter's policy. Your lease should indeed restrict the use of the property for any commercial enterprise. If there is some exception, such as the tenant's being a writer or similar professional, that can be added and designated as a specific exception in the lease.

Pets

People love their pets. They are passionate about them and consider them part of the family. People also take great offense if you are not a pet lover and don't share their familial attachment to a pet. Once again, business is business. The fact is, many residential properties don't allow pets of any kind. I recall one condominium that was so strict you couldn't keep goldfish in your unit, and the residents accepted it. Other buildings do allow pets but have size and weight restrictions and regulate on which elevators the owners may take their pets and where on the property the pets may be walked. This is all perfectly legal (except possibly the goldfish; I have lots of issues with that). The first question is, what is a pet? Dogs and cats come to mind as the obvious examples. Is a goldfish, strictly speaking, a pet? Does a bowl of water containing a squiggly little creature the size of a piece of sushi, and with the life span of a library book withdrawal, constitute a pet? It's more like an ornament. What about an aquarium full of tropical fish that takes up a whole wall and has air tanks and filters and feeding tubes? Collectively, are those pets? Do you want a contraption like that in your house or apartment? What about a lion or an ocelot (a cross between a tiger and pussycat favored by *femmes fatales* in old movies)? Can you keep a shark or snake in your bathtub? Can you keep a horse in the backyard?

When you talk about pets in terms of landlord-tenant relationships, you are really talking about what are commonly referred to as "domestic animals" or "household pets." It may very well be that your house is in a rural area with lots of land and even a barn, and you don't care what kind of animals the tenant keeps. But for average landlords whose properties are located in and about urban centers, we will deal with animals that reasonably can be construed as "household pets."

Basically, dogs, cats, tropical fish, and nonpredatory birds (a hawk is not a household pet) are generally considered domestic animals. Since the house in our current scenario has a yard and is in a suburban area, more than likely, you would be unduly restricting your pool of applicants if you did not allow pets. But you are entitled to charge a pet deposit to cover damages from dogs and cats. Further, and with all due respect to pet owners, the fact is that non-pet owners can be very sensitive to pet smells, which often remain after the tenant vacates the property. I knew of one tenant who kept several dogs and cats in his unit. When the tenant moved out, the landlord spent the pet deposit and more to repaint the unit in order to remove the pet odors. Depending on various factors, such as the durability of your house or apartment, pet deposits run from about $50 to one month's additional security. Of course, common sense should govern, and requiring pet security for a goldfish or a caged bird is clearly unnecessary.

Utilities

When we talk about utilities, we mean items such as telephones, water, and electricity. The simple answer is to always transfer the utilities to the tenant, irrespective of the term of the lease. Don't fall for this famous argument: "Look, Mr. Landlord, I'm only going to be here six months. Why not keep the phones and utilities in your name, and when you get the bills, I'll pay for them?" For one thing, when the tenant moves out, do you really want to track him or her down for the phone bill? What if the tenant was from Europe and called home every day for hours and ran the air-conditioning 24 hours per day, at the highest setting? Either your security deposit won't cover it or state law may force you to return the security deposit before the final utility bills arrive. Also, utility companies have a nasty habit of not allowing the new occupant to open an account until the old account is settled. This could complicate your subsequent rental and cost you money. There is really nothing else to discuss in this regard. All utilities should be transferred to the tenant and your name removed.

It pains me to admit that my wife and I actually fell for this argument early in our careers. We owned a small beach apartment, which we rented to a couple from abroad for six months. The couple paid the full six months in advance plus one month's security. Everything was fine, but the couple asked if we could keep the phones and electricity in our names because it was difficult for them to open accounts in the United States for such a short time. We agreed. Everything was fine. Each month we sent them the utility bills and they paid them. The final month came, and they moved out. At that time, Florida law required that we return the security within fifteen days (it's now thirty), and we did so, since the unit was impeccable. A couple of weeks later the utility bills rolled in, and we called the tenants and told them the amount. They replied that they thought those bills were exorbitant, that I had a nerve asking for this money, and that they weren't going to pay a dime more. Further, they demanded to know if I had sent them their security deposit refund. My heart sank. We were stuck! We had already mailed them the security deposit (which, of course, didn't cover the bills anyway), and we had to pay the utility bills to clear the accounts. To add insult to injury, I also had to swallow an additional long-distance call to Europe to learn I wasn't going to get reimbursed. The story did have a happy ending of sorts, though. When I sent the security deposit refund to the tenants in Europe, I mistakenly used a domestic stamp instead of an international one, and several months later, the envelope with the enclosed security deposit refund check was returned for lack of correct postage.

It is true that some utility companies may still require the account to be cleared prior to allowing the new tenant to open an account. However, since the bills are in the tenant's name rather than in yours, it is their credit involved, and thus, they are less likely to engage in that sort of nonsense.

Anybody can buy a form lease, throw an ad in the newspaper, and stick a tenant on his or her property. Those are the people who keep real estate lawyers employed and the court system busy. The purpose of this book is to help you understand and appreciate the complexity of the landlord-tenant relationship from the viewpoint of the landlord. It's not the forms that make you successful—you'll get plenty of forms in this book—it's understanding the content of those forms and thinking about the transaction itself and how you progress with each step that will make you a successful landlord. Certainly, no book can substitute for twenty years of experience as an attorney, real estate broker, and landlord, but those experiences are the core of this book and will help you on your way to a better landlord experience. The real issue is if you want to trust (and pay) others or if you want to understand the system yourself.

Altering the Property

What if your tenant wants to remove a wall or replace a bathroom? What if the tenant wants to build an addition to the house or add an alarm system? A good lease will require that any alteration must be with the written consent of the landlord. In some cases, you may want the tenant to make the improvement, provided it is at his or her expense and the improvement remains with the house after the tenant vacates the premises. But there are hidden dangers here. Let's suppose the tenant wants to install an alarm system and asks your approval. Sounds good, right? Maybe, but consider this. The alarm system the tenant wants to install is the type that is connected to a monitoring company. The company requires a contract with the tenant. When the tenant moves out, your choice is either to renew the contract or have the alarm not function. Of course, you can try to pass the expense on to the next tenant, but I'll bet you that the new tenant will want you as the landlord to include the cost of the alarm in the rent. Furthermore, what if the area where your house is located is a very safe and secure area, but the previous tenant was a person who merely felt better with the added security? Now your home and the community have the appearance of being unsafe.

Consider this example. Your tenant loves trees and requests to "improve" your backyard with a little more landscaping. You eagerly agree because it sounds great (and the tenants can't take the trees with them when they move out). At the expiration of the lease term, you inspect the property and discover that you now own a veritable jungle paradise. It's beautiful, but you quickly realize that it is going to take maintenance to keep it that way and you can't let it deteriorate. Now your expenses are increased and you must maintain it at your own expense, remove it at your expense, or try to pass the expense on to the new tenants. First of all, the new tenants may not want all the foliage, and the increased costs of keeping up this jungle may send you over the market value for rentals. So you can't pass the costs on to the tenants. Lease agreements should state that no alterations should be performed without the express written consent of the landlord. When the request comes, you need to consider all aspects of any proposed alteration. A good landlord is proactive in his or her considerations. Try to anticipate issues in advance.

Repairs

Another area that causes numerous problems is the issue of repairs. Leases often stipulate that major repairs not due to the negligence of the tenant are the responsibility of the landlord, while so-called minor repairs are charged to the tenant. The question is, what is a major repair? Local statutes may offer some general guidance if they designate such items as heating or water as "essential services" that the landlord must supply, but what about a washing machine or a dishwasher? How about a refrigerator—is that a major appliance? There are several ways to deal with this type of situation to avoid conflict. The first and most effective way is to merely stipulate a dollar amount in the lease that differentiates a major versus a minor appliance. I usually use $100 as a base figure. Anything over $100 should be the responsibility of the landlord, and anything under, that of the tenant. Of course, you can raise that figure, depending on the area and appliances on the property. You should also specify other items such as swimming pool upkeep and repairs, as well as gardening and lawn maintenance. Damages to the property itself are discussed below.

The second solution, which can be used separately or in conjunction with the first and is highly advisable, is purchasing an appliance repair contract. These are relatively inexpensive and cover the major appliances, including heat and air-conditioning. Plumbing is usually extra. If the dishwasher breaks, the tenant calls the service, which repairs or replaces the item. There is one caution, however, and that is that these service contracts don't abrogate the landlord's responsibility to repair an item. For example, the water heater breaks and the cost to repair is $200. Under the terms of the lease, it is your responsibility as the landlord to make the repair. No problem—you call the service company and report the item. Unfortunately, the service company doesn't arrive for three days and has to order a part, which takes six weeks, and it turns out to be the wrong part, causing further delays. Your irate tenant is threatening to move out under the theory of constructive eviction (we'll discuss that later) and wants to sue you for damages. "But I called the company; it's not my fault," you argue. Wrong; the tenant is at best a third-party beneficiary of a contract between you and the service company. This may give the tenant some cause of action against the company in a lawsuit, but it doesn't relieve you of your responsibility to provide hot water to the tenant, probably under a state statute, if nothing else. Certainly, the repair sum is more than $100, and that binds you according to the terms of the lease. In Chapter 1, we discussed the fact that the landlord must be decisive in complying with his or her duties and must take care of these responsibilities quickly. This is a prime example of when the landlord must be prepared to act. Are there any other issues that bear consideration?

Selling the Property

The law states that a leasehold interest is not extinguished by the sale of a property. The new owner takes title to the property *subject to* the leasehold interest, unless you specify otherwise in the lease. Thus, if you sell your property, neither you nor the purchaser can evict the tenant solely because there is a new owner. This is one exception where the leasehold interest outweighs the owner's rights with regard to the property.

Here's another question for you. What happens if the lease is going to expire in six months and you now want to place your property for sale with a broker? Can the broker come and show the property while the tenant is still occupying the unit? The answer is, maybe. Many leases address this issue. You may place a clause in the lease indicating that during a certain period of time prior to the expiration of the lease, a "for sale" sign may be placed on the property and with 24 hour's notice, the property may be shown by your agent. If you are planning on selling at any time during the term of the lease, you may wish to settle the terms of showing the property up front, but be prepared to reduce your rent as an incentive for the tenant to cooperative. A good legal concept that you as a landlord should be aware of in this regard is the principle of "quiet enjoyment" of property.

Quiet Enjoyment

Quiet enjoyment of property is a fundamental concept in real estate law that applies to owners as well as tenants. It means that the lawful residents of a property are entitled to occupy and enjoy the premises free of interference by other parties, including you, the landlord. Here are a couple of examples that illustrate this point.

In the first case, Tim and Tanya Tenant have rented your apartment in Gigantic Towers Condominium. Harry and Harriet Hardy own the unit directly above Tim and Tanya. Harry and Harriet Hardy are a very sociable couple who love to party. In fact, Tim and Tanya once received an invitation from them stating (you guessed it) *party hearty at the Hardy party.*" The first party, which took place on a Saturday night, was very noisy, but it ended about 1:30 a.m., and Tim and Tanya did not complain. The second "Hardy party" was on a Wednesday and lasted until 5:00 a.m. This time Tim and Tanya complained to the management association of Gigantic Towers, but nothing was resolved. After the third party, which lasted from Sunday noon until 6:00 a.m. the following morning, you, the landlord, get a phone call from Tim and Tanya stating that if you don't solve this problem, they are moving out.

After that cold, sinking feeling in your stomach subsides, you begin to plot a course of action. The first issue is, do you have to resolve this issue? The answer is yes, for two reasons. The first is, if you don't, your tenants are going to move out, and the second, it really is your legal responsibility as the landlord to ensure that your tenants have quiet enjoyment of their property. But how do you solve the problem? I recommend that you first check the law in this situation. The town or city zoning regulation will state at what time noise must be curtailed.

It is usually somewhere between 10:00 p.m. and midnight. The second thing you need to check is what your condominium or homeowners' association rules and regulations state about loud noises in the building or development. They usually mirror the zoning rules and call for no disturbing noises after a certain hour. Since the Hardys' parties are unreasonable in any event, your best course of action is to insist that the management fix the problem. I usually don't advocate direct contact with the offending persons for safety's sake. You are not a neutral and detached person, and you should avoid direct confrontation. Of course, if you want to try a polite phone call to see if the offending party is reasonable, you are welcome to make the attempt, but don't count on it. After all, if they were considerate, you wouldn't have a problem. In the case of the Hardys, if the management office can't solve the problem, you may need to take legal action. Generally, a strong lawyer's letter to the management and the offending party solves the problem without exorbitant legal fees.

Inspections

The second example involving the concept of quiet enjoyment concerns inspections of the property. As the landlord, you have the right, from time to time, to inspect your property to verify that the tenant is upholding the terms of the lease. There is usually some notice provision in the lease that addresses the landlord's rights to inspect his or her property. Many generic leases state that the landlord may inspect the property during reasonable hours or with reasonable notice. The problem is, what is reasonable to the landlord may not be reasonable to the tenant. State statutes often stipulate the terms for landlord inspections, but if they don't, the lease should clearly define the landlord's right to inspect. Usually, once every six months with 24 hour's notice is sufficient unless the landlord has a reasonable belief that the lease is being breached or the property is in danger of imminent harm or other emergency. Remember that if you enter the premises unlawfully during the leasehold, you could be technically guilty of trespassing. If you do enter without the consent of the tenant, make sure you document your actions in case the tenant complains later. Let's put some of these concepts together with a slight variation in the facts.

Several years ago, Nora and I leased our condominium unit to an elderly woman who in her younger days was a concert pianist, or so she claimed. In any event, we began to get calls from the management office of the condo-minium association saying that our tenant was playing the piano and disturb-ing the neighbors.

"Playing the piano is not a crime," I replied.

"It is if you're playing a Hungarian Rhapsody at 3:00 a.m.," countered the manager, somewhat tersely.

"Why, do you have something against Hungarians, or is it just rhapsodies in general?" I joked.

"Look, you and your wife are listed as the owners of the unit, and it's your tenant. If you don't get her under control, we'll send the matter to the associ-ation attorneys."

That pretty much ended the conversation. Notice the twist in the facts. This time it is the neighbors who are complaining to the management office, and they are the ones who are seeking a resolution from you. But how does quiet enjoyment figure in this example? Are you obligated to guarantee quiet enjoy-ment for the whole building or neighborhood, as the case may be? Indirectly, you are. Your tenant, as the inhabitant of your property, is entitled to quiet enjoyment of the property. But the other residents are equally entitled to the quiet enjoyment of their property, and your tenant is causing the problem. So how did we handle the situation?

First, we called our tenant and advised her that we would be stopping by to check our unit. She was hesitant and indicated that it was not really conve-nient. My wife, who at times can exercise remarkable patience, explained that we had received noise complaints from the association and threats of litiga-tion against us. Further, under the terms of the lease, we had the right to inspect the unit to see if there was any truth to these allegations. Reluctantly, she conceded and we made an appointment to see the unit.

When we arrived, we saw the biggest piano ever created. This was not a baby grand but a super large grand piano. We didn't even want to think about how she got it into the unit. The other problem was that this tenant, who was about 80 years old, was tough as nails. This was going to require some diplomacy. First thing we did was request that she favor us with a small concert, and she readily obliged. She was excellent. It was actually quite amazing to watch her play. She was astute, too. She assumed (correctly in this case) that we were not classical music aficionados and stuck to a program of classical music favorites that most "lay" people are familiar with. At the end, we were quite taken with it all.

But business is business, and we had to get back to reality. All this talent was fine, but not at 3:00 in the morning. At this point we simply explained that she could not play after 10:00 p.m., which was in the condominium rules, and that if we got any more complaints, we would be forced to ask her to leave or take the appropriate legal action (much to our regret, of course). We also explained that we could not control the condominium association and that it could take action independent of us. Leadership prevailed, and she assured us that the nocturnal concerts would end.

There are a couple of footnotes to this story. The first is that during the conversation, she asked us a question that frankly caught us off guard.

"Where does it say in the lease that I have to obey the rules and regulations of the condominium association?" She asked this looking me straight in the eye. I checked the lease (which I had brought with me), and sure enough it didn't directly address this issue. I did find a clause that talked about obeying "state and local laws," and she accepted that argument. In addition, I reasoned that when she rented the unit, by implication, she accepted the rules of the association. However, when you rent to someone, be sure that whatever lease you use clearly states that the tenant will obey whatever rules govern your property, be it local ordinances, homeowners' association rules, or condominium association rules and regulations. What may be obvious to some are cogent arguments to others. And it's one less problem to debate. Also, if there are rules for your property, be sure to provide them to the tenant.

The other footnote is that several months later we received a letter that appeared to be from the tenant's son. "Uh oh," we thought, the poor woman must have died. We nervously opened the letter, only to find that it was indeed the son who was writing to advise us that his mother would not be renewing the lease. She had married the gentleman who lived in the penthouse and would be moving in with him. But the story doesn't end there. About a year later we got another letter from her son. "Oh, poor woman, this time she must have passed away, but why is the son writing to us?" Again we opened the letter, this time to find that the son was requesting, on his mother's behalf, if she could lease our unit again. Apparently, she and her gentleman friend had divorced. We called the son to advise him that, unfortunately, the unit was not available, as it had already been leased.

"Why did they get divorced, if you don't mind my asking?" I inquired. "Oh, the fellow couldn't stand her piano playing. Can you imagine that?" I believe I could!

Termination of Agreement

Are there any other lessons that can be learned from this experience? There are several, actually. What would have happened if the woman had actually passed away? Would that have terminated the lease? Arguably it would, because the basic purpose of the contract no longer exists. Practically speaking, if the tenant dies, you are well advised to move on and lease the unit as soon as possible. If your lease has a clause that specifically indicates that the intent of the agreement is to bind the "heirs and assigns," then arguably, the deceased tenant's estate may be liable on the remaining portion of the lease. Where would such a consideration come into play? What if you lease a property to a person who discloses that he or she has a terminal illness, but doesn't know how long he or she has to live? Several years ago, we were in that same situation with a relative who was dying. We disclosed it to the landlord but made it clear that the risk of her passing was not going to be absorbed by us. The lease did have a clause about "heirs and assigns," and the landlord did make an attempt to enforce it. However, because there was an addendum in the lease that addressed this very issue, he quickly backed off.

Discrimination

This brings us to a very important consideration that every landlord needs to be aware of, and that is whom you should consider for a tenant. The answer is simply, anyone who is ready, willing, and able to pay the rent. There are federal and state antidiscrimination laws that relate to certain "protected classes" of people, the main categories being race, creed, color, national origin, and religion. I would also add sex (including gays and lesbians) and age, as well as disabled persons and family status (i.e., persons with children or couples

55 and over). Volumes have been written on discrimination, and this is not a book on constitutional law. The message I wish to get across is that whatever your personal prejudices are, keep them private. Your job is to rent the property.

Further, there may be a few lawyers reading this book, and it is not my intent to get into complex issues of whether a private individual who owns a single property that he or she wants to rent is subject to federal or state antidiscrimination laws. It is arguable that a landlord who owns a single property and wishes to rent it is not subject to the Civil Rights Act of 1968, which includes the Fair Housing Act, which protects against the various forms of discrimination outlined above. The 1968 act applies to persons who own four or more properties, excluding the property that is owner occupied. However, the original Civil Rights Act, which was passed in 1866, unqualifiedly prohibits discrimination along racial lines. My question is simply this: Do you want the aggravation and cost of becoming a test case for a constitutional issue, or do you want to rent your property and make money? Besides, if you lose the case, the penalties can be severe. In addition, real estate agents are subject to strict antidiscrimination laws through federal and state statutes and will not discriminate, so don't ask them to. In the next chapter, we discuss credit and background checks. That should be your only yardstick, legally as well as morally. If the background check indicates that your prospective tenant has a criminal record, especially where child molestation is concerned, you should consult with a qualified attorney for advice, as each state has different laws relating to these issues.

The issue of discrimination can be tricky. What if the prospective tenant arrives for an interview and is dirty-looking and smells awful? Dirty, smelly people in and of themselves are not a protected class of individuals, so you can politely tell them you'll let them know and proceed with your search. But what if that same tenant is dirty and smelly but is also a member of a protected class? Now the issue is not so clear. Are you dismissing that prospect because he is sloppy or because of discrimination, and can you prove that it is the former and not the latter if you are challenged? This is why the demonstrated ability to pay rent is the best gauge. It takes personal feelings out of the equation. Would you rather have a neat tenant who pays late every month or a slob who's like an atomic clock when it comes to the rent check? Personally, I'll take the latter every time.

Americans with Disabilities Act

There is one other law that you need to be cognizant of that is related to the issue of discrimination described above, and I want to touch on it before we move on to other matters. This law is called the Americans with Disabilities Act. This is a law that prohibits discrimination based on the disability of the consumer. Basically, you cannot discriminate against a person who is handicapped. The ADA, as it is called, is a federal law that is not *per se* aimed at the single-unit owner who wants to lease his or her property, although it could theoretically apply. However, many states have enacted state Americans with Disabilities Acts that specifically affect the single-unit landlord. Florida, for example, requires that landlords, regardless of how few or many properties they own, make reasonable accommodations when it is practicable to do so that would afford a handicapped prospective tenant access to a property offered for lease.

You needn't be too nervous about these issues. Remember that the time to consider all of this is before you meet the prospective tenants. If you are well prepared, you should be fine.

Let's return to some more common types of situations and introduce new legal jargon that you may need to know. We are now going to discuss "joint and several liability." In discussing this concept, you will also see how discrimination may become a factor.

Joint and Several Liability

As the term implies, joint and several liability involves situations where more than one person is a party to a side of the transaction. In this case, let us propose that a couple responds to your advertisement and wishes to lease your property. They are going to split the rent and live together as roommates. Who is going to be a signatory to the lease? The answer is, both of them. You want both parties to be responsible, both as a group and each individually, for the whole amount of the rent, hence the term "joint and several."

A common situation with roommates is that after a few months they fight, one gets married, or one runs into financial trouble and moves out. The remaining tenant, who cannot carry the rent on his or her own, asks for time to pay it or find another roommate. That is your choice, but the answer should be "no" to any rent delays. If the roommate can find a substitute, it is up to you, not the tenant, to approve any change in the lease and any new tenant. Please recall our discussion of subletting earlier in this chapter.

If the tenant finds a new roommate, he or she must be subject to a complete credit check and be added to the lease at your discretion. If the new roommate checks out, there is probably no reason not to continue with the lease. Do you remove the "offending" tenant's name? Theoretically, you don't actually have to, but if a new tenant replaces the party who left, most states would not allow you to "stack" your damages if you ever tried to collect from the former tenant. Legal theory aside, in the real world, the roommate who breaches the contract is generally gone and out of the picture.

In cases where the roommates approach you as the landlord and request a substitution of one of the parties, if the new roommate meets your qualifications, you should do a formal substitution of parties as an addendum to the lease. Don't worry! I'll teach you how to do that later. For now, a few more points on joint and several liability and its relationship to our earlier discussion on discrimination. Let's look at the issue of husbands and wives.

A husband and wife (or, where permitted by law, same-sex spouses) are basically roommates with a secular and, in most cases, religious document legally sanctioning the union from a secular legal as well as a moral or religious foundation. Thus, a formal marriage creates certain secular legal rights in the union as well as the ecumenical or religious sanctioning of cohabitation (i.e., sex). This is a very delicate issue from a variety of viewpoints. However, I believe it would be wrong to avoid the issue simply because it's controversial, as some of the readers of this book may encounter this issue. Also, recall that the purpose of this chapter is to highlight and discuss items that you, the landlord, should consider before you lease your property. You may wish to review our earlier discussion on discrimination before reading on. So here's the scenario:

A young couple of legal age answers your ad to lease your house. Clearly they are living together but are unmarried. You, the landlord, are a clergyman or a person with strong religious beliefs and do not want unmarried people living in your house. Can you turn them away?

a. Yes, because they are living in sin.

b. Yes, if you believe that it is morally wrong and they are not otherwise members of a protected class.

c. No; business is business, and your religious beliefs should not be a factor.

d. Yes, but if you do lease your property to them, be sure that both parties sign the lease.

e. Yes, if you can demonstrate that your sole consideration in turning them down is based on your personal beliefs and that such beliefs are nondiscriminatory in nature.

What do you think the *best* answer is? My answer would be choice *e*. I believe this to be the best of the choices provided. Let's analyze them.

Choice *a* is too general a response. Landlord-tenant decisions are based on secular law. Since premarital sex is not illegal between consenting adults, there is no secular legal basis for turning them down "purely" (no pun intended) on the basis that they are unmarried. Choice *b* is a good answer and one that we should consider. Choice *c* is not technically correct, because, as we shall see, you may be able to turn them down. Choice *d* is correct but doesn't factor in the issue of protected classes. Choice *e* is the *best* answer because it is the most complete. Regardless of what the technical legal rules are with regard to discrimination, you really want to avoid an appearance of an impropriety. You need good tenants and not problems. If you are going to deny parties the right to lease your unit, you need to be able to show that you had a lawful, nondiscriminatory reason for turning prospective tenants away.

Let's change the scenario just a bit. What if the couple is married but wants to smoke marijuana in your house? What if they claim it is part of their religion or for medicinal purposes? The first question is easy. If it's illegal, you can deny their request without any further consideration. Part of the lease stipulates that the tenant shall obey the law. If they claim it is part of their religion, it has to be a *bona fide* religion that is recognized and accepted under state or perhaps federal law. The same applies for use of marijuana for medical purposes.

Returning to the example, what if a nonmarried interracial couple wants to lease your unit? The fact is, you had better be able to prove that the reason you are turning them down is based on your personal belief that unmarried couples, *irrespective of race*, should not be living together. If it is because you don't approve of interracial couples, married or not, that is racial discrimination. If you run into these situations and you have a doubt, it is best to consult with a local attorney. As I indicated earlier, as a landlord you should be in the business of leasing property. Keep it on a business level and you will be legally safe and profitable. Now, let's return to joint and several liability.

Let us suppose that a married couple wishes to rent your house. Both have good jobs, and there is every indication that they can pay the rent. The husband says, "There are *issues* with my wife's credit (or vice versa); just put the lease in my name." That is a red flag. I would still insist on placing both parties on the lease (if you decide to lease to them) because both parties are going to live in the unit. The rule of thumb is, whoever is living in the unit, who is of legal age, should be on the lease and be held jointly and severally liable for the rent irrespective of marital status. After all, what if there is a divorce during the term of the lease? Why should you, the landlord, suffer? In addition, you may also wish to place a third party with good credit, not living in the property, on the lease as a guarantor, if necessary. We will talk more about this issue when we discuss credit checks in the next chapter.

Right of First Refusal vs. Lease Option

What if the tenant says, "Look, I really want to buy a house and I like yours, but I'm not ready to make a commitment yet. I want to live in it first to see if I like the house and the area." You are interested in possibly selling the house and wish to consider this. How do you deal with it? There are two concepts that govern this type of transaction; each has its own set of rules and must be specifically delineated in the lease. The first is the *right of first refusal*, and the second is the *option to purchase*. Most people confuse these two concepts. Make sure you don't. We will start with the right of first refusal.

Right of First Refusal

The right of first refusal means that before you can finalize a contract to sell your property to a third party, you must inform the tenant that you have a contract offer for purchase and give the tenant the opportunity to make the purchase at the same price and terms. An offer of first refusal must be clearly spelled out in the lease agreement. The two key issues in the right of first refusal are:

1. The amount of time the tenant has to consider whether he or she wants to make the purchase

2. The tenant does not need to pay "added consideration" to the landlord for the right of first refusal.

In plain English, the tenant does not have to pay extra to have the right of first refusal in the lease, although there is nothing to prevent you from negotiating it into the lease.

If the lease is silent on the time element, the tenant has a "reasonable time," usually about two weeks, to make a decision. However, you would want to stipulate a much shorter time, about 48 hours at best. Any longer and you run the risk of losing your purchaser.

Lease Option or Option to Purchase

An option to purchase, also known as a lease option, differs from a right of first refusal in that it does *legally* require "added consideration" to be a valid option. In an option contract, the landlord and the tenant agree on a purchase price, a time for execution of the option, and any other terms that may be relevant, such as credit for monies already paid as rent. At the stipulated time, the tenant has the right to exercise the option at the negotiated price and terms. However, if the tenant elects not to exercise the option, the money paid to the landlord for the right to the option is lost. Option money can be as little as "$10 and other good and valuable consideration" but should really be a significant sum of money. "Good and valuable consideration" is merely a legal term that refers to whatever else in the contract is the subject of the sale besides the stated sum of money. The phrase often appears in legal documents, and I put it in so that you will recognize it. But what you need to be concerned with here is the actual amount of the option money. For example, if you are granting a purchase option on $150,000, the option money should be between $7,500 and $15,000 or 5 to 10 percent of the agreed-on purchase price. In this way, you know you have a serious purchaser. Even real estate agents often confuse these concepts. In our sample lease, we include option language as well as a right of first refusal clause, should you need them.

Payments in Advance (Bulk Sums)

There are two final points that I would like to discuss with you before we move on to the next chapter and the issue of credit and background investigations. Staying with the original scenario at the onset of the chapter, let us suppose that a prospective tenant answers your ad and agrees to lease your unit for one year. His offer is this:

1. "I'll take the house. I like that you can hunt and fish and my kids can skate in the winter, and my wife is an avid skier. Tell you what, give me the house for $1,300 per month and I'll pay you six months' cash in advance plus your security deposit."

2. The second request goes something like this: "One other thing, Mr. Landlord, aside from paying in advance, I would like to lease the house under my corporate name—tax reasons, you know—no problem, right?"

What do you think? Is this a good deal? Should you accept? In my experience, the answer is "no." Let's analyze each separate request, starting with the payment of six months' rent in advance.

Receiving bulk sums of money is tempting. You get a large chunk of money up front. I would recommend resisting this temptation, however. Although you should always consider the present value of money, it depends on how badly you need a large sum of money up front. By accepting this offer, you are paying a premium of $200 per month for the privilege. If the property could indeed command the $1,500 per month and the market were robust, you might not wish to do so. However, what you need to be concerned about here is the intent of the tenant to actually complete the lease. It has been our experience that people who want to pay in advance sometimes do so with the intent of breaching the lease at the end of the prepaid period. Legally, there is absolutely no basis for this, but psychologically, many tenants think that they somehow are justified in breaching where a prepayment of rent is involved.

Furthermore, even if the tenant merely paid in advance for the sake of convenience, why should you grant a premium unless you need the money? In our example, you have some clues. The tenant has lots of cash, which most people will not encounter, and he has stated that your home is good because of its proximity to certain sports. It is likely that the family plans to engage in winter sports and maybe get early hunting and fishing in when the season opens. If this can all be accomplished in six months, it is a pretty good bet that they plan to cut and run at the end of the six-month period with a discount on the rent.

Also, in prepayment cases, that last month's rent tends to be forgotten. We'll talk about why getting the last month's rent is significant in our discussion of security deposits. Let's say you turn down the six-month advance payment. What is to prevent the tenant from breaching at the six-month period anyway? The answer from a legal standpoint is, absolutely nothing. If the tenant is going to breach the lease, he or she will breach it either way. But at least you didn't give the tenant a $200 per month discount for six months. Remember that we already established that seasonal tenancies command a higher rental price than long-term tenancies do, so in this case, if the tenant breaches in six months, you are getting doubly cheated.

Psychologically, most prospective tenants are pretty straightforward when it comes to paying rent. You agree on a price and terms, and the norm is that the agreed-on sum will be paid monthly for the term of the lease. I'm always suspicious of fancy deals, and you should be as well. In a short-term or seasonal rental, where six months is the term of the lease, you will want all of the rent money in advance. In the case of the short-term rental, where you know the tenant is strictly seasonal, it is obviously safer to get the money up front. But the tenant doesn't get to pay less for that privilege. The tenants' privilege is the fact that they can have a short-term rental. Seasonal tenants pay for that right. They don't get credit for it.

The Corporate Identity

The next scenario involves the use of a corporate identity. The conversation generally goes something like this:

"Look, Mr. Landlord, I like the apartment and I'm going to take it, but I need to put the lease under my corporation—tax reasons, you know."

You nod your head sagely and make humming noises in agreement, as if you really understand what he or she is talking about. After all, it's tax reasons. It must be all right.

Maybe it is. If the tenant has a legitimate business reason to lease a house in your area and can write it off his or her taxes, fine. But that is not your concern. Your concern is getting paid. One of the benefits of a corporation is liability protection for its officers. Remember what I said earlier. If you are of age and you are living in the unit, your name has to be on the lease. When banks and credit card companies issue corporate credit cards, you as an employee sign that you will be personally liable for the card as well as the corporation. If you are accepting a corporate entity as a tenant, why shouldn't the same protection be afforded to you? It is if you spot the issue and make sure that you have the tenant sign as a personal guarantor. The corporation would be the legal entity that is officially (and legally, for tax purposes) leasing the unit, but the tenant himself or herself would be personally liable on the lease in case the corporate entity defaults.

The other aspect of leasing to corporations is that a corporate property may be just that, a property used for corporate employees. True, your lease states that the property will not be occupied by more than "x" number of people (let's say x = 2). However, if the lease is in a corporate name, there is no presumption that the two people are the *same* two people. Once again, do you want your property used as a hotel or a timeshare? If all that is disclosed up front and there is no objection by the building management (since the use would not be, strictly speaking, residential use), maybe you don't mind. However, the level of care in these types of uses is generally minimal and, in the long run, they may not be a good deal for a landlord. Thus, when faced with the corporate client, you need to look carefully at these issues. If the client is willing to pay for the privilege and there are no other objections, maybe it is a good deal. If you understand the issues, you can effectively negotiate.

A different twist to the corporate use situation is where you get a response from what is commonly known as a "relo" office. "Relo" is short for "relocation." Big corporations have these offices to help employees who are transferred from one area of the country to another. Great, you think, I'm contracting with Mammoth Giant Corporation, so there can't be a problem. Wrong! You are contracting with whoever rents the unit. Mammoth Giant Corporation is simply acting as a leasing agent. Consequently, you need to take all the steps outlined above in consideration of this tenancy. The only difference is that if the tenant creates a problem, you can threaten to call the relocation agent at Mammoth Giant Corporation because the employee will probably not want the situation reported to his or her employer.

Spotting the Issues

In this chapter, you have been presented with a great many concepts and information. Some of those concepts can be books in and of themselves. The key is not to know everything about landlord-tenant relations in one chapter, but to be able to spot issues that arise during the process. I can't tell you how many times I've heard the same questions and engaged in the same dialogue with various tenants. During your career as a landlord, you will anticipate and know what the tenants are going to propose before they finish their thoughts. For the novice, just being able to spot the issue puts you way ahead of the game. Generally, you will not get all the problems presented in this chapter from one tenant, but at least one or two issues discussed above will arise, and you will be prepared. Spotting the issues and knowing what questions to ask is 95 percent of the battle and will save you time and money if you have to consult an attorney or other professional on a legal or other point of controversy.

You are now ready to advertise for your tenant. You place your ad and wait for the results. A few days pass, and the phone rings. It is a prospect. A husband and wife want to see your house. You are ready to go. In the next chapter, we discuss what to do if the prospects like your unit and are prepared to sign a lease. Don't worry—you are going to be well prepared.

CHAPTER 4

Prelude to the Lease

Checking the Prospective Tenant (Legally)

This is the moment you have been waiting for; a tenant is ready and willing to lease your property. But is he able? How do you find out? This is the topic of discussion in this chapter. How do you legally investigate the background of the person or persons who are going to occupy your unit?

The first and most important rule in checking your tenant is the old saying "don't judge a book by its cover." In our years in the real estate business, some of the most elegant people we have ever encountered turned out to be the biggest deadbeats and vice versa. We have also had some really woebegone-looking people who paid on time month after month, and when they finally moved on, left the unit in better shape than it was when they received it.

Conversely, I recall an incident when our business card found its way to a young fellow living in a beautiful condominium in Miami. The person contacted us, and several days later, my wife and I presented ourselves at his unit. We were instructed by an unidentified individual to wait in the living room, and we were further advised that our host would join us shortly. On the coffee table were several yachting magazines, which you might expect to find in the homes of very wealthy people or those aspiring to seem so, or in medical offices that have these magazines in the waiting room. Several minutes later, the young fellow made his appearance. The unidentified friend strategically disappeared into the kitchen, whereupon the young man explained that he wished to move to a larger unit on the beach but required access to docking for his boat. Hence, the yachting magazines. We told him we could get him such a rental without any problem. We asked what he wished to pay for rent, and he responded that money was no object and that he was in fact the nephew of one of the world's wealthiest men. He then proceeded to show us the yacht he was buying. Naturally, it was on the cover of one of the magazines. I can't disclose whom the young man was related to, but you may be sure it was a well-known celebrity. In any event, we told him we would show him several units and agreed to call him at the end of the week with a list of suitable residences.

On the way out, we stopped by the front desk, where a friend of ours was the concierge. "You went to see so-and-so?" he asked. "Good luck working for him—he's being evicted for nonpayment of rent, and I know several other lawyers are looking for him also. If you don't believe me, check with the last broker who dealt with him." We did, and it was true. "You mean he's a fraud?" we asked the broker in shock. "No, no," she replied, "he's the real thing; he just doesn't pay his bills."

Do you want to rent to this guy? Of course not! It doesn't matter who he is or who his uncle is or how much money the family has. If none of it is going to you, who cares about his background? So what is the first thing you do after the prospective tenant agrees that he wants to lease your unit? Very simple; you go over the terms you desire, and if the prospect agrees to those terms, you present a questionnaire to fill out, along with a consent form to allow you to perform a credit and background check on anyone who is planning to occupy the unit. If it is two people, each should get the forms.

Questionnaire

What questions do you need to have answered? The first and most important thing you want to know is the prospects' histories as tenants. Were there any problems with them in the past? So the form is going to ask for the names and addresses of the last three places they resided in. Three should be enough. You will need the addresses, the names, and the phone numbers of the respective landlords or management companies. If they were homeowners, you need to know that as well, because you may need to focus your investigation on other aspects of their histories.

You also need to find out about their financial background. You should know how they manage their money. To do this, you need information about at least one bank account. So your form will ask for the financial institution with which they do their banking and their checking account number.

Other things you need to know are car registrations and criminal records. Were they ever convicted of a crime or served time in prison? Granted, these are highly personal questions, but then again, these people are going to be living in you home. Where do they work? Certainly you would want to know what they do for a living.

What is the address and phone number of their employers, and who are their supervisors? All of these are relevant questions if you are going to trust a total stranger to live in your property and pay you rent. To get this information, you are going to need their Social Security numbers. You will also need the Social Security numbers to run a credit check on the party or parties.

A quick trip to the phone book will reveal various agencies that perform land-lord-tenant background checks. They will give you forms for your prospective tenants to complete, and the background check usually takes a week or two to complete. This cost is usually passed on to the tenant. If you own a condominium, the management will often do the background check for you through its investigative agency. If you are a condominium owner, you should check with the building manager, and he or she will explain the association's procedures in this regard.

Is this search legal? Sure it is, if the prospective tenant agrees. That is why you have the prospect sign various consent forms that accompany the request for information. You really shouldn't have too much trouble in this regard, as most people who are used to renting are accustomed to these background and credit checks. However, if prospects do complain or otherwise balk at filling out the forms, calmly tell them that it is a condition that must precede their signing the lease, and it is not negotiable. If they refuse, then you are under no obligation to proceed with the transaction, and you should move on to the next prospect.

What Are You Looking For?

What are some of the signs of a good application? A quick review of the application will indicate if the prospect has lived in several homes over a short period of time or was relatively stable. The work history should also be a clue to his or her stability. Did the prospective tenant hold many jobs over a short period of time or just one or two? Does the person work for a corporation, or is he or she self-employed? Self-employed people are a bit harder to check because there is literally no supervisor to call. However, as you have no doubt guessed, the most important factor in the background check is the prospect's credit. That is still the most telling factor about how people conduct their financial lives and is the best indication of how much of a risk that person is to do business with. For those who don't know exactly how a credit check works, I'll discuss it now.

Credit Check

Most people have had their credit checked at one time or another. When you apply for a credit card, finance your home, or buy or lease a car, a credit check is performed. To be sure, if you ever leased an apartment yourself, a credit check was performed on you. Some banks are now running credit checks on prospective clients prior to allowing them to open an account with the bank. If they do it for their business, so should you as a landlord. There are basically several major credit bureaus whose business it is to maintain credit histories on individuals. These bureaus are also known as consumer reporting agencies. Equifax, Experian (which was formerly TRW), and Trans Union are the three big agencies. I have provided contact information for these agencies in the Action of Lease Application response letter, which you will find in Appendix C. When you send in the consent form and the party's name and Social Security number (and the required fee), the reporting bureau will issue a report on the individual with a detailed report on his or her financial history. This includes the person's outstanding loans, credit cards, payment histories, and an overall score. The score reflects the person's relative standing. A higher score indicates a better credit rating. However, these reports may also include information concerning criminal convictions, lawsuits, and other outstanding judgments.

The most important aspect of a person's credit score is usually the payment history, followed by the amount of outstanding debt the person carries. Banks look very carefully at this when they are considering granting a loan to an individual, and that is what you, as a landlord, should consider as well. If the credit report shows a history of late payments or, worse, defaults, there is no reason to believe that you, as a creditor, will be treated any differently. In addition, if the applicant has a high amount of debt, his or her income to debt ratio may not allow the applicant to become further leveraged. In this case, that would be the monthly debt to you in the form of rent. The reporting company takes these and the other aspects of a person's credit history and calculates a score.

There are many different types of scores, but one that is commonly used in real estate transactions is known as the *Fair, Isaac & Company* score (FICO). These scores range from a low of 400 to a high of 900, with a score in the high 600s being desirable. With Internet online access to credit histories, it is relatively easy to obtain a person's credit report as long as you have the required information and his or her consent. The problem is that these reports are often complicated with various codes, which are not always easy to interpret. In addition, the Federal Fair Credit Reporting Act (FCRA), which governs credit reports, has numerous laws to protect the privacy rights of individuals.

For example, if you were to deny a party a lease based on poor credit, you would technically have to give, in writing, the name, address, and telephone number of the reporting agency that provided the report on which you based your decision. This gives the applicant the right to dispute findings in his or her report with the reporting agency. Therefore, it is easier to find an agency that professionally conducts these searches to represent you, and it will advise you on an applicant's history as it specifically applies to leases. Most of these investigative agencies will not tell you what to do with regard to granting or denying an application. That is your decision as the landlord. However, a good agency will discuss specific aspects of the applicant's history so that you will be able to make an informed decision. I provide a sample letter for you in Appendix C, Authorization to Release Records, to send to an applicant in case you are forced to deny a person a lease based on his or her credit report.

Why is it so important to go to the trouble of doing a credit check? Let me give you a couple of "war" stories. These are two of my favorite scenarios because they happen more often than you think. The first I call the "Cool Car Client" and the second the "Old Smitten Story."

The Cool Car

The Cool Car Client is someone who drives a really nice car and tries to use it as credentials for his creditworthiness in lieu of a more formal credit check. We know a landlord based in New York who needed help in leasing his condominium unit in Florida. Apparently, he had placed an advertisement in the newspaper in New York, and someone responded. Since the landlord could not come from New York to Florida and admitted he really didn't know what to do anyway, he asked for our help. "Fine," we responded. "The first thing we do is run a credit check, and then if everything is okay, we'll write a lease."

"Look, Ken," he said, "do we have to complicate this deal? My unit has been empty for months now, and I don't want to lose these people. Besides, the guy drives a really nice Mercedes."

You get the idea. The landlord assumes that because the prospect drives a luxury automobile, he or she must be rich, and if the prospect is rich, he or she will pay the rent. We have already seen that there is no basis for the latter two-thirds of that argument. Let's consider the first part, that the prospect drives a nice car. So what? First of all, how do you know that the person owns the car? It could belong to a friend, it could be a lease, or it could even be stolen. It could also be 95 percent financed. A credit check will probably let you know the status of the car. This should be obvious, yet I hear this from so many clients. Forget about what kind of car a person drives. It's how they pay their bills that counts.

The Old Smitten Story

The second scenario is the Old Smitten Story. This is one of my favorite stories because it is one of the few instances in my twenty-two years of marriage and business partnership with my wife that I could say, "I told you so." We leased a unit to a really sweet lady. She was middle-aged, soft-spoken, and claimed to work with underprivileged children. She drove a "nice car" and was just dotty enough to be charming. She had a very pleasant, almost hypnotic voice and was attractive in a motherly sort of way. I don't know why, but for some reason every instinct I had told me she was a phony.

Our client strongly disagreed with me. "This is a saint," he said. "If you don't want to handle this case, I'll get another broker." My wife, who is usually more suspicious than I am, took the client's part. "You lawyers are all alike, you don't trust anyone. If everyone were like this woman, the world would be a much better place." It sounded like she was about to erupt into a chorus of some song from the 1970s. I remained unconvinced, especially as I learned the sainted lady had bounced a check for the $100 application fee that the condominium charged for a credit check. This was not a good sign. But she calmly explained that she was switching accounts and the bank must have made a mistake. Also, it was her sister's account, and her sister was always overdrawn. Of course, both my wife and my client agreed that this was logical.

"But look at the check," I pleaded. "The name on the check, the signature on the check, and the signature on the application are different. Doesn't that strike anyone as being a teensy bit odd?"

My wife not so calmly reiterated, as if talking to a moron, that it was the sister's account and they signed each other's names. She also made it clear that she did not appreciate having to explain this to me twice. "You just don't like her, and it's not logical. Besides, the client is satisfied and doesn't want to investigate her, and, yes, I did advise him to investigate."

"But the names, the names are all different, she's signing different names, don't you see?" I cried. But they just stared at me. They were mesmerized. A few days later, the security deposit bounced in our escrow, along with a check for the first month's rent. We notified the client, who informed us that he and his wife had dinner with the tenant the other night and that they decided to let her move into the unit without signing a lease. After all, the woman was a saint. On further investigation, we discovered that she had changed the locks on the door and that our passkey didn't work. In addition, we got a call from the locksmith who changed the locks complaining that she had paid for the new locks with a check and that the check had bounced. She referred him to us for payment.

We called the tenant, and she advised us that all matters must be taken up with her lawyer. We called the number she gave us for the lawyer and found the number was disconnected. I checked with the Florida bar, and it had no listing for the name given as her attorney. This was serious, and the landlord was beginning to panic.

Whom had he let into his unit?

Fortunately, the problem resolved itself. The valet from the building called to tell me that he had helped the woman move out and she had paid him with a check that, as you may have guessed, bounced. We later discovered that the car she was driving was stolen as well. Actually, there was a happy ending of sorts. The client stayed out of our business from that time on, and my wife baked my favorite dessert and let me choose the next four movies. It really does pay to be right.

The Moral of the Story

The moral of the story is that it really doesn't matter what kind of car a person drives, how sweet the person looks, or any other concocted story he or she comes up with. What is important is what the credit history shows. Sometimes, a tenant will admit to having bad credit and ask you to make an exception. Case in point. Several years ago, my wife and I were going to rent one of our condominium units that we had purchased for investment purposes. It hadn't been empty very long, but we were still anxious to lease the unit as quickly as possible.

Our advertising yielded a well-dressed couple who drove up in a new BMW. They looked at the unit, liked what they saw, and offered us the price we were asking without much negotiation. When we told them we would have to run a credit check, they admitted that they had bad credit due to several investments that hadn't turned out well. However, they indicated that they were back on their feet, as evidenced by their new automobile, and were certainly in a position to carry the rent. We told them that we would have to run the credit check nonetheless, and they consented.

Their report was about what they had predicted. It showed that during the time they indicated they were having financial problems, their credit cards went unpaid and were charged off, and they did have a bankruptcy. The BMW was financed, but payments were made on time. We advised the tenants that although they seemed very nice people, we really could not rent to them based on their credit history and followed it up with the required letter, which I will discuss in detail later in this chapter. The husband called back and countered by stating that he understood our position, but that bankruptcy was a business decision. In his case, it did not really reflect their true economic position. We countered by pointing out that such an argument may be true if you are talking about a major airline that needs time to reorganize, but in the case of individuals, bankruptcy usually means that there is no money to pay debts, and that is a bad thing. They persisted, and we finally stated that we would lease our unit to them if they found a guarantor, a third party with good credit who would be jointly and severally liable. The tenants concurred, and the husband's brother, who had excellent credit and an impeccable background, agreed to be added to the lease. As it turned out, this was a good thing because it was this brother who had to pay the last four months of the lease, as the couple disappeared one night, never to be heard from again.

Let's try a multiple-choice question. An applicant tells you he has bad credit but wants to lease your property for one year. Because of his credit problems, he will pay you six months in advance plus security. Which is the *best* answer?

a. Lease the property because he is paying in advance.

b. Lease the property but run a credit check anyway.

c. Don't lease the property.

d. Require the full year's rent plus security and run the credit check.

If you chose *d*, you would be right. That is the best answer. Answer *a* gives you six months rent and no further guarantees. Answer *b* is good, but you already know he is going to have bad credit, and so the result is the same as answer *a*. Answer *c* is a good answer but not necessarily the best answer, because there still may be a way to lease the property. Answer *d* is the best answer because it fully covers you. If the applicant can give you the entire year's rent in advance, you are covered in terms of the rent. You would still run the credit check to determine if there is any other relevant background information, such as a criminal history, that you may require in making your decision. I have already noted that where a criminal history is uncovered, you may be wise to talk to a local attorney to ascertain what the rules are in this regard. However, there is one specific law that we should discuss, which is known as Megan's Law.

Megan's Law

Megan's law is a federal law that requires law enforcement agencies to maintain and disclose the addresses of convicted sex offenders. The law was passed after Megan Kanka, a seven-year-old, was killed by a convicted sex offender who had lived across the street from her and her family. The family did not know the individual had a criminal record. Unfortunately, the law is a bit complicated in terms of disclosure. If you, as the landlord, fail to disclose to your tenant that there is a convicted sex offender in the community, you could potentially be liable to the tenant for failure to do so if his or her child is injured or killed by that person. The tenant might have to prove that you knew or should have known of this person's background, which may be a difficult hurdle to overcome, but you don't want be placed in a position of having to defend such an action.

If you lease your property to a convicted sex offender, you could be liable to other families in the community if their children are injured or killed. For that reason alone, there should be no hesitation about conducting a credit check on an applicant.

The best way to handle this situation is to provide a disclosure statement advising tenants about Megan's Law and suggesting that if they are interested, they should contact the local law enforcement agency to find out if any sexual predators or sex offenders live in the community. In that way, the onus of investigating the issue is transferred to the tenant. Such a disclosure is provided in the sample lease at the end of this book (Appendix B). Obviously, if you discover that your prospective tenant falls under the Megan's Law category, you would be within your rights to reject the person as a tenant.

Renting Is a Business

As I've argued consistently in this book, when you become a landlord, be it for one property or a dozen, you are in business, and you need to conduct your affairs in a businesslike manner. In fact, you have done nothing more than any other business does in conducting its affairs. If you shop at a department store and it offers you a discount on goods purchased if you obtain a store credit card, the store will run a credit check on you prior to issuing the card. You consent to this when you agree to accept the card. You probably don't even think about it. Actually, you should, because as a consumer, each time you allow your credit to be checked, it lowers your overall credit score, but that is another story.

We are here to discuss being a landlord. What are you doing that is so different? You are inviting someone to live in your home, and you need to protect yourself. The only difference is that now it is you who are doing the investigating, and that may be somewhat unsettling. But rest assured that people are used to credit checks, and it won't have a chilling effect on your ability to lease the property. Quite the contrary; if a person objects to a credit check, that is a red flag that you should move on to the next applicant. Remember that the leasing of property is based on the laws of supply and demand. It is a function of the market.

South Florida, where we are based, had gone through a period where the normally robust rental market was weaker than normal. There were several reasons for the weakness. The first was that interest rates were very low, and so it was an opportune moment to buy a property and finance the purchase rather than pay rent, which yields no equity. Add to that the fact that South Florida has a condominium market where purchasers are generally part-time residents or specifically make the purchase as an investment for rental purposes, and so there was competition for the available supply of tenants. But as we indicated earlier, it only means that you as the landlord have to make a reasonable decision as to rental amount. At a given price, everything will sell or, in this case, rent. It depends on what you are willing to accept. However, once you accept the "market value" for your property as a rental, there is no reason to otherwise lower your standards in terms of choosing a tenant. Desperation should never factor into your equation as a landlord, or you will just make matters worse by getting a bad tenant. In the end, that will be a major loss to you in time, damages, and possible legal fees. It all translates into money.

The other point is that running a credit check is not complicated once you have gone through the process. The applicant merely fills out some forms that he or she has probably filled out many times before, and you pay a nominal sum to a rental research agency to run the check. The fact is that most of your applicants won't be master criminals and will have decent credit. You have taken the wise and precautionary steps in a businesslike fashion. But it is not over yet. There is still some research you need to do before you can proceed to rent the property, and the investigative agency generally handles this for you as part of its check. I am referring to calling prior landlords and references.

Getting References

I know you are wondering why the background check isn't enough. Sometimes a person can have excellent credit and still be a pain in the butt, and that may factor into your decision to lease to the applicant. I recall a case where the tenants had excellent credit. They paid every bill on time, all the time. They were never late on any payment, and their credit score was through the roof. They had enough credit to lease all of Florida, not just an apartment in Miami, but the whole state. The landlord was ecstatic, and I, as a fellow landlord, was just a little jealous. Unfortunately, the story didn't end there.

In response to the reference section of the application, we received a response from the applicant's boss indicating that he was a first-rate executive who hadn't missed a workday in five years of employment and always met his sales projections. "Let's sign him up, what's the delay?" the landlord kept screaming. "Well," we said, "the report indicates that the management company of the last building the applicant lived in was not overly enthusiastic about the tenant but was reluctant to cooperate with the investigator." "So what?" asked the landlord impatiently. "You once told me that most of these references never say anything bad because they are afraid of being sued." That's true, and I hate it when a client throws back my own wisdom at me. "But you can damn with faint praise too and you can't be sued for it," I replied. The investigator suspected there was more to this story.

I called the prior landlord and after a brief discussion discovered that the tenant did in fact pay his rent on time, but to the clerk of the Court's Registry, because he had sued the management company of the building. The case was later settled out of court. No details of the settlement were forthcoming. I then called the second referenced landlord, who recalled the tenant and, with a little more coaxing, offered that although the tenant did pay on time, he was constantly complaining and literally drove the landlord to distraction. It got so bad that the landlord elected not to renew the lease.

"But he pays his rent," the landlord continued to argue. "Can't we work this out?" We called in the applicant and told him what we had discovered. He told us his side of the story, which, quite frankly, was unconvincing. Basically, his argument amounted to the fact that he was paying top dollar on time like an atomic clock, each and every month. For that consideration, he demanded that the landlord provide service to the letter of the lease based on the tenant's interpretation of that document. Any perceived deviation, no matter how slight, would not be tolerated.

Sounds convincing on the surface. But is it really? The applicant argues that because he pays on time, he is entitled to strictly enforce the terms of the lease and takes the high moral ground at the onset. He is also establishing himself in a leadership role. However, his argument is totally without merit, because paying on time is what he is legally supposed to do. You don't get extra points for performing your part of a bargain.

Criminal attorneys often use this type of argument. "Your honor, members of the jury, my client has always obeyed the law and been a good citizen; this is his first double homicide." A variation of this argument goes like this: "Your honor, members of the jury, my client always did a good job at work; this is the first time be embezzled 11 trillion dollars." The argument sounds good but is based on a false premise. It is our duty to be good citizens and obey the law. When we hire an employee; it is presumed that he or she will do a good job. Nobody hires an employee to do substandard work. It does not mitigate the crime that you previously did something you were supposed to do in the first place.

The second part of the argument is equally without merit. The applicant states that he is entitled to strict enforcement of the lease. Strict enforcement as opposed to what, sloppy enforcement? A lease is a contract, and its terms should be as clear as possible; each side has a duty to follow its terms. If the lease is fundamentally complete, most issues, such as which party pays for what expenses, should be clear. We advised the applicant that the landlord was willing to lease the property to the applicant, according to the terms of the lease that we were prepared to go over in as great a detail as necessary. Basically, the landlord was willing to lease the property to the applicant in an "as is" condition, and the tenant was to be responsible for all repairs and maintenance. In addition, we crafted a lease with five pages of addendums that literally dealt with every issue we could find that the tenant previously had engaged in with his prior landlords. We didn't flinch. The applicant had a simple choice: Accept the terms and behave or find another property. We knew very well that the landlord had reluctantly consented to this tactic, and if it failed, we would have been fired. We also knew the applicant liked the unit and wanted to lease it.

The applicant responded, "I'm not going to sign this lease; this is an outrage. It's discrimination; I'm calling my lawyer. I'll have your licenses for this." My wife stood up and told him to do whatever he felt he had to, and we were preparing to walk out when we noticed that the applicant's wife gave him what had to be an extremely painful elbow shot in the ribs. "Oh, for pity's sake, sign the damn thing; you are not going to put me through another crazy lease. I want some peace. If you don't rent this, you're going to buy me a condominium, and not some cheap one either." After a brief negotiation on some of the finer points of the lease, they signed it for the next three years, and the landlord had excellent tenants who finally bought the unit.

Was it discrimination? No, it was not, for this basic reason: While it was true the couple were getting a lease that was more complex than those offered to other tenants, it was not based on race, creed, color, national origin, religion, sex, age, infirmity, or any other protected class of individuals. It was based on a well-founded belief (documented by several very complete memorandums for record in our files indicating our conversations with the prior landlords) that this was a litigious and difficult tenant. It was within the landlord's rights to protect his interests and clarify his position vis-à-vis the rental. Were we scared? You can rest assured that we were. But we were convinced that it would have been worse if we hadn't zealously represented our client. As the landlord, you are your own client, and you need to zealously represent yourself.

Other Background Checks

Another variation on a background check could arise where the prospective tenant literally has no credit. This is not all that unusual in many parts of the United States, where new immigrants arriving in this country tend to settle. In other cases, a person may have had his or her credit "cleaned up" and now is in the process of establishing new credit. Others, weary of the problems associated with credit cards and debt status, simply pay cash (or use a debit card) and thus have no credit history. A lack of credit is not *per se* an indication that you should not lease your property to the prospective tenant. It just means that you must be more thorough in your investigation. We have already discussed some of the other clues that can be of help. For example, here is a situation where automobile ownership could be a factor. Does the tenant own his car? Has he leased property before?

In some nations, such as Canada, which maintains close telecommunication ties with the United States, these issues can be checked. If the client is from Europe, it may be more difficult. What about a bank reference? No matter where the tenant comes from, unless he or she keeps the cash under the proverbial mattress, you are going to at least have a checking account to investigate. The next issue we need to discuss is what happens when you get the report back.

Confidentiality

The first thing we need to stress is that these reports are strictly confidential. Don't sit around the bar or the local restaurant and discuss these things with your friends. "Gosh, Mary, you should have seen the credit report on this guy; he actually charged a tummy tuck to his credit card." This is highly improper and can get you into serious legal problems if the prospect ever finds out. Similarly, don't show these reports to anyone or pass them around. Place them in a file where they should remain during the course of the lease. Be sure the file is secure. After the tenant moves out and the file is closed out, you are best advised to destroy them.

Although we touched on this subject earlier, it bears repeating. With the current wave of identity theft crimes, many prospects may be reluctant to hand out their Social Security numbers. The law does not require anyone to provide his or her Social Security number. Conversely, you have the right not to do business with that person if he or she doesn't provide the information. By assuring your prospects that you understand the law and that you will secure their information properly, you will help to alleviate their anxiety. You may also point out that each time they charge a credit in a restaurant, write a check in a supermarket, or order a product over the phone or via the Internet, they are giving out confidential information to a stranger. The fact that the person works for a company doesn't change the fact that he or she has access to your personal information.

The basic problem is that, fundamentally, our economic society operates on an intellectual dichotomy. In order to do business, we must all to a certain degree operate on trust. We give total strangers our private economic information in order to make purchases, do the most basic banking functions, and even pay our bills. But when it comes to the granting of credit, we operate on distrust. We check and investigate. It is curious that people are willing to give out their personal information over the Internet or through an 800 number in order to purchase a video on improving a golf swing or the latest weight loss fad. However, those same people are equally averse to giving out personal information to secure a loan or a lease. We are all human, and this is just part of human nature.

Television or the Internet lends a type of legitimacy to a product. The fact that it may very well be a fraud doesn't generally occur to people. I recall that I purchased a weight-loss devise through an infomercial. I paid by check (a mistake) and never received the product, although my check was cashed. It was a small amount and not worth the time or effort to pursue, but it bothered me nonetheless. However, a landlord with one unit to rent does not present an air of legitimacy. You're not a major corporation or television personality endorsing some product. You are not a multinational management company that owns rental property all over the world. You are a person, just like the applicant, except that you are asking for some highly personal and confidential information. In reality, whether it is given to a corporate employee, a cashier at the local supermarket, or a landlord, personal information is being given to a stranger. It is the perception of legitimacy that makes the difference.

You can create the perception if you present yourself professionally. We have talked about this from the onset. Have your forms ready, be prepared to discuss why you need the person's Social Security number, and explain that everything is confidential. If you set yourself up to be the same as any other corporate landlord, the fact that you own one or two units, or even just an upstairs bedroom, will give you the air of legitimacy you need. Having done so, if the applicant still refuses to give the information, that may be the red flag that tells you to move on in your search.

As indicated earlier, the desire to get information is part of the adversarial nature of the landlord-tenant relationship, and your ability to get it is also part of your initial role as the leader. Leadership is vital to presenting your air of legitimacy. Here is an example of where this actually worked in reverse, with a result that nobody quite expected, except the applicant.

Several years ago, a landlord we know had an applicant who wanted to purchase an expensive condominium in Miami. The prospect was a partner in a major corporation in Latin America and owned at least twenty cars that the landlord was aware of; the landlord also saw his credit card bills, which indicated that he spent more in a month on his social life than most professionals earn in a year. Unfortunately, he also had absolutely no patience and could not be bothered with such minor details as filling out the required loan questionnaires and agreements or providing the mortgage company with the myriad documents required to verify his wealth.

He kept on saying, "Leave me alone with this nonsense, I'm a millionaire many times over, I can't be bothered with this stuff" (although I'm not sure "stuff" was the exact word he used). He gave three months of credit card statements, indicating that he made the payments, and said that if he didn't get the loan, he would not make the purchase. The landlord was ready to move on, thinking the deal was over, but, lo and behold, the bank approved the loan and the deal went through.

What happened was simply that by force of authority, by setting himself up as the leader, by presenting an air of legitimacy, the prospect was able to convince the bank to forgo its normal procedures. "Of course," you say, "sure, he was rich and could get away with it, but what about the rest of us?" The fact is, the bank or mortgage company did not have any hard information on this fellow except three credit card statements, which, if you analyze it carefully, did not mean a whole lot. It simply indicated that he spent lots of money and the bills were paid. It didn't prove anything about the individual or his capacity to repay a loan on the property. Sheer audacity and not much else consummated this deal. Those in sales know that a fundamental principle of salesmanship is to establish your command of the customer. This is especially true in car sales, where the customer is very defensive and walks in with the comment, "I'm just here to look; I'll get back to you if I see something I like." Haven't you ever said that when you walked into a car dealership? A good salesperson takes command of the situation and the customer so he or she can show the customer the cars and try to make the sale.

Libel and Slander

In situations where you, as the landlord, require a credit check, you have to take command. You need information about your prospective tenant, and by being professional and formal, you should get it if the prospect has nothing to hide. But now, let's return to our discussion of permitted uses of the information you receive on a prospect. We've already noted that the credit report is not a proper subject for gossip. But let's pose a question. What if you get an applicant's credit report and it turns out to be negative? You make your notifications, and the case is closed. Then a problem arises. Your friend Bob calls. Bob is also renting his apartment, and the same prospect you rejected now wants to rent from Bob. Somehow, Bob knows he's been to see you and asks why you didn't rent to him. What do you say? To answer this question, let's talk about the laws of libel and slander.

First, let's define our terms. The essential difference between libel and slander is that *libel* is a written defamation, while *slander* is oral. An easy way to remember the difference is that slander, with an "S," equals spoken, also with an "S." Defamation is the wrongful tarnishing of a person's character or reputation. What you tell Bob will determine whether you have met the elements required of defamation. Since you are conversing with Bob on the phone, any wrongful statement would be a slander. Probably, you recall the legal adage that truth is an absolute defense. Obviously, if you tell Bob that you got the prospective tenant's credit report and he is an absolute deadbeat, and Bob repeats this to the prospect, you may have a serious legal problem.

The Elements of Defamation

Let's look at the elements of defamation. The first element is that the defamation be published. Since you called the prospect a deadbeat on the phone, the law can consider that a publication. Bob is another party, which is the second element, and the remark was directed at the prospect, which is the third element. Those are three elements of the case: publication to another party concerning the defamed party. The fourth element is whether the statement was false. In this case that would be a key issue. Was the prospect really a "deadbeat," or was his credit just not up to par? This can be a crucial question, because the only defense here is the truth of the statement, presumably made without malice. Since Bob will no doubt deny the prospect's application as a result of your conversation, the prospect is injured, which is the last element required for a successful case.

So what do you do when Bob asks the question? You could argue that there is some sort of legitimate business need to discuss someone's credit, but I don't think such a discussion would include calling an applicant a "deadbeat." Use of such language may remove any potential defense to a defamation action that you might have. In any event, you don't want to spend your time and money on an attorney to defend such an action. If Bob calls, tell him that you really can't discuss it and that he has to run his own credit check and draw his own conclusions and let it stand at that. You'll be much better off.

Our society allows investigation of people's past and present to a certain degree as regulated by law. As long as you remain within the law, there is really nothing to worry about. It is when you step outside the law's protection that problems can begin. Actions such as defamation and slander of credit, which is an offshoot of the defamation action, can be tricky and expensive to defend. But the rules that can keep you out of trouble are relatively simple if you follow them.

Confidentiality is the key, along with a brief letter explaining why you are turning the applicant down. If bad credit is the reason, you need to advise the prospect which reporting agency generated the report that you relied on, along with a contact address and phone number where the prospect could receive further information or contest the report. In the form section in Appendix C, Action of Lease Application, I have provided you with a sample letter. In most cases, the applicant already knows his or her credit is bad and will tell you about it up front. If you turn the prospect down, he or she will generally expect it and not complain, but it is prudent in these types of situations to follow the rules carefully.

Surprise Questions

Sometimes, you will get a question straight out of left field that will take you completely by surprise. On occasion, it will be because the issue is so obvious to you that you couldn't imagine anyone not understanding the point, or perhaps you just missed the issue. I'll give you an example of one that caught me by surprise. Nora and I were preparing a lease for a small beachfront condominium we had purchased, and all was going well. The transaction was proceeding, and the tenant, who was paying us one full year in advance, was going out of the country for a few months and would return at the commencement date of the lease. In the course of conversation, he innocently asked if he could put some of his "belongings" in the unit prior to the official commencement term of the lease. This is actually not so unusual in sales of property, but in rental transactions people pretty much understand that you move in with your belongings at the start date of the lease.

We replied that we would have to think it over. After a brief discussion, we agreed that as long as the tenant made the payment in advance, he could put a few things in the unit. Sounds reasonable, right? Usually, these requests have more to them than the requester lets on. In this case, the tenant wanted to put his belongings in the unit right away, as in prior to making any payments and prior to his credit report coming back. As it turned out, he was leaving for Europe on business the following week, and his current lease expired at the same time. Unfortunately, the answer to the tenant was changed to a "qualified yes," subject to certain conditions. The first condition was that prior to any placement of belongings in the unit, a complete inventory of what was going in had to be performed. The second condition was that a waiver of liability for the belongings be added to the lease. A waiver of liability simply means that the tenant agrees that the landlord is not responsible for any damage or loss of the items while they are in the unit. Finally, the advance money *had* to be paid prior to any entrance by the tenant under any circumstances. In this case, the deal seemed pretty firm and the client agreed to pay the money in advance, but normally a landlord is well advised to resist efforts to "occupy" the unit prior to the stated term of the lease. In these situations, you have to make a call, and sometimes it can be wrong!

Think Before You Speak

We have just looked at a situation in which the tenant has asked you a question you may not be prepared to answer. The simple response is, don't answer it. There is no law that says that because a prospect asks you a question, you must give him or her an immediate reply. My father always cautioned me to think before I spoke. If you are not sure what you want to do, merely respond that you will have to get back to him or her on the issue. Just say that you'll let the prospect know. It is much better than giving a quick answer that, on further reflection, you may have to retract later.

The Zen of Landlording

Many of the "how to" books that I have read over the years contained what I like to deem "arcane wisdom." The author, the subject matter notwithstanding, feels it is his or her duty to impart some mystical truths akin to the true meaning of life while teaching you how to tune your car, lose weight, or, yes, rent your property. The fact is that everything we do has some greater lesson, perhaps even some meaning attached to it. So what can I impart to you as the "Zen of Landlording"? I thought about this and came up with "being a landlord is not like a martial arts movie." All right, so it's not Voltaire. If you've ever seen martial arts movies, the plot is not the main attraction in 99 percent of these films. It's the fight scenes. The fluid action, the kicks, punches, jumps, and whatnot. But it's all choreographed. Have you ever watched a kickboxing match on television? The two combatants in the ring basically box and throw a few kicks. That's more or less all there is to it. The opponents are scored on their technique and how well the punch or kick connects with the other fighter. I'm not saying it's easy or not dangerous; in fact, it requires great skill and is very dangerous, but there is no leaping through the air or any other acrobatics. Of course, if you've ever seen a real, nonprofessional street fight, or, worse, been involved in one, it is pretty much a free-for-all, with punches, kicks, and wrestling all rolled into one sloppy affair. Being a landlord is being in business, and some would argue that business is a form of combat.

I have argued that the landlord-tenant relationship is inherently adversarial. Whatever it is or is not, it's real life, and you can't choreograph it. Running credit checks and garnering background information are attempts to choreograph a perfect situation with regard to renting your property. You have to try to do this. But you must also recognize that there will come a time in your career when things will go wrong or you will make a mistake.

Several years ago, we rented one of our units to a young couple. Both had good jobs and excellent credit. They had no children and no pets. The background check was impeccable. Several months into the lease, the rent started to come late, but when it did come, they paid the $50 penalty, and a little note of apology was attached. This went on for about three months. Because the rent was only a week late at the most and the penalty was paid, we didn't bother contacting them. Then things started to get worse. The couple ran a month late. We sent them a letter and the rent came within the stipulated three days, but without the late payment penalty. There was no polite note attached. The following month the rent did not arrive and there was no response to our late notice letter. An attempted phone call revealed that the line had been disconnected, which of course meant that they had vacated the premises. The place was left in immaculate condition with a note on the refrigerator stating only "we're sorry." We never heard from them again, and we made no effort to look for them.

The point of the story is that there will be times when no matter how right you do things, they can go very wrong. We did not attempt to hunt the couple down. What was the point? How much are you going to spend, as opposed to concentrating on leasing the unit again? Sometimes you just have to write it off and move on. The issue of default is discussed in detail in Chapter 8, but the teaching point for now is that nothing in life is perfect. There will come a time when a landlord-tenant relationship will go sour in spite of your best efforts at screening. You will also make mistakes. There will be situations that were not adequately addressed in the lease, or you will allow the tenant to do something you may later regret. It's all part of the game. Don't beat yourself up over it. Press on. The next tenant could be a pleasure.

There is an exception to the above discussion on credit and background checks. If you purchased an income property of a nature, or in a geographical area, where running background checks on your tenants is clearly not apropos, that is the nature of your investment and you assume the risk of such a venture. My father owned a low-income building in Manhattan where his tenants would not have passed a credit check, and there was no point in running them. Oddly enough, I also recall that he had very few problems with his tenants or in collecting the rents. Most of them lived there for years, and many without leases. When he passed away, several tenants came to the funeral to pay their respects. However, low-income housing is a specific type of real estate investment that is outside the scope of this work, and my father's situation was not typical of that type of investment.

In the next chapter, we discuss in detail the lease agreement. This is the blueprint for your rental operation. It is also the written evidence of the terms and conditions of the transaction. So take a break and rejoin me as we look at the lease agreement.

PART TWO

CHAPTER 5

The Lease

"Oh, No, More Documents to Sign"

While many lawyers and real estate brokers would argue that the lease is the single most important document in the real estate transaction, that is technically not the case. We have already seen that there are a variety of components involved in the lease transaction. However, once the tenant moves into the property, the lease becomes the center of attention because it perpetuates the terms of the transaction. The complexity of the lease agreement should depend on the nature of the property being leased.

In this chapter, we discuss in detail the lease agreement and its contents. We start by discussing the general legal background of the lease agreement and then proceed to a specific discussion of the contents. Thus, at the conclusion of the chapter, you should understand that what is important is not finding the perfect lease, but rather understanding the nature and content of your lease agreement and how it fulfills your specific needs as a landlord. I hope that you will also understand that the true purpose of a lease is not to act as a sword against the tenant, but as a document whose essential requisite is to clarify the terms of the agreement for both parties in order to avoid disputes later on. First, let us explore the legal background of the lease agreement.

History

Generally speaking, U.S. laws are created by legislatures and put in writing or "codified." These codes are also referred to as statutes. A federal legislature, the U.S. Congress, enacts federal laws. At the state level, state legislatures enact the laws of your particular state, and so forth down to local town ordinances enacted by the local government. If a law is challenged, it is up to the courts to determine if the law is constitutional. When you read or hear about the Supreme Court declaring a law unconstitutional, it is telling the legislature that enacted the statute that it violates the Constitution and must be either rewritten or struck from the books. But the system doesn't end there. Our legal system is based on what is known as *stare decisis* or "precedents."

Thus, a statute may refer to "reasonable hours" for inspecting an apartment, but what is "reasonable"? That is the other function of our court system. The courts interpret the statutes, and their interpretations become part of the law. Let us propose that your state landlord-tenant statute reads that landlords may inspect their property during "reasonable hours," and your lease contains the same language. You interpret "reasonable" to be either on weekends, when you don't work at your normal job, or after work at 8:00 p.m. Your tenant, who is retired, interprets "reasonable" as between 10:00 a.m. and 4:00 p.m. on Tuesdays and Thursdays only (which are the days the tenant doesn't play golf). If your tenant refuses to allow you to inspect the apartment at 8:00 p.m. on Monday, and you file a lawsuit against your tenant for breach of the lease, your attorney will look up prior cases to determine what previous decisions or "precedents" have been decided on your issue.

In this example, each state has numerous case law decisions that have considered what constitutes "reasonable hours" in terms of landlord inspections. If the courts have not previously considered your issue, then it is deemed "a case of first impression" and the court renders a new decision that then becomes the new precedent for future similar cases. While this is a simplification of an extremely complex system, for our purposes it is enough for us to proceed with our discussion of the lease agreement. We now need to see how the lease interacts with the codified law.

Recently, a friend of mine asked me to witness his lease agreement. The entire lease was one short paragraph and contained only the names of the parties, the address of the property, the amount of the rent, the amount of the security deposit, how often the rent was to be paid, and the period of time the lease was to run. I cautioned him that there were many other issues to consider, and he simply replied that the "law covers it" and this was all that was needed.

Actually, he was right to a certain extent. On major issues, state law will resolve such matters as what essential services a landlord must provide to a tenant. For example, under most statutes, you cannot rent an apartment that has not got sufficient plumbing. The ability to have running water is an essential element of a residential property. However, most statutes don't resolve who pays the water bill. The parties to the lease agree on that issue.

I have given many examples throughout the book of disputes between the landlord and tenant that are resolved by interpreting the lease. While it is entirely possible and lawful to have a short, one-paragraph lease that outlines the terms of the tenancy and rely on state law to do the rest, I don't recommend it. In fact, the clearer the lease, the less it will be necessary to rely on the judicial system to interpret the language, should a dispute arise. A general rule of contract law is that ambiguities in a contract are interpreted *against* the drafter of the lease. In plain English, this means that if it is your lease and a clause is unclear, the court will try to interpret that clause in favor of your opponent (the tenant) rather than you. Since you are the landlord, and, presumably, it will be your lease that is being used, you are considered the drafter. Therefore, it is in your best interest to have as clear and unambiguous a lease as possible.

The Lease Clauses

Let us now discuss the specifics of the lease agreement. In the "forms" section of the book (Appendix B), I provide a model lease. This discussion follows the outline of the model. Remember that no document can be all things to all people. There may be an issue in a specific situation that is not covered by the terms of the lease. There is space provided for you to cover those situations. You don't need to be a lawyer to insert a clause that clearly resolves an issue. Such issues as "tenant is responsible for maintaining the lawn" or "cleaning the pool" indicate clearly what the initial responsibility of the parties is with regard to that specific issue. Of course, the word "maintaining" is subject to interpretation, so you may wish to define that word. We discuss this in greater detail later in the chapter. However, at this point, we begin our analysis of the lease agreement.

Try to read the applicable paragraphs of the model lease agreement provided as you follow the discussion in this chapter. It will help you understand the document that you are going to offer to your tenants. At the conclusion of the chapter, reread the lease in its entirety, and you will find that you have acquired quite a bit of knowledge in landlord-tenant law and a coherent understanding of your lease agreement. You should feel a sense of accomplishment because you will have mastered a difficult legal document. You will also find that it is an interesting document as well. You will have the urge to try your hand at changing or adding clauses. Be careful in the beginning, but as you gain experience, you will be able to tailor your lease agreement and make changes. Let's begin.

Initial Page

The initial page of the lease should provide the date the agreement is signed and the parties to the agreement, as well as the address of the landlord (which is where the landlord may be contacted for a variety of reasons, including, but not limited to, payment of rent). Of course, the address of the rental property should be next, because that is the subject of the lease.

Term of the Rental

The next item you should define is the term of the rental agreement. When does it commence and when does it terminate?

Amount of the Rent

Directly thereafter, you state the amount of rent. This is the essential element of the transaction, and you want it to be clear at the onset.

Where to Send the Payment

You also want to state clearly where the rent is to be paid so that there is no misunderstanding as to where the check is to be mailed. If the money is to be paid by electronic or automatic deposit into your bank account, this is the place where you would insert such instructions and directions for such deposit.

Due Date

Next is the "due date of the rent." Obviously, you want your rent paid promptly at a certain time of month, usually on the first. I would recommend always stipulating that the rent shall be paid on the first of each month. It is simpler and easier to track. If the tenant insists on moving in on the twentieth day of the month, simply prorate the payment, that is, determine how many days of rent the tenant owes for the month based on the daily rate (divide the monthly amount by 30 or 31 days). Then proceed normally from the first day of the month thereafter. These additional details would be stipulated in the lease in the "miscellaneous clauses" section provided. Simply write in the additional details.

Payment

If payment is to be made by check, you should state who the *payee* is to be. Generally speaking, you the landlord are the payee, unless your broker or management company is receiving the funds. If you have trouble understanding terms such as *payor* and *payee,* remember that the *payor* is the "oweor" of the money, and the *payee* is the person who receives the *"monee."*

Recently, we rented an apartment to a client who wished to pay the entire rent term in advance. This is fine, although it is a situation that you will probably not encounter too often. We received the check, and it was made out directly to the landlords, a brother and sister. The sister lived in Europe, and although her name did appear on the lease, as she was an owner of the property, the brother was handling the transaction, and it was cumbersome to forward the check to his sister in Europe for her signature prior to deposit. The lease stipulated that the check should be made to us as the brokers in care of our escrow account, and we were instructed to pay the brother. However, the client stated that his friend, who was a lawyer in South America, had told him to make the check out only to the landlord. Since the tenant had given a "cashier's" or bank check, it would have been difficult to undo the transaction because in the case of bank checks, the money is debited imme-diately from the payor's account.

Also, as a business philosophy, if someone wants to give you money in an attempt to comply with an agreement, it doesn't make much sense not to accept the funds if at all possible. In this case, a bank check is almost the same as cash. Even though the tenant did not strictly speaking comply with the terms of the lease, we accepted the payment (with agreement from the land-lords) based on that old adage that "a bird in the hand is worth two in the bush." However, technically speaking, the landlords would have been well within their rights to insist the check be made out as per the lease agreement, and had it been a regular check, we would have insisted on the check's being properly written. The lesson learned here is that with a properly drafted lease, the landlord is placed in a greater position of strength because the lease is clear and unambiguous on virtually any point contested by the tenant.

Penalties

Of course, you want your rent paid on time. Good faith and intention aside, what is the incentive to make that extra effort to get the rent to you promptly? A penalty for being late is the accepted method. The next paragraph of the lease indicates that a penalty of $100 shall be applied to the rent check if the landlord receives the rent payment more than five calendar days late. While this may seem a bit extreme, the idea is that some tenants may be willing to incur a minor penalty for the privilege of paying late, and that a higher penalty will discourage this behavior.

We had a tenant whose bank in his native country gave him a very high rate of return on his savings accounts, much higher than any bank paid in the United States. The late fee in the lease was $25. As a result, the $25 penalty did not bother him, and he gladly paid us any late fees on his rent because his money made more remaining in his bank account than paying on time to avoid our penalties. In all other respects he was the perfect tenant. He took excellent care of the property and never bothered us with problems. But every month it was a battle to get the money out of him, even though we knew he would eventu-ally pay. But we needed to meet our expenses and couldn't live on his sched-ule. When it came time to renew the lease, we raised the penalty to $300 for late fees. He complained bitterly about how unfair this was, but in the end he signed the lease and paid on time each and every month thereafter. While having such a $300 penalty is unusually high, $100, while significant, should not discourage anyone from signing a lease and provide sufficient incentive to pay on time.

Automatic Payment

One good way to ensure prompt payment is to try to get the tenant to agree to automatic payment into your account. This is also known as *electronic funds transfer* or "EFT" and may be set up through an agreement between your bank and that of the tenant. With this method of payment, the funds are taken by the tenant's bank each month and automatically deposited into your account. Of course, the tenant must still have sufficient funds in the account, or it is the same as bouncing a check. But assuming he or she has the funds available for payment, promptness is no longer an issue.

Bouncing Checks

What happens if a check is "dishonored" by your bank? A "dishonored check" is the banking term for a check that bounces.

If the check bounces for any reason, the lease states that the tenant will pay the administrative fees that your bank charges you, and these can be significant. For example, my bank charges $50 for a bounced check. In addition, as I am a long-standing customer with good credit, my bank will give me provisional credit against checks deposited rather than hold the checks anywhere from twelve hours to two weeks before I can draw funds against them. If I write a check against these provisional funds and the deposited check ultimately bounces, my bank will pay on the checks I wrote against those funds but will charge me added fees over and above the bounced check charge for "covering" or paying on my checks. The bottom line is that the bank is lending me money to cover my expenses because someone bounced a check on me. At the end of the month, these bank charges can really add up. There is also the added time, effort, and expense of paying back the bank and collecting on the bounced checks.

Certified Checks

To solve this problem, the lease shall also say that the landlord can require all future payments to be made by certified checks (which are similar to cashier's or bank checks) if the tenant bounces a regular check. Certified checks are checks (also known as drafts) that the bank "certifies," meaning that the funds are available and the check won't be dishonored or "bounce."

Rent Increases

Where the lease is a multiple-year lease, the rent may be increased as negotiated by the landlord and tenant on expiration of each yearly period. A specific amount of increase should be stipulated. Try to avoid such general phrases as "the increase shall be based on the cost of living." If the cost of living were to actually decrease, you could find yourself on the losing end of an argument for decreased rent. A 3 to 5 percent increase is generally acceptable, although landlords often try for more. Just indicate in plain language that the rent shall be increased by "x" dollars each yearly term.

Thus far, the lease has been a logical progression of events concerning the transaction. You know the principles, the term of the lease, how much the tenant will pay, to whom the check will be made, how it is to be paid, and what happens if the tenant pays late. Thus far, there are no problems and not much that requires any complex interpretation. The next paragraph deals with security and advance payments.

Advance Payments

Advance payments, as the term implies, deals with payments made by the tenant to the landlord that are made prior to the tenant's taking possession of the property. For example, the most common forms of advance payments are first month's rent, last month's rent, and security. Most landlords will require payment of the first and last month's rent and a security deposit for damages. If you are leasing a condominium, keep in mind that a "move-in" fee may be required by the association to cover damages to the common elements of the building, such as the elevator or hallways. While you can collect that money on behalf of the building, it is better to leave that to the tenant and not get involved, since it is not your money at stake. Be sure to check the relevant portion of the lease indicating move-in fees and who is responsible for collecting such fees, to avoid any possible disagreement with the tenant or the building's management company.

State statutes will advise you as to how advance payments must be held, and you need to check these out. You can call the local chamber of commerce or check at the local courthouse that handles landlord-tenant cases. It will likely have a pamphlet outlining state law regarding these and other issues peculiar to your state. Additionally, the pamphlet should be written in layperson's terms and be easily understood. Some states require that all advance payments be kept in a separate account (either interest or noninterest bearing) until such time as the money may be transferred to the landlord's personal funds in accordance with the lease.

Some states stipulate that only the security deposit is to be specially maintained. Other states may be silent on the issue. The problem is that if you as the landlord do not comply with your state's regulations on maintaining advance payments, you may lose your rights with regard to those funds. Security deposits are usually the greatest source of controversy, so we will now look carefully at what that deposit is, how it is to be maintained, and how you may withhold it if necessary.

The Security Deposit

A security deposit is an advance payment that the tenant pays to the landlord as a form of "insurance" against damages to the property that may occur as a result of the tenancy. Usually, it is equal to one month's rent, but where the landlord furnishes the apartment, it may be more. If no damage occurs, the landlord returns the money at the termination of the lease. State law usually provides the method for this transaction. In many cases, the landlord has thirty days to inspect the property and notify the tenant in writing that he or she intends to withhold a portion of the security deposit to pay for damage to the property. If the landlord fails to inspect and notify the tenant within the stipulated period of time, then the landlord loses his or her right to withhold the security deposit.

The landlord could still file a separate lawsuit to collect the funds, but, obviously, it is much simpler to comply with the law and simply withhold the security than to file a lawsuit. In some cases, the security may not fully cover the damage, and so the landlord may still have to resort to court action. Generally, where there is a dispute over the security deposit, the landlord has to show that he or she properly maintained the funds in accordance with state law prior to arguing that those funds could be properly withheld. That is why it is important to know and follow the law.

Some states also require that you notify the tenant within a certain period of time, and in writing, what bank the funds are being held in and whether the account is interest bearing or not. If the account is interest bearing, the law will state how the interest is to be divided between the landlord and tenant, if at all. States on occasion also require that the funds be held within the state where the rental property is located and not in the state where the landlord resides. Unfortunately, most landlords tend to disregard these rules and simply deposit the security deposit in their personal accounts. The experienced tenant (or the tenant's attorney) will challenge the landlord on this issue if he or she attempts to withhold a security deposit, irrespective of the reason for doing so. It is silly to lose on a technicality that can be easily avoided.

Normal Wear and Tear

The majority of disputes regarding security deposits arise because people don't understand the phrase "normal wear and tear excluded." Simply stated, normal wear and tear refers to the amount of use an item (such as carpeting) receives by reasonable people using the item for the purposes it was designed for. Landlords think that any damage is chargeable against the security, and tenants believe that every damage is normal wear and tear. Carpets wear out because they're walked on. People tend to spill food on carpets, and they are often soiled or stained. Sometimes they have to be replaced. What about a situation where a tenant spills ink on the carpet and leaves a big blue or black stain right in the center of the living room? Can you withhold the security and charge the tenant for replacing the entire carpet? The landlord would argue that ink stains on a carpet are not normal wear and tear because reasonable people don't spill ink on carpets. That sounds right. So we can with-hold the security, correct?

Let's look at the tenant's side. His argument is, "Look, Mr. Landlord, nobody's perfect. Carpets are on the floor, and things spill on them. That is a function of gravity. I own a fountain pen, which is not illegal. I was filling it with ink and accidentally spilled the bottle of ink on the carpet. I'm so sorry, but that can happen to anyone. I paid good rent to live in the unit, and an accidental spill is part of life. In fact, Mr. Landlord, I paid for a professional carpet clean-ing company to try and remove the ink stain, and what you see is the best they could do. You can't make me pay for a new carpet. After all, I'm sure you have had an occasional accident in your time. That is the risk you assume when you rent your unit. It is part of doing business." Uh oh, that sounds pretty good too. So we don't charge the tenant? This is a case that arises more often than you may think, and court decisions have yielded some frankly weird results.

I recall a case where a landlord told me about a dispute involving this type of situation. The lease had expired, and the tenant had badly stained the carpet to the point where it had to be replaced. The landlord withheld the security deposit in accordance with state law, and the tenant objected and filed suit in small claims court (that particular state had no specific landlord-tenant divi-sion). The landlord created an impressive display showing the stained por-tions of the carpet as opposed to clean portions, as well as a report from a carpet cleaning company indicating that the carpet could not be restored to acceptable levels of cleanliness. She also had properly documented pho-tographs showing that the carpet was clean at the onset of the lease. It seemed that the case was extremely well presented, and I advised her to go forward.

Several months later, the landlord contacted me again. "How did your case with the carpeting go?" I asked. "Oh that," she replied. "Not very well. The judge asked me how old the carpet was, and when I told her, she said that if you depreciated the value of the carpet, it was of a value below that of the security deposit, and she made me return the money to the tenant. Is that fair? After all, the carpet was in perfect shape when the tenant got the apartment, and I still had to buy a new carpet. What difference does it make if it was old? It was in perfect shape."

I agree. It shouldn't have made any difference, because the nature of security is to protect the landlord from unreasonable damage by the tenant based on reasonable use and to fund replacement of the damaged item in order to make the landlord whole. It was not intended that the landlord be required to factor in such items as product life and depreciation when deciding to withhold security.

In other words, a security deposit should not be subject to normal legal remedies. I believe that if the carpet was clean before the lease and dirty beyond reasonable wear and tear at the end, the landlord should be able to withhold security. Unfortunately, that is not always how the law sees it, as evidenced by the story above.

The judge's decision was the one that counted, and she depreciated the value of the carpet. The landlord was looking to have the carpet not merely cleaned but replaced and therefore withheld the entire security deposit. Since we are now talking about replacement cost, the judge could rightly have considered the depreciated value of the carpet and did. This does not mean that all judges, in all states, will decide in the same fashion, but it is one of the many ways these issues may be resolved by the courts. Below is a more in-depth discussion of what are known in the law as "remedies" available to the landlord and tenant when a dispute occurs, and we explore the issues of depreciating carpeting and other items in the following chapter on security deposits.

The moral of the story is that you have to be careful in withholding security deposits. As I already indicated, few tenants will agree that they left the property in anything but pristine condition. My advice is not to go crazy over security deposits. If the property is in reasonably good condition, return the deposit and move on. Remember that the property will have been lived in for a period of time for which you, the landlord, received income. There is a cost for doing business, and wear and tear on the unit by the tenant is part of that cost. I'm not suggesting that you should always return security deposits or spend countless hours considering depreciated costs of items. But what I am suggesting is that you have to be realistic about what you are doing. Security deposits are designed to cure damages beyond what is reasonable use by the tenant. It is not designed to ensure against receiving a less than perfect apartment or as additional income, or, worse, revenge. "I'll get them, I'll withhold their security" is a phrase I hear all too often from landlords. Don't fall into that trap.

Another common example occurs when the tenant moves out and the walls are dotted with holes from where pictures once hung. Landlords think that because they have to plaster and repaint they can withhold security. Is that okay? Probably not! The landlord repaints most properties every few years. If you leased your apartment for three years, you would probably have to repaint anyway, so you can't charge the security deposit. That is a normal cost of doing business. What if the paint job was still good but there are holes in the walls from the pictures. So you hire someone to spackle and touch up the paint. Do you withhold part of the security for the paint and labor? You should ask yourself if it is worth the time and effort to fight over that cost. Doesn't the tenant have the right to hang pictures on the wall?

Unusual Wear and Tear

But let's change the scenario a little. What if the tenant uses extra large nails with special properties to hold tapestries on the walls? The tenant removes the nails, but the nails leave huge gashes and holes of Swiss cheese proportions in the walls. This is not normal wear and tear, and you should withhold the cost of spackling and touching up the walls.

Broken windows, fixtures, and appliances not covered by insurance or other clear damages of such nature are usually ripe for withholding part or all of the security deposit. Also, you need to be prepared to prove the cost of the repairs, so be sure to document everything with bills and invoices. If you have to repair a light fixture, that is the amount of the cost you should withhold. Don't decide to upgrade the unit with a new light fixture based on the security deposit. If the fixture can't be repaired and you have to replace it, do so with a like fixture at as close to the cost of the original fixture as possible. In this case, I doubt if depreciation costs would be factored in, but again, it is possible, depending on the nature of the damage and what you are withholding. Clearly, don't upgrade a damaged item funded by the tenant's security deposit.

The best advice in security withholding cases is to consider carefully why you are withholding the money and try to be objective. You rented your property and received income. Security deposits are not designed to ensure perfection. The rule of thumb is that, with rare exceptions, most tenants will not treat a rental property like it was their own, simply because it isn't. The tenants paid you to live there, and if they paid on time each and every month and didn't completely trash the property, you are probably ahead of the game. Accept it and you save yourself time, money, and aggravation fighting over the withholding of security deposits. If you cannot accept this principle, you may be better advised not to be a landlord. Remember, they paid you $1,000 per month for three years. So what if you have to spring for a cleaning service or a paint job? Is that really such a bad deal? What is your time worth? Do you want to hang around court all day long waiting for your ten minutes to talk to the judge? What if you have to pay a lawyer? All I ask is that you consider carefully all sides before you decide to withhold the security.

I am often asked if it is necessary to film or photograph the property prior to the tenant's moving in. Sure, if you want to, but the lease will contain a clause that the tenant inspected the unit and stipulated that it was in good condition. Also, you don't need an Oscar-winning film crew to take a few pictures. Use common sense and good judgment. Better to screen your applicants as thoroughly as you can than to prepare for litigation, which is what taking pictures is really all about. In any event, in the "forms" section of the book (Appendix C), I have provided a sample letter for you, the Security Deposit Letter, should it be necessary to withhold the security deposit.

The other thing to consider is that withholding the security deposit may not be the only avenue, or indeed the proper avenue, of redress under the lease. There are other clauses in the lease that may better address a situation. So let us continue with our discussion and see what other lessons are to be learned. The next paragraph discusses occupancy and use of the leased property.

Occupancy and Use

There are several factors that you want to consider in this area. In earlier chapters, we have already touched on the fact that you, as the landlord, have the authority to decide the number of people you want occupying your unit. Remember that your decision will also affect the marketability of the property. The model lease used in this book provides for stipulating the number of people who are the principal tenants and any other authorized parties such as children.

Guests

In addition, the lease stipulates that if the tenant has guests for more than two weeks, he or she must notify the landlord in writing. These clauses are self-explanatory and require no in-depth discussion other than to state that the landlord should maintain some degree of control over his or her property in terms of occupants.

One landlord we know required a clause stating that the tenant could not hold parties on the property unless the tenant was present at all times during them. Actually, the tenants in this case were a retired couple who wanted only to live quietly in the property and never had any intention of having wild parties. But it was something that concerned the landlord, and so a clause was inserted into the lease agreement. This brings us to the discussion of the uses of the leased property.

Use of the Property

The most important aspect of the "Uses" clause is that the subject property shall be used only for residential purposes. This is not a commercial lease, which carries very different rules and regulations. You don't want clients coming to the apartment or inventory stored in the garage or to have the property used as a corporate retreat by different members of the tenant's business firm. If you are leasing a condominium, the association could become involved in this discussion as well.

Subletting and/or Assignment

Next is the clause indicating that the tenant may not sublet or assign the lease agreement to another party without your prior consent. Remember that if they are living in the property, they should be a signatory to the lease. One of the biggest problems in landlord-tenant cases is where roommates break up and one moves out. The remaining party cannot afford the lease alone and tries to find another roommate. This cannot be done without your consent. It is your property, and you, the landlord, control who resides in your property and under what conditions.

Again, we are going through a logical progression of events within the lease agreement. We have now determined how many people will live in the unit and under what overall conditions. We should then specify particular categories and items, such as who will pay for utilities and how and by whom the various components of the property should be maintained.

Utilities

Unless there is some specific technical reason for not doing so, all utilities should be paid by the tenant. Be sure to contact the various utility companies prior to the tenant's moving in and again before he or she moves out to make sure there are no outstanding bills. We have discussed this issue previously, and the concept should not require any further evaluation. If it is a short-term rental, or there is some technical reason for not wanting to switch utilities, then be sure to obtain a sufficient security deposit to cover the cost of the utilities as well as general damage to the property. The next paragraph deals with the condition of the property.

Condition and Maintenance of the Property

Landlords sometime feel the urge to document the condition of the property with all manner of new digital photographic technology. In many cases, this is just an excuse to play with a new toy, but others feel that it is important to document the condition of the property at the outset in anticipation of court action. The fact is that television portrays the court system in slow motion. Most landlord-tenant and small claims courts move very rapidly, with the judge hearing the case and passing judgment. There are no impassioned pleas to a jury with dramatic endings as the foreman announces the verdict. Evidence, including photographic evidence, must be properly admitted before the judge can consider it.

In other words, you have to prove when the photographs or film was shot, among other prerequisites. It is not necessary to spend thousands of dollars in equipment unless you are leasing a mansion filled with antiques and art treasures. In this regard, let's look at the "Conditions" clause of the lease.

Conditions

The "Conditions" clause simply says that the tenant inspected the property and has agreed that the property was in habitable condition, and that all appliances and any other fixtures or items of the property are in working order. If there were a problem, this would be the time to note and correct it; otherwise, the tenant has acknowledged that the property is ready for occupancy. As a reserve military officer, I have sometimes been given a government vehicle to use for official business during my active duty tours. Prior to accepting the vehicle, the contractor, the transportation person, and I check it for dents and damages, and we all sign a form indicating the inspection and its results. When I return it, the car is re-inspected. This is not a complex situation and works well. It works equally well in rental situations. The "Conditions" clause of the lease is also a good place to discuss who is responsible for repairs to the property.

Repairs

Whether you lease a house or an apartment, eventually something breaks. An appliance requires repairs, the plumbing gets backed up, and so on. Who is responsible for these repairs? Sometimes the statute will address repairs to such big-ticket items as heat and water as the responsibility of the landlord. Check to make sure the law applies to you. For example, it sometimes applies only to a landlord of multiple dwellings (usually at least four or more units). Some leases list the major components of a household, and each item is checked off in terms of either landlord or tenant responsibility. I find that to be an untidy way of accomplishing this objective. Lists tend to be cumbersome and often incomplete. I find that it is better to divide the responsibility based on some negotiated sum of money. For example, the landlord needs to deal with anything costing more than $100. Anything under that sum is the responsibility of the tenant. This is why landlords should have an appliance contract. An appliance contract is a type of insurance policy that is relatively inexpensive and that covers such items as repair or replacement of kitchen appliances, air-conditioning, and, depending on how much extra you wish to spend, possibly plumbing, electricity, and maintenance of other various household components. However, you can always tailor the lease to specify certain areas of responsibility, such as lawn maintenance or pool servicing contracts.

Willful Misuse

Willful misuse by the tenants or their guests is always the responsibility of the tenants. You can't purposely destroy other people's property. Thus, if, in a drunken state, the tenant takes an ax to the washing machine, obviously it is the tenant's sole responsibility to replace that item. If you get stuck with such a tenant, I would advise that communication be in writing rather than in person. However, as stated in the lease, regardless of whether or not there is a repair contract in effect, you cannot leave your tenant without a refrigerator for weeks on end until the part arrives from heaven knows where. You still have to solve the problem for the tenant.

If the appliance repair contractor fails to take care of the problem quickly, you need make the repairs for your tenant and try to get the costs back from the appliance contractor later on. You would argue that the appliance contractor failed to meet the terms of the contract and caused you damages. In most cases, the contractor will cooperate in some form of reimbursement if it was clear that it didn't meet its obligations. The next paragraph of the clause deals with emergency situations.

Emergency Situations

When time permits, all situations can be resolved calmly, but when the pipe bursts and the water is flowing, the situation must be dealt with immediately. The landlord may not be available, and the tenant may not be able to wait. In those situations, the tenant must be allowed to at least address the immediate problem without fear that he or she will not be reimbursed by the landlord. The real problem usually occurs when the tenant calls the plumber to stop the water from running and proceeds to order new state-of-the-art copper and gold plumbing for the entire house as a preventive measure.

Clearly, the tenant has overstepped his or her bounds. The landlord should be given the opportunity to choose a contractor to effectuate the repairs because he or she is responsible for major repairs and is paying for them.

Reimbursement

The other issue that comes up is the method of reimbursement. Tenants usually want to simply withhold the money from the following month's rent. Often, the landlord will agree because it is easier than writing a separate check. This is not a good idea. From the landlord's perspective, it is a bad habit to let your tenants get into. In most states, withholding of rent is unlawful unless the rent is placed in a registry or escrow maintained by the courts. The tenant must file a civil action prior to being able to exercise this option. So why, as the landlord, would you encourage your tenant to do something not favored by the law?

Also, as a bookkeeping function, any repair you make on a leased unit is an expense that can be deducted from rental income. We will discuss taxes in greater detail further on, but for now, documenting your expenses is far less complicated if you don't take the easy way out. Finally, it establishes the concept of the "inviolability" of the rental payment. "The rent is the rent" should be your motto. If you allow your tenant to make deductions for agreed-on expenses, you may find you have empowered him or her to start taking extra liberties. If you owe the tenant a reimbursement, write him or her a separate check.

Force Majeure

Actually, you are probably already familiar with the concept of *force majeure*. If you look at your insurance policy, it talks about acts of God such as hurricanes and floods. "Acts of war" is another category that falls under *force majeure*. Thus, the concept here is, if the property is rendered uninhabitable by a *force majeure* condition, that is, a condition not the fault of the landlord or tenant but an act of God, the lease is terminated and rent is prorated to the date the property became uninhabitable. That is the only way the tenant may not be liable for rent during the lease term. Insurance becomes a major player in these types of situations, and this area is also dealt with in greater depth later in the book.

Alterations and Improvements

On signing the lease, many tenants refer to the leased property as "their home." If the tenants have lived in the property for many years, they may have established a relationship with the landlord (which we have already noted is not a good idea). However, both legally and morally, it isn't their home. By nature, tenants are transitory. At the expiration of the lease, they can leave. It is you, the landlord, who own the property. You, the landlord, pay the taxes and have the ability to transfer title (sell the property) to another, not the tenants. As such, the tenants may not make any alterations or improvements to the property without your express consent. If they do, the remedy is that they must restore the property to its original condition.

Can you withhold security? I would say yes in this case because an unauthorized change is a breach of the lease and a technical damage to the property. What about the case where the alteration is an improvement? My first comment would be to define improvement. We have already discussed a situation where the tenant transformed a garden into a tropical jungle. Was that an improvement? Not to the landlord who now had to maintain it. Before granting rights of improvement or alteration, be certain that you and the tenant agree on the specifics. You should put the agreement in writing. The writing should then become an attachment to the lease agreement. I realize that all of this seems like a big pain, but in the long run, if a dispute arises, you will benefit greatly from taking the extra time on these matters. At this point, all parties to the lease should fully understand their rights in the property. But there are still a number of other issues that require consideration. One interesting aspect is a pet.

Pets Revisited

Pets can be a very controversial issue, because pet owners consider their pets to be members of the family. We have already had a discussion of pets in Chapter 3, so for now, it is time to reduce our conclusions to the lease agreement. In the "Pets" clause, you finalize in writing your decision regarding what pets shall be allowed in and about your property and whether or not you require a pet deposit. For our purposes, we have defined domestic pets or animals as animals commonly found in a household, such as a dog or cat. A python would not qualify.

Default

Now comes the discussion of the default clauses of the lease. The important thing to remember, and I have stressed this, is that defaults can occur on both sides. In the first chapter of the book, I stated that a lease is a two-sided agreement, and there are rights and obligations on both parties. Therefore, it is important to define default from both the landlord's and the tenant's obligations. Default means that one party refuses to comply with part or all of the agreement. This is known as a "breach" of the agreement. The other party to the agreement may then declare default, meaning that the subject of the agreement is at an end. If it is a lease agreement and default is declared, the lease is over. At that point, the default remedies will kick in.

The default remedies tell the parties what happens now that the agreement is over. Strictly speaking, default is not automatic. If the landlord does not declare the tenant in default (or vice versa), the lease continues. Sometimes, if the case goes to court, the court will decide if a party is in default. The most common default occurs when the tenant fails to pay the rent.

Tenant Default

Unfortunately, the equally common reaction from the landlord is to place a padlock on the property and confiscate the tenant's personal property until the tenant pays. While this may seem very proactive and even satisfying under the "revenge is sweet" principle, locking out tenants or taking their personal property is against the law in most, if not all, of the United States and other nations. Basically, we are a society of laws, and self-help is not an option in these types of cases.

The plan in a default case is to give the offending party the chance to "cure" the default or comply with the lease. In many states, the law requires a notice to be sent that stipulates a certain number of days to cure the default. See the sample default letter in Appendix C, Late Notice. In our sample lease we have named three business days as the time required for curing the default. The letter should describe what they did wrong and should refer to a specific paragraph of the lease. The letter should be sent by certified U.S. mail, which provides a return receipt requested, or by any other form that can provide proof of receipt. Most private couriers such as United Parcel Service (UPS) and Federal Express (FedEx) provide these services. However, for legal purposes, the courts most easily recognize certified mail as the accepted form of proof of mailing. You will have to check the landlord-tenant laws of the state where your property is located to find out the rest of the procedure. This includes damages you can claim.

If the tenant cures the breach, the lease continues. Some breach of lease cases are examined later in this book, but for now, it is important that you understand the terms of the contract that you are going to give your tenant. It is equally important that you are able to explain your lease to the tenant. In this respect, let us look at the default clause for the landlord.

Landlord Default

In the case of the landlord, we are a bit more liberal. There are several reasons for this. If you consider the various default scenarios, tenant default cases usually involve some activity that can be cured within three days. But in the case of the landlord, there is usually more required. For example, some non-emergency repairs may take longer than three days. Therefore, in the case of the landlord, the tenant's obligation is to notify the landlord of the breach by certified mail or the equivalent, and the landlord is then given a reasonable time under the circumstances to cure the breach. We discuss such issues as constructive eviction further on, but in terms of the lease. For now, the lesson is simply that you as the landlord can be in breach of a lease as well as the tenant. Be aware of state laws that govern breach of contract.

Jurisdiction and Venue

The lease should also state jurisdiction and venue. These are terms that define which state laws apply and in what location a legal action will take place should it become necessary. If your property is located in New York State, the laws of the State of New York apply. If the property is located in the borough of Queens, the venue is Queens County.

This portion of the lease is also a good location to place a sentence about which party to the lawsuit pays the attorney's fees and other costs such as filing fees, serving documents, or, when necessary, the hiring of private detectives, which are often a part of a lawsuit. This is called prevailing party fees. Since costs and attorney's fees don't always automatically go to the party who loses the case, it is always best to state specifically in the lease that, should legal action be necessary, the losing party pays the winner's costs and attorney's fees; the court will usually honor that clause.

Termination

The first paragraph of the "Termination" clause of the lease deals with surrender of the property.

Surrender of the Property

This does not mean that the tenants have to wave a white flag and come out of the property with their hands raised high. The paragraph merely specifies the fact that on a specific day the tenants must give the keys back to the landlord or landlord's agent and that the property should be in the same condition that the tenants received it, normal wear and tear being excluded. No conceptual problems here, other than the issue of normal wear and tear and damages, which have been discussed earlier in this chapter and will be revisited in Chapter 9. But what if the tenant doesn't move out? What if the appointed day comes and the tenant remains? This is known as a "holdover tenant."

Holdover Tenant

In the case of a holdover tenant, the state laws are pretty unified. Let us say you open your mailbox on the last day of the lease expecting to find a set of keys and instead you find a check for next month's rent. What do you do? The answer is, it depends. If you don't care if the tenant remains, you can deposit the check, creating what is known as a "month-to-month tenancy." This means in most states that the law requires you to give the tenant at least fifteen days' written notice that you intend to terminate the tenancy, or the lease continues on a month-to-month basis as long as the tenant continues to pay rent and you accept it. All other terms of the lease remain in effect. If you want the tenant out, and he or she refuses, when the lease expired, the tenant would be technically guilty of trespassing and you could call the police and have him or her removed. State law may require you to go through an eviction proceeding. The police will tell you if they cannot handle the situation. We know what happens if the tenant remains after the lease, but what about a situation where the tenant leaves prior to the lease's termination? This is known as "abandonment."

Abandonment

Abandonment occurs when the tenant leaves the property and, of course, ceases to pay rent. If state law does not govern the situation, then the lease usually stipulates that the landlord may enter the property. Any item left behind becomes the property of the landlord. Again, state law may modify or override this provision.

Advertising the Property

What about a situation where the tenant does not wish to renew the lease and has notified you that he is going to move out? When can you advertise the property for a new tenant, and can you show the property while the old tenant still occupies the property? The answer to this question is found in the next clause of the lease.

Many tenants are reluctant to allow strangers into their apartment during the term of the lease. This is part of what we earlier referred to as "quiet enjoyment." Some tenants don't want the landlord to lease the apartment to a new tenant so they can negotiate a better deal at the last minute. That's not fair, but it is also a fact of life. The best way to handle this situation is right up front in the lease. Clearly stipulate the terms whereby the landlord or his or her agent may show the property to prospective tenants. Again, try to avoid interpretive phrases such as "during reasonable hours." Specifically delineate the times acceptable to the tenant for showing the property. The usual standard is 24 hours' notice to the tenant during the period from 9:00 a.m. to 5:00 p.m. on weekdays. You can try for weekends, which is when many people like to see real estate, but that is also a time when the tenant may wish to relax, and that is his or her right as well. If the prospective tenant is serious, he or she will find the time to take a look during the stipulated hours.

Selling the Property

The general maxim of law is that a sale of the property is subject to the existing lease. That means that you, as the landlord, cannot terminate the lease if you want to sell the property, and neither can the new owner. In terms of the tenant, the only thing that will change is the name and address of where he or she pays the rent. However, there are instances where the tenant's rights are not above other situations that may arise. Subordination is one such issue that landlords and tenants should be familiar with.

Subordination

The "Subordination" clause simply states that any "leasehold interests," which is a legal phrase for someone who has a lease, are subordinate to or less important than any liens or encumbrances that are in effect upon the property or that could be made in the future. For example, when you borrow money by taking a mortgage and using your home as collateral, the bank places a lien on your property. This means that if you try to sell your house, your bank can insist on being paid before you can transfer title to the new owner. Since a lien is something that could prevent a transfer of ownership, it is often referred to as an "encumbrance." Think about this for a moment. In most cases, a property is not owned by the landlord outright; there is a mortgage with a bank. Imagine, if you will, the bank's not being able to foreclose if you fail to pay your mortgage, simply because you have a tenant living in the property. Banks would never make loans unless their mortgages were primary to any other interest. That is stated in your mortgage documents, and nothing you place in a lease can change that.

Here is another variation. What about a situation where you do own the property outright and you want to get a mortgage because the rates are favorable? The bank will not lend you money if your tenant's interests are greater than its. Sometimes, a shrewd tenant will ask what would happen if the bank were to foreclose on the mortgage. The tenant would have to move out and would have no choice but to pursue you, the landlord, for breach of the lease and hope that he or she would be compensated.

Some tenants will want to verify if the landlord is current on his or her mortgage payments, does not owe money to the condominium or homeowners' association, or has paid his or her real estate or income taxes. Is the tenant within his or her rights to ask these questions? Sure; after all, didn't you check the tenant's credit? Why shouldn't he be afforded those rights as well? It is because a tenant's lease is, legally speaking, less important than other potential claims on the property, such as a mortgage lien, that the tenant bears a risk with his or her landlord, much along the lines that the landlord bears a risk with the tenant. It is a basic obligation of the tenant to pay his or her rent on time, but it is an equally basic obligation of the landlord to meet his or her financial requirements on the property that the tenant occupies.

While I was a condominium manager, I recall that each year I would get a phone call from a seasonal tenant. He would ask if his landlord, the owner of the condominium unit that the tenant leased during the winter months, was current on his monthly maintenance assessment. The tenant wasn't being nosy. He understood that if the landlord was not current, the condominium association could foreclose on the unit and the condominium association's foreclosure interest was greater than the tenant's leasehold. So don't be insulted if the tenant asks you if you are current on your payments with regard to the property.

Do you see how the lease continues to flow with regard to the subject matter? Each phase of the lease is dealt with in turn. If you recall, it begins with the identification of the parties, then moves on to the money, then to taking care of the property. After that, it deals with things that could go wrong in the transaction, default by either party being the primary example. It then proceeds to delineate the termination portion, the end of the lease agreement, and the various ways landlord and tenant could part company. Looking at the lease in phases makes it easier to understand. It begins to read almost like a story with a beginning, a middle, and an end, rather than a complex document of boilerplate language of intimidating legalese. However, there are a number of miscellaneous clauses dealing with the rights of the parties that don't neatly fall into a storybook category. These types of clauses are discussed in the next chapter.

CHAPTER 6

The Lease Continues

We ended the last chapter by comparing the lease to a story that has a beginning, a middle, and an end. Now we are going to look at parts of the lease that don't fall neatly into that story but nonetheless must be dealt with. The first issue is that of interpretation and effect.

Interpretation and Effect

This clause states that the agreement between the parties applies not only to them, but extends to their heirs as well. Thus, if either the landlord or the tenant were to die during the leasehold, the estate of the deceased party and the heirs would have to honor the lease. There are some exceptions to this paragraph, and should there be an unfortunate incident involving a tenant, you should consult an attorney for further advice. However, the lesson learned here is that a lease can sometimes literally extend beyond the life of the tenant, although I wouldn't really push this too much.

The other matter dealt with in this clause is the notion that grammar won't be taken literally. Additionally, the clause notes that should one paragraph of the lease be deemed invalid, the rest of the lease still remains in effect. These are technical legal points, but they need to be mentioned in the body of the lease. For example, let us suppose that the lease indicates that the landlord can enter the property anytime he or she wishes. State law says that the landlord can enter a lease property only with 24 hours' notice to the tenant. In such a case, the state law would govern because it has priority over individual leases. However, the rest of the lease would still remain in full force and effect. This is a very nice lead-in to our next point in the lease, the landlord's inspection rights of the property during the term of the lease.

Inspection

In the best of all scenarios, the landlord will lease the property for a year or two and receive a check each month on time from the tenant, have no problems, and not need to visit the property until the termination of the agreement. As landlords, this is what we hope for, and in the vast majority of cases, if we do things right, this is what we get. Unfortunately, there are times when disputes arise. The classic example is when the tenant hasn't paid the rent and won't respond to any communications. Perhaps you get a call from a next-door neighbor complaining about "wild parties and strange smells coming from your unit." What do you do in such a case? We know the tenant is entitled to "quiet enjoyment" of the property, but if it's not so quiet, or, maybe, not so legal, you certainly have the right to investigate.

"Quiet enjoyment" notwithstanding, recall that in the beginning of the book I said that the landlord has the "superior interest" as the owner of the property. As a landlord, you have the right to protect that interest. Inspection is one way to do that. You have the right to visit the property to ascertain that it is being lawfully used and maintained. How the landlord accomplishes this is outlined in the "Inspection" clause of the lease.

In many cases, state law will serve as a guide to how the landlord may inspect a property. Some statutes require 24 hours' notice, while others waive the notice right of the tenant if the tenant is not current in his or her rent payments. If the law is silent on this issue, I suggest that the tenant be given 24 hours' notice of the right to inspect. The paragraph in the sample lease (Appendix B) states that the tenant shall not withhold the right to inspect the property. The paragraph further states that where an emergency exists and the tenant cannot be contacted, the landlord has the right to enter the property.

Unfortunately, some landlords tend to use this clause to harass tenants. That is not its intent, and the wrongful use of the inspection right may breach the lease for failure to provide "quiet enjoyment" of the property. I know of one tenant who became involved in a dispute with his landlord. The tenant attempted to allege "trespass" against a landlord who entered the property without his consent. The idea was to use the trespass theory as a cause of action to transfer his dispute from the County Court, where landlord-tenant cases were heard in that jurisdiction, to Circuit Court, which is a higher court with a higher threshold for damages. Generally speaking, actions in higher courts are more complex and require the assistance of an attorney if any success is to be derived. This became a much more expensive proposition for the defendant landlord, a fact not overlooked by the tenant, who happened to be an attorney. Therefore, it pays to use the "Inspections" clause according to the rules set forth either by the law of the state in which your property is located or by the lease, whichever is applicable. Another topic that needs to be specifically addressed involves dealing with military members.

Military Personnel

Many states have enacted specific laws regarding when and how military personnel on active duty may break a lease. In most cases, a military member who is transferred, on presentation of valid military orders, may break the lease with thirty days' notice. As a Reserve officer, I support such clauses because the nature of the military occupation is to go where the member is needed, and that move is beyond the control of the military member. In most cases this isn't a problem, but this issue should be dealt with up front to avoid the problem for both the military member and the landlord. In other cases where the tenant is transferred, unless the tenant specifically negotiates the settlement procedures in advance, there is no requirement that the landlord allow the tenant to terminate the lease. Now, let's look at some of the disclosures that the landlord should give the tenant.

Disclosures

Disclosures are items that you want to let the tenant know in advance. The concept is that the tenant, when renting the property, should know everything about the property that could affect his or her health or welfare. Disclosures also protect the landlord because he or she cannot later be accused of concealing relevant information.

In the sample lease, we try to touch on the major types of disclosures. The disclosures we have selected here are quiet enjoyment, radon gas, Megan's Law, lead-based paint, security deposit notification, and a blank space for any other miscellaneous clauses that the landlord needs to impart to the tenant that are not otherwise considered in the lease. Even if you told the tenant some fact about the property, put it in writing so it won't be your word against the tenant's, should a dispute arise. I can assure you that during a dispute, your memory of the events and that of the tenant will be very different. The first of the disclosures is the concept of "quiet enjoyment."

Quiet Enjoyment

We have already discussed the meaning of quiet enjoyment and its significance to the landlord-tenant agreement. It is not, strictly speaking, a disclosure, as it is a basic tenet (no pun intended) of the landlord-tenant law. However, as the lease is a bilateral agreement, the rights of the tenant should be noted as well as those of the landlord, and the "Disclosures" section is an appropriate place to do so.

Radon Gas

In a number of states, such as Florida, radon gas is a problem and, depending on state law, must be disclosed to the tenant. As indicated in the lease, radon gas is a radioactive gas formed in the ground that, given sufficient time, can accumulate in buildings and cause health risks to the occupants. In Florida, for example, this is a problem in certain areas, and the law decrees that the tenant must be informed of this fact. However, since Florida law does not require an inspection for radon, if the tenant is concerned, he or she must conduct a test for the gas at his or her own expense.

Radon exposure must be over a long period of time for it to be harmful, and opening the windows and airing the property generally keeps radon from accumulating enough to cause a health problem for the occupants. In addition, the higher the floor, the less likely that the radon gas will reach the unit. But once the problem is disclosed, the landlord has fulfilled his or her responsibility unless he or she actually knew or should have known that there was a problem with radon gas. If your next-door neighbor died from cancer caused by exposure to radon gas, that is probably a good clue that your property is in danger as well, and in such a case, you should conduct the test and disclose the results. As a landlord, you need to check if your state requires a radon gas disclosure clause.

Megan's Law

Another clause required in some states is what is often known as the "Megan's Law" disclosure. Megan was a seven-year-old girl who was attacked by a released sex offender who, unbeknownst to her parents, had taken up residency across the street. Where required, Megan's Law mandates that the public be notified of their right to contact local law enforcement agencies to determine if recently released convicted sex offenders are living in the community. Again, the onus is upon the tenant to launch the investigation unless you, the landlord, know or should have known that such a person lives in the neighborhood.

Lead-Based Paint

Lead-based paint is another disclosure that is mandated, but this is by federal law and applies in all states. Although modern house paint does not contain lead, in the 1970s and before this was not the case. Where the paint was peeling, children apparently found it tempting to eat the paint chips, which were, of course, poisonous. The problem became so bad that the federal government stepped in and passed legislation that, among other things, requires disclosure in homes built prior to 1978. If the landlord owns four or more units, he or she must disclose if the walls contain lead-based paint. The law does not require that the landlord attempt to abate the risk, but only disclose the fact. Risk abatement generally requires repainting the walls with nonlead-based paint. I always use a lead-based paint disclosure on any unit built prior to 1978, regardless of how many units the landlord owns.

Security Deposit Notification

Another disclosure that could be placed in a variety of areas within the lease agreement is the security deposit notification. Some states specifically require that a letter be sent to the tenant within a stipulated period of time indicating in what bank the security deposit is placed, if the account bears interest, and what the legal requirements are for its return to the tenant at the termination of the lease. The sample lease states that deposits shall be held in accordance with state law. You should check the individual state statutes to determine your own procedures and follow them carefully.

Add Your Own (Miscellaneous) Disclosures

The final clause is left blank and gives the landlord the opportunity to fill in any other matters that he or she should disclose to the tenant that would "negatively impact on the tenant's quiet enjoyment of the property." For example, let us say that your tenant is renting your apartment because it overlooks a beautiful lake. In fact, that is the main attraction of the property, and the tenant has remarked several times that the only reason he has selected your property is because he wants to sit on the terrace and look at the lake. You have heard rumors that the owner of the property directly in front of the lake has sold to a developer and that the developer plans to build a high-rise building on the property that would obstruct your tenant's view of the lake. Do you have to tell him? As in most cases in the law, it depends. If it is just a rumor and there is no reason to believe the property will be sold, there may be no reason to "kill your deal." But what if you read in the newspaper that a permit was issued to a developer to build on that piece of land the very next week? Do you disclose it then? Morally, you certainly should, and probably even legally.

The fact is, if you are in a position to know that the essential factor behind your tenant's rental of your property is to enjoy the lake view and if you know for a fact that the view will definitely go away, you should make the disclosure. What if your advertisement said, "Glorious view of lake" as part of the description of your property? Does that now make it more incumbent on you to disclose the new construction? While you are not the guarantor of a view, if you know, or perhaps should have known, of the impending change in the view, you may be under an obligation to disclose it.

Most states now require full disclosure of relevant facts. If you are not sure whether a fact is relevant or not, it is best to err on the side of disclosure. What about a situation where you own a condominium apartment that has a noisy neighbor who plays the television far too loud at all hours of the night? Do you have to disclose it? Again, it depends on how big a problem it is. If you are an unusually light sleeper and the average person isn't disturbed, you should not have to disclose it. But if that person keeps half the building up all night and it is a problem that the management is dealing with, possibly through litigation, you should disclose it.

My wife and I once lived in a building that had motorized toilets. When the resident in the unit above flushed, you would hear it throughout our unit. I recall one evening when my wife and I were having guests for dinner, and during the main course, a *whooshing* sound resounded throughout the unit. "What was that?" inquired a startled guest. "Oh, that's just the sound of the ocean," my quick-thinking wife responded, not wishing to ruin our guests' dinner. "Imagine," said our guest, "you can hear the ocean way across the street." What if your guest had been a prospective tenant? What would have been the proper response in that case? Here you have a real dilemma. The problem is obviously not one that is specific to your unit but is building wide. Let us suppose that there are upwards of 150 apartments in the building, and 30 percent are tenants. Let us also suppose that none of the other landlords disclosed the "atomic toilet" problem. As everyone knows, life is full of moral dilemmas. In more cases than not, the law does not offer a clear-cut answer. At best, it offers some guidance. My advice is to try to do what is morally right and things will tend to work themselves out in your favor legally, at least most of the time. In the case of our atomic toilets, while everyone complained about the noise, in most cases it was in a joking manner. Nobody moved out or sold because of the toilets.

At the board meetings, discussions were held about having a special assessment to replace all the toilets, but nobody was willing to pay to have it done, so the assessment was never passed. When we rented a unit in that building, we disclosed the problem with the toilets and never lost a customer because of it. I advise full disclosure up front, which is better than having the tenant discover the problem on his or her own. The tenant will be happier and trust you more, and you'll have fewer problems in the long run. Now, let's move on to some special circumstances.

Special Requests

There are often special requests that the tenant will make that should be stipulated in the lease agreement, including those listed below.

Right of First Refusal

One of the most common is the "right of first refusal." As we have already discussed, the right of first refusal simply indicates that should you sell your property, you agree to offer the tenant the same contract you are offering your buyer. The terms of this right are spelled out in the clause and are self-explanatory. However, many people confuse a right of first refusal with an "option to purchase." A right of first refusal is simply the right of the tenant to be offered the chance to purchase the property at the same price and terms as the landlord contracts for with a third party. With an option to purchase the property, the tenant actually contracts the right to purchase the property at a given time and at a certain price that is stipulated. However, in order for an option to be lawful, there must be consideration. In other words, the tenant must pay a nonrefundable sum of money for the right to secure an option. When a tenant asks for an option to purchase, in nine out of ten cases, he or she is really thinking of a right of first refusal. If the tenant is truly considering "locking in the price" with an option, an attorney should draft this. The other clause that often turns up is a variation of the military clause that is known as the "opt out" clause.

Opt Out Clause

Opt out clauses are generally used in multiyear contracts where the tenant wants to be locked in on a multiyear price but wants the freedom not to extend the contract for another period. This is strictly a business decision on your part. This type of clause is conceptually akin to an "option to renew" the lease. You may, but are not legally required to, negotiate added consideration, that is, added money, for this right. A variation of the opt out clause is a breach clause similar to the military clause discussed earlier. Businesspeople like this because it allows them to "opt out" of the lease if they are transferred to another location. Where you have a breach clause of this nature, the terms of the opt out should be specified. For example, "If tenant is transferred more than 100 miles from his or her current location, upon presentation of proof of transfer and 30 days' written notice, the lease shall be terminated as of the next full rental month after the 30-day notice." In this fashion, the tenant must give 30 days' notice and, subsequent to that notice, must pay a full month's rent rather than merely prorate the rent 30 days from the date of the notice.

Ambiguous Language

Now that you have followed the lease along with your reading of this and the preceding chapter, reread it alone and be certain you understand it. There is a certain logical flow to the lease. It begins with a description of a transaction between you and another person or persons who are going to live in your property and pay you money for the right to do so. It discusses when and how they will pay you that money and what your and their rights and duties are with regard to this tenancy. It also advises what will happen if either party does not adhere to the agreement. There is nothing magical about a lease agreement. It doesn't matter if it is written on legal- or letter-size paper, in 12 point Script or 10 point Times New Roman lettering. What is important is that it reveals as clearly as possible the intent of the parties. Where the intent is not clear, it may be up to a judge to figure out what he or she understands the intent of the agreement was, and that judge may not come to the conclusion you desire.

As I mentioned earlier, ambiguous language usually hurts the drafter of the lease's case if there is a dispute. Since you are the landlord and it is your lease, any ambiguity in the lease will be construed against you. As a result, it is in your best interest to be as clear and unambiguous as possible.

It is just as important to say what you mean as to mean what you say. If you and the tenant reach some agreement that needs to be transcribed into the lease, make it as clear and complete as possible. Be specific and avoid such subjective terms as "reasonable." As we have already illustrated, "reasonable" means different things to different people. The most important lesson, though, is that a lease should not be a weapon of the landlord to subjugate the tenant. For one thing, most tenants won't sign them if they are too one-sided. There is a lot of property out there, and yours will generally not be the only one on the market.

Contracts of Adhesion

Agreements that are too one-sided are known as "contracts of adhesion," because whatever the terms are, no matter how bad, you are stuck with them. There are many examples of adhesionary contracts. A bank loan agreement is one such case. An automobile sales contract is another. I actually argued some fine print or "boilerplate" language once, but this is unusual and you have to know what you are doing. These contracts are basically the "take it or leave it" variety. You don't have to sign them, but if you don't, you won't get your home loan or new car. In addition, every bank and car dealership has the same basic language, so what are you to do? If you have ever read the contract you receive prior to opening a new software program, you may be surprised at what you have agreed to. But you have no choice. Either you agree or you don't use the program.

In the case of your lease, you as a small business landlord do not have the power to provide adhesionary contracts, nor should you. Even if you find someone naïve enough to sign one, sooner or later he or she will realize what you have done and resent it. In the end, you will have an enemy living in your apartment, and if you should find yourself before a judge, you may have a hard time defending it in court. Over the years I have heard many debates over which party the court favors in landlord-tenant disputes. Landlords complain that the courts favor the tenants, while tenants generally argue the opposite. The fact is, the judge will listen to the dispute, hear the arguments, look at the lease, and apply the law. Later on in the book, we look at how to prepare for court, but for now, your lease agreement, if done properly, should be clear enough to prevent, rather than catapult you into court, where frankly, you don't want to be.

Actually, court can be an interesting experience, since it is part of our culture, but this is business and not social studies. Preparing for and going to court waste time and time is money, so it is best to avoid court actions if you can. For now, I would like to focus on the positive. You have a signed lease and the tenant is getting ready to move in. What do you do now? Find out in the next chapter.

Chapter 6
Case Studies

CASE STUDY #1

The Stubborn Landlady

Laura Landlady had it all, or so she thought. She had an interesting job, an active social life with congenial friends and companions, and a beautiful condominium apartment. In fact, the apartment, although only 850 square feet consisting of one bedroom and one bath, seemed quite roomy by most standards in the city. The kitchen was small but modern and complete, and the apartment had a bayfront terrace with one of the most beautiful sunset views imaginable. Laura was fond of saying that only "heaven and earth" could move her from that apartment. As it turned out, heaven and earth came in the guise of a job promotion and a rather hefty salary increase. The only condition was that Laura had to move to another city to accept the position. A friend of hers, Annie Agent, who was a real estate broker, advised her not to sell the apartment yet, as its value was still increasing, but rather suggested that Laura rent the unit. Annie felt that Laura could get more than enough income from the rental to cover the mortgage payment, the monthly maintenance fee, and the property taxes. In fact, there might even be enough money left over at the end of the year for a nice vacation. Meanwhile, the unit was appreciating in value, and it would cost Laura nothing to carry it. When she did sell, it would be pure profit. Annie offered to list the unit for Laura, but Laura was determined to handle the matter herself. "I bought it on my own and I will rent and manage it on my own," she told her friend. Annie recommended several good books on leasing, but Laura would hear none of it. "I know what I'm doing. I don't need any help at all."

The next day Laura placed an advertisement in the local newspaper which read:

Great apartment, excellent view.

Unfurnished

$1,200.00 per month

Call Laura at 555-555-7755 for more information.

Laura did not get any response the first two weeks. Her friend Annie, who had seen the ad, called to tell Laura that the list price was too expensive for a one bedroom and recommended some changes in the advertisement. Laura would not hear of it. "My mother told me to ask $1,200 per month, and Mom was in real estate too," Laura reminded Annie. "Besides, this ad is expensive enough. If somebody is looking for a unit like mine, they will pay the price, and I'm not making any changes," Laura continued to argue. Annie sighed but knew that once her friend made up her mind, that was it. Annie could not help but mention that Laura's mother had been in real estate in a different state and that she had been retired for 25 years. "It is possible," Annie suggested in her most diplomatic voice, "that your mom may not be up on our local real estate market." "Nonsense," replied Laura, "rentals are rentals. It's a one bedroom and mom knows her stuff. She was a top producer for 5 years in a row." Annie sighed again, wished her friend the best, and hung up.

About one week before Laura was scheduled to move, she got a call from a prospect who was coming into town and needed a one bedroom. Although Laura wouldn't admit it, she was getting really nervous and was ready to grab just about any tenant who literally walked through the door.

Tony Tenant was on time for his appointment with Laura. A middle-aged man who looked fit enough, he checked the apartment thoroughly. "Can't be too careful," he told Laura. "I work constantly and I can't be distracted by problems at home." Laura could understand this and assured Tony that the apartment was first rate. "It had better be for the price you are asking. Tell you what, I'll offer you $900 per month, take it or leave it." Laura was flabbergasted; this was much less than she had anticipated. In fact, she wasn't really planning on negotiating her price, but then again, the movers were coming the next day.

"Okay," she said. "$1,100 per month and its yours," she countered, trying to control her nerves.

"All right," replied Tony, "but don't bother me with first, last, and security and all that rot. I'll give you a check for $1,100 for the first month right now. I'll move in next week."

Laura felt a bit uncomfortable but figured that she really didn't have time to fool around. Her friends in the legal department had warned her about being sloppy and told her to insist on a security deposit, but what the heck, they weren't the ones under the gun to rent. Besides, it was an empty apartment, what could this guy break? She pulled out the lease she had bought at "Office Universe" that stated in bold print that this was a legal document in all fifty states and that all one had to do was fill in the names of the parties and the price. Laura filled in the blank spaces provided for the names of the parties to the lease and the amount of the rent. They each signed, and Laura began to pack. Soon she would start a new life.

When she arrived at her new job, her company gave her two weeks to find a place to live and put her up at a good hotel. She used the time wisely and located a very suitable apartment with a good view of the park. The rent was $2,000 per month, which was more than Laura wanted to pay, but she could afford it. She signed the lease, gave the new landlord the first month's rent along with the last month's payment and one month's security deposit. She also gave an additional $30.00 to cover the credit check on her. As she walked out of the leasing office, she couldn't help but think how much more organized and professional the company was compared to the way she leased her own unit. It did everything the way her friends in the legal department had told her to do it.

"Oh, well," she thought, "that's a building of 200 units. I'm only a single unit owner, and Tony seemed O.K. I'm just making myself crazy."

Laura had taken Tony's check with her and used it to partially open her new bank account. She was informed that it would take as much as two weeks to clear because it was an "out of state" check. About one week later, Laura received a letter from her bank informing her that Tony's check for the first month was being returned for insufficient funds. It was like being punched in the stomach. She tried to calm herself. Fortunately, she had Tony's cell phone number and called him immediately.

"Uh, Tony," she tried to sound calm, "it's Laura. I just called to see how everything was going?"

"Everything is fine, Laura. Thanks for calling."

Laura thought she detected a slight annoyance in his tone of voice. "Did I catch you at a bad time?"

"No," Tony replied. "But I am embarrassed to have to tell you that the $1,100 I gave you will probably be returned. I was transferring funds to a new account here in town and my bank closed my account before clearing the check. I was furious."

"Well, actually, it was returned, and I was a bit concerned," replied Laura, who was now feeling calmer. After all, it seemed like a legitimate reason. "Well, Tony, when can I expect another check?"

"Not to worry, Laura, I'll send one right away, as soon as the bank gives me my new checks, should be a few days. I'll call you when I mail it so you'll expect it. Got to run, your apartment's great. Bye." With that, Tony hung up.

Laura was dumbfounded. She didn't know what to do. Why didn't she ask him to wire the funds to her new account? She would wait a few days and call again. Yes, that is what she would do. She forced herself to calm down and prepared for her new job and new life. Everything would be fine, she told herself again and again until she believed it.

Laura's new job was exciting and challenging. It was an executive position, and the time seemed to fly. Each day was filled with meetings, decisions, and reports. It was so engrossing that Laura didn't realize that a whole month had passed and Tony hadn't sent her a new check. In fact, the second month's rent was already past due by several days. Laura made a note to call Tony again if the check hadn't arrived in the day's mail. At the end of her workday, Laura took the bus home to her apartment. She stopped at the mailroom and opened the box, where several letters and magazines were neatly piled. There it was, an envelope bearing her old return address. Laura opened the envelope and found a check from Tony for $600. Along with the check there was a bill from APEX PLUMBING Company for $1,500. The bill was itemized at $1,000 for materials, including such items as pipes and a new commode, and $500 for installation and miscellaneous labor. There was also a note from Tony stating that "there was a problem with the plumbing in the bathroom" and he made the repairs.

"That son of a b———, how dare he?" Laura was inflamed. "We'll see about this."

The next day, Laura took a copy of her Office Universe standard lease, good in all fifty states, and marched into the legal department of her company. One of the perks of the job was that she was entitled to legal assistance, and an attorney from the department was provided for such purposes. The attorney read Laura's lease and noted the following:

A. The lease states that the rent is due and owing on the first of the month, but there is no provision for late payments or penalties if the rent is paid late.

B. The lease states that major repairs are the responsibility of the landlord but doesn't define what constitutes "major repairs."

C. The lease does not address the issue of when the tenant can effectuate repairs on his or her own initiative and does not state whether or not a tenant may withhold rent to cover the costs.

D. The "default clause" of the lease covers only nonpayment of rent.

"Your problem," explained the corporate attorney, "is that based upon the loose language of the lease agreement, and the fact that you have been presented with what appears to be a legitimate bill for parts and services, it appears that you are responsible, so you cannot say that your tenant is in breach of the lease. Of course, you can ask for any fees in connection with the check he bounced, but he probably won't pay it. Just take it off the security when he moves out. The lease doesn't indicate it, but you did take a security deposit?"

"Sure, of course I did; thanks for your help," Laura said as she gathered her paperwork and somewhat sheepishly marched out of the legal office.

In the months that followed, Tony's tenancy did not get any better. Rent continually came late and always with deductions for this repair or that. A few checks bounced and had to be redeposited. Finally, around the sixth month, Tony disappeared. Fortunately, he didn't appear to have used the apartment much, and the building manager reported to Laura that her place was in pretty good shape. The manager also remarked that her toilet seat seemed much bigger and more comfortable than the standard seats.

"Yeah," replied Laura, "people don't know how important it is to have a good toilet seat."

The next day, Laura bought a book on how to be a successful landlord. She knew the matter of Tony's rental could have turned out a lot worse, but with all the aggravation, she enjoyed the idea of being a landlady and getting income from her property. She was determined to lease the unit again, but this time she would do it right.

Questions for Review

1. Was Laura correct in electing to lease her unit as Annie Agent advised her?
2. Review the case study and list the mistakes Laura made in leasing her property. Then compare your list to the list provided in the answer section immediately following these questions.

3. Do you think the lawyer was correct in advising Laura that she was basically stuck with Tony as a tenant and she really couldn't do anything about it?

Answers and Analysis

1. Yes. This is the classic example of how a property should be utilized to its highest and best use. Laura was given an opportunity that

required her relocation to another area. The condominium that she owned was increasing in value, or "appreciating." In addition, the rental market in her area appeared to be active. Laura was advised that the rent the unit could command would cover her expenses and even throw off a profit while the property was appreciating.

2. Laura made numerous mistakes:

   a. *The newspaper advertisement.* It is no wonder that Laura did not get any response to the ad except for Tony. Reading the ad, we are told only that the unit is a great unit with an excellent view, and we are also given the price. But there is no description of the unit. How many bedrooms; how many baths; where is it located; besides the view, what if any are the features of the apartment, the building, or the area? Is it close to transportation or shopping? Does it have a swimming pool or a gymnasium?

   b. *The price.* According to Annie Agent, the price was too high. When pressed by Annie to justify asking such a price, Laura responded by stating that her mother told her to list it. Her mother's qualifications were that in the 1970s she was a top agent in another city. Annie is correct in pointing out that Laura's mom had no knowledge, let alone any current knowledge, of the rental market in Laura's city. Obviously, Laura had no basis for asking $1,200 per month. While it has been said that you should always listen to your mother, in this case, Laura would have been better advised to do the research herself or listen to Annie, who was familiar with the real estate market. The fact that Tony responded to the ad and accepted $1,100 as a rental amount is not indicative of the true rental value of the unit because he had no intention of paying the full rent or, apparently, remaining in the unit for the term of the lease.

   c. *Not insisting on first month's rent, last month's rent, and security.* These should never be negotiable items except in a case where the tenant offers to pay the full term of the lease in advance, and even in that circumstance, the security deposit should never be waived. There is a great tendency for tenants to "live through" the security as the last month's rent. As a landlord, if you accept the first month's rent and a security deposit without the last month's rent in advance, the temptation you offer the tenant to "live through" his or her security deposit and not pay that last month's rent is too great for most tenants to resist. However, where you hold the last month's rent, a tenant will generally not try to "live through" the security payment by not paying rent on the eleventh month. In Laura's case, when Tony accepted the $1,100 per month but no last month or security, that should have been a red flag for Laura to send him on his way, pack her bags, and list the property with Annie Agent, as she was out of time.

A related general lesson that applies to all facets of real estate, including the rental of property, is that real estate is not liquid. It's not like having cash in the bank or stock. With cash or stock, if you need money, you simply withdraw it from your account or you sell your stock and "cash out." In the case of real estate, while appreciation is often greater than for other investments and rental income the highest return, capital recovery takes time. Unless you give the property away at bargain prices for a quick sale, a real estate transaction takes time if it is to be done right. If you are pressed for time, or in dire need of money, you should never count on real estate sales or rentals for such purposes. The facts of the case study indicate that Laura was getting a big salary increase, which means she probably could have carried her property a few months before running into trouble. This should have been more than enough time to lease it. However, Laura created her own deadline by insisting that she would rent the unit herself before she left town. Aside from the fact that she didn't do the correct research in terms of price, the fact that she was pressured further reduced her negotiating position and literally forced her to accept Tony, not because she wanted to, but because he was there at the right time. That should never be a reason to accept a tenant.

d. *Failure to perform a credit check.* This was also a function of the fact that Laura was in a rush to conclude the transaction. It is doubtful that Tony would have even submitted to a credit check, and that would have "red flagged" him as an unsuitable tenant.

e. *Acceptance of Tony's check and failure to immediately deposit it.* Laura took Tony's check with her to her new city, trusting that it would clear. All this trust was apparently based upon her one meeting with Tony for a few minutes. Laura should have run to her local bank to deposit that check. In today's security-conscious atmosphere, many banks won't verify funds even to another bank, nor will banks "freeze those funds" pending arrival of the check as a bank-to-bank courtesy. Whether or not a bank will verify funds of one of their depositors depends on the individual bank's policies, so it is always worth insisting that your bank attempt to verify funds for the check being deposited. However, Laura should have demanded a cashier's check, or "bank check," good old cash, or that Tony wire the funds bank-to-bank before giving him the keys to the apartment. Those are all acceptable options when time is tight with regard to a move-in date. As she did not, she should have at least tried to get her local bank to verify funds from Tony's bank. But to carry the check with her to help fund her new account was a mistake, and it cost her time, effort, money, and possibly good credit with her new bank.

f. *Laura's use of a "universal lease."* This is a bit of a "red herring." A red herring in mystery stories is a false clue. The writers of the lease used by Laura claimed that it was good in all fifty states. This may sound like a bad thing, but it is fine provided the form lease addresses all of the issues. The mistake was not Laura's use of a universal lease, but that she failed to read the document to see if she understood it. There are numerous form leases available as well as do-it-yourself legal software kits that contain all sorts of preprinted documents on everything from preparing wills to getting divorced. The problem is that you can't just use forms in a vacuum. It requires at least some technical knowledge of the subject matter. In Laura's case, she may not have even had enough knowledge of the subject matter to determine if the lease was suitable. We don't know, because Laura never read the document. When Tony deducted the $1,500 plumbing fee, Laura took the lease to her legal department. The teaching point is, you learn about the forms before you use them or you go to a lawyer. The time to learn about a legal document is not after the problem occurs, but before you sign it.

In this and the preceding chapter, you have been provided with an analysis of each clause of a lease. After completing and mastering this chapter, you should have enough technical knowledge to evaluate a basic lease agreement. With experience, you will also be able to tailor those agreements because you understand the contents of a lease and the nature of the transaction. For whatever reason, Laura insisted on leasing her unit on her own, yet she failed to even attempt to comprehend what should have been the basic foundation of her transaction, the lease agreement.

A friend of mine who owns a building recently showed me a commercial lease and asked me if he could prevent one of his lessees from assigning the lease to a third party. The relevant clause in the tenant's lease stated that the landlord must consent to the assignment in writing, but such consent should not be "unreasonably withheld." My friend told me that he had gotten the lease from a neighbor who also owned a building. Neither my friend nor his tenant had actually ever read the agreement they both signed. The tenant had been in the property for years, and there had never been a problem before. Basically, the answer, which my friend didn't want to hear, was that unless there was a good reason for withholding consent, the lease could probably be assigned. Moral of the story: "Read and heed" whatever you sign.

g. *Failure of Laura to insist on immediate payment of the bounced check.* Although already at a disadvantage, Laura should not have accepted further stalling by Tony on making good his rent payment by waiting for checks to arrive or any other excuse. At this point, Laura should have sent Tony a "due demand" letter (an example of such a letter is found in Appendix A) that would begin the eviction process. Instead, Laura continued to wait and hope that everything would work

3. Was the lawyer correct in his advice to Laura? Although lawyers don't like to readily admit it, the law is more of an art than a science, and often there are no real clear "yes" and "no" answers. However, it appears that the lawyer was correct in his analysis. The lease that Laura used did not clearly deal with the situations that Tony Tenant presented. In addition, Tony had evidence of serious problems in the apartment. While the evidence strongly suggests that Tony was not the most forthright of people, it is still his word,

and, probably, the word of the plumber who wrote the bill, that Tony had an emergency. The fact that he deducted items each month may not be morally right and may be extremely annoying, but it does happen in the real world, even with the nicest of tenants. That is why these situations must be dealt with in the lease agreement. The lease that is proposed in this book specifically states that except in clear emergency situations, the landlord must be given the opportunity to cure first. It also sets a sum certain that defines the parameters of responsibility for repairs between the landlord and the tenant.

Conclusion

Laura was actually fortunate that Tony did not complete the term of the lease. A bad tenant can be one of life's aggravating situations. However, even in the situation where you get a bad tenant, there is always a positive side, at least in the United States.

In the United States, contracts, including leases, in order to be legal, must have a termination provision. Even those contracts that do not have a specific date of termination but simply state that they renew automatically if one party does not cancel in writing renew for only a specific period of time. They are subject to an end at each period if a party to the lease makes his or her intention known. In other words, at some point, the lease will end and the tenant must move out, willingly or not. At the end of the lease, you may negotiate a new lease, if you choose not to renew with the current tenant.

Laura's whole approach to the landlord/tenant transaction was wrong from beginning. Her concept of leasing a property was that you put an advertisement in the newspaper and the offers come rolling in. The lease agreement itself appeared to be some sort of formality. Please note that Laura, who also became a tenant, was subjected to a credit check and payment of a security deposit and the first and last month's rent. I can also assure you that the lease she signed was very complete and favored, to the largest degree possible, the landlord.

As I have stressed and will continue to stress, being a landlord is not an intellectual exercise. It is a business, and a business where you can own a property, watch it appreciate in value, and have income from that property while it is appreciating in value. A wonderful investment like that deserves the investor's time and attention.

CASE STUDY #2

The Good Tenant: Laura's Revenge

After her experience with Tony Tenant, Laura was determined not to make the same mistakes again. She read the lease that she had signed for her new apartment and was amazed at how it almost totally protected the landlord and granted her almost no rights at all as a tenant. She literally could not hammer a nail into a wall without the written consent of the landlord. "This is good," she thought. "I'll copy it and use it for my next tenant."

The next day she placed an ad in the newspaper. It read:

Beautiful One Bedroom, One Bath For Rent

Large Apartment, Beautiful Views

All It Needs Is You

Priced to Lease at $1,100 per month

Call 555-222-3322

This time Laura got numerous responses. She called each enquiry back and arranged appointments to view the apartment during the following weekend. She made the appointments at 15-minute intervals between 10:00 a.m. and 2:00 p.m. She figured that this would be long enough for people to look at the unit, and they would probably see the next appointment coming in. This, she figured, would create a sense of urgency. This is a good marketing ploy. Laura also arranged to have a friend with her so she wouldn't be alone and also to assist with other prospects if they arrived early. Laura also copied the application form from her new residence and made enough copies to hand out to interested parties. She added that a $30.00 fee for a credit check was required with the application. She located a national credit reference company and secured its forms (sample copies of these forms are located in Appendix A).

Laura took the week off and stayed with her friend who was going to help her rent the unit. Laura then checked the apartment, and although Tony had left it in good shape, she hired a painter to "freshen the walls" and a carpet cleaning company to steam clean the carpets. She cleaned the windows herself, and with a little air freshener, the place looked great. On her way home, Laura noticed a repair van with the sign, WE FIX-IT FAST APPLIANCE COMPANY. Laura got a business card from the driver and secured an appliance contract for about $150. "Excellent, if something goes wrong, the tenant can just call the Repair Company. Next time, I'll make that a condition of the lease and make the tenant pay for it." Laura was practically grinning. She would not have a repeat of the Tony Tenant affair.

The weekend arrived, and Laura and her friend greeted the prospective tenants. The day went remarkably well, and Laura received several offers to lease the unit. Laura had given each an application with an envelope to mail back the application if they decided to lease, but Luke and Linda Lessee filled the application out and returned it to Laura with a $30 dollar check. They did tell Laura that they could only pay $950 per month. Laura reviewed the form and it was complete in every detail. The check was drawn on a local bank. Laura sent the forms to the credit company, and the applicants checked out perfectly. They had rented in two previous locations and always paid their rent on time. In addition, the prior landlords gave glowing reports. Laura called Luke and Linda and told them that she would rent the unit to them at $1,100 per month and that there were several other qualified applicants, "so take it or leave it." Laura figured that based on their application, both Luke and Linda were employed, and they commanded salaries sufficient to pay the rent at full price. They were just haggling, and she would have none of that. Besides, there were two other parties who had expressed interest in renting and filled out applications, but one hadn't given the $30 application/credit check fee and the other had a shorter rental history than either of the other two applicants. After a brief and highly dramatic pause, Luke and Linda agreed, signed the lease, gave Laura a check for first month's rent, last month's rent, and a security deposit equaling one month's rent, and moved in. The rent checks came on the first day of the month, each and every month, like clockwork. "This is great," thought Laura.

Five months into the lease, Luke called Laura and told her that Linda had just lost her job and they were struggling a bit. He explained that it couldn't have come at a worse time because their car needed expensive repairs that weren't covered by their warranty. Luke asked if they could pay the rent a few weeks late this month. Laura replied somewhat tersely that he could have until the 15th of the month provided he pay the $100 late fee provided for in the lease. Luke reluctantly agreed and hung up without a "thank you." "Not very grateful," thought Laura. She quickly typed a letter to Luke and Linda that read:

This confirms our conversation of 25 August 200__. You may pay your rent not later than the 15th of September 200__. The late payment fee of $100.00 in paragraph ____ of your lease is NOT WAIVED. If the late payment is not included, you may be in breach of your lease or payment will be deducted from your security deposit.

> Signed
> Laura Landlord

On the 15th of September, Luke and Linda's rent check arrived with the $100 penalty included. There was a short note included, which read:

> Please note that I have accepted a position with Newman, Newman, Newman, Newman and Newman, Attorneys at Law, as an office manager. My salary has been increased by 5 percent. Please note the change in your records. Mr. Sam Newman, senior partner in their real estate division, has agreed to review our lease.

> Signed
> Linda Lessee

Suddenly, Laura had a sinking feeling in her stomach. She checked Linda's application, which noted that she was an office manager for Jones and Jones, Certified Public Accountants. It hadn't occurred to her that Linda could switch jobs and become the office manager of a law firm. That sounded scary. "So what?" she thought. "I'm within my rights, and I won't be intimidated by anyone. If she thinks I'm going to be impressed by a bunch of Newmans, I'm not. Besides, a major leasing company used that lease. It's rock solid."

On the first of the month, the rent check arrived on time. Laura was proud of herself. She was tough in a tough world. Her triumph, however, was short-lived. Two days later she received a certified letter from S. Newman, Attorney at Law. It read:

> Dear Ms. Landlord:

> Please be advised that this firm represents Luke and Linda Lessee, tenants in the above-described property. Mr. and Mrs. Lessee advised us that the air conditioning system is not functioning properly. Your appliance company advises us that the compressor in the system is about to fail. An improper air filter placed in the unit by you caused this failure. Therefore, the company has refused to effectuate repairs. The estimated cost of replacing the compressor is $2,500. Please advise the undersigned as to method of repair and payment by close

of business Friday, or we will have no recourse but to take any and all appropriate legal action.

Signed

S. Newman
Attorney at Law

Laura started to panic. "They're going to sue me?" Laura was about to grab for the phone and call her legal department but then thought better of it. "I'm an executive," she said under her breath. "I deal with crisis situations every day. This is no different. I'm just not being objective because I'm the one being attacked personally. I can deal with this."

Laura pulled out her lease agreement and read it carefully. "I've got them," she screamed triumphantly. "I'm not going to lose again."

The next morning, Laura called the repair company and demanded to speak to a supervisor. After identifying herself, she placed the supervisor on hold and called Mr. Newman.

"He's in conference right now," responded Mr. Newman's secretary. "Can he call you back?"

"Not if he doesn't want his new office manager to be without air conditioning for the next few weeks," said Laura.

"One moment please," came the response.

The next voice was that of Mr. Newman. "Newman here."

"Mr. Newman, Laura Landlord. I have on the line a supervisor from the appliance company. Here's the bottom line. You indicated that the air filter causing the compressor to fail was the original filter in the air conditioning unit found by your clients, and that that is why I am responsible for repairing it. I have in front of me a certificate of inspection from the appliance company saying that they inspected the air conditioning unit and approved it for repairs. Obviously, if that was the original filter, and it was incorrect, then the appliance company should not have approved it. Hear that, Ms. Supervisor? Your inspector should have noted that the filter was incorrect. That was your mistake. And as for you, Mr. Newman, your clients didn't bother to change the filter in the air conditioner for six months. Ask your clients if they read the message on the cover of the air conditioner, which says in bold letters, FILTERS MUST BE CHANGED EVERY MONTH. So even if the wrong filter was in the unit, your clients didn't properly maintain the system. I'm not a lawyer, but I know a few, and I've discussed this issue with them. They agree that if this case went to court, the judge would not make me pay for the repairs."

Laura hoped she sounded naïve enough to be convincing, yet give the impression that she had solid legal opinion behind her. "I really don't care which of you pays for the repairs, but I can tell you it is not going to be me."

"I think we can solve the problem." The voice was that of the supervisor. "The repair order says that the compressor is about to fail, but it hasn't as yet. We can clean and repair it without replacing it, and your unit should work fine."

"I don't know," said Mr. Newman. "I think that my client should get a new compressor."

"Absolutely not, sir." Now the supervisor was assertive. "Our repair people maintain that the unit can be placed in proper working order by cleaning the compressor and that is all we are legally obligated to do, and that is all we will do."

"Well, I'll confirm with my client, but I think that will be okay as long as the unit functions properly."

"It will. We'll repair the unit by 5:00 p.m. today. Please have someone available to let our technician into the apartment."

With that, the supervisor hung up, and so did Laura. She was jubilant; she had won a huge victory. She had faced down a lawyer and the appliance insurance company. This was unbelievable. "What power a landlord has if he or she does things right," she thought.

Luke and Linda continued to pay their rent on time each month for the remainder of the lease and never had any further contact with Laura. At the end of the lease term, they notified her that they were moving out. Laura inspected the unit, and it was perfect. Laura found out from a neighbor that Luke and Linda rented a similar apartment in the building for $1,150 per month, as Luke also got a promotion and an increase in salary.

Questions and Analysis
How would you critique Linda's behavior as a landlord? Was she really a winner?

As the title of the case study suggests, Linda has reacted to her unpleasant experience with Tony Tenant by "clamping down" on her next tenants. In my opinion, she has overreacted. All the evidence indicates that Luke and Laura were good and reasonable tenants who ran into a tough situation. Their credit history was impeccable, and they paid their rent on time. A good tenant is money in the bank, and when Luke asked Laura for some consideration, she should have granted the request. I probably would have suggested that if Luke paid by the 15th as promised, then Laura would forgo the $100 penalty. In this way, the penalty still serves its purpose as an incentive for the tenant to pay his or her rent on time and Laura is not waiving her right to receive it for that month. On the other hand, it softens Laura's position and makes her seem less of a villain and more of a reasonable person who is giving the benefit of the doubt to her tenants, who may have run into some bad luck, but have otherwise acted properly. If the tenants missed the payment as promised, Laura could have reassessed the situation and then got tough if the situation called for it. If the tenants made the payment on time, Laura then appears as a reasonable person and a good relationship with the tenants is maintained.

Laura's Problem-Solving Ability

In dealing with Mr. Newman and the appliance company, Laura showed outstanding analytical and leadership qualities. What she did was very difficult to achieve in a real-world situation, but it is possible with the proper research. Laura was prepared in terms of both the facts and the law as it applied to the case. She managed to bring the parties together and, in the face of the facts, presented a compelling argument to both sides to find a solution to the problem, because ultimately, she would not bear the burden of responsibility. There was an excellent bit of bluffing involved as well. Although Laura hadn't spoken to anybody, she managed to strengthen her argument by stating that several attorneys with whom she had consulted backed her position. Laura understood that in some cases, the perception of power can be effective even if you don't actually possess that power. Laura made it seem as though she had an army of lawyers behind her, when in fact she had none. But was Laura the winner?

The answer to the question lies in what you believe the goal of a landlord is. I have argued that the ultimate goal of a landlord is to have tenants who pay their rent on time and respect you and your property. In this case study scenario, Laura won every victory along the way against her tenants, including a rather stunning coup against Mr. Newman and the appliance company. However, at the end of the lease term, the tenants moved out and rented a similar unit in the same building for more money, leaving Laura to start her search for a tenant once again. Laura won every battle but lost the war because she lost good tenants. The lesson learned here is to first give people the benefit of the doubt. If they disappoint you, then all bets are off and you take whatever legal steps you must to protect your interests. But at least when you take action, you do so knowing you tried to resolve the issue on a friendly basis first.

Laura's Tyrannical Approach

After her experience with Tony Tenant, Laura's toughness is understandable but not defensible. As I have stressed, you are in business. To learn from your prior mistakes is a positive thing. It is another to exact revenge for revenge's sake. Laura's whole approach was, "I will not be taken advantage of by unscrupulous tenants again." Not every tenant is unscrupulous, and each case should be assessed on its own merits. Just because Tony was a bad tenant, you don't take out your frustrations on the next tenant. Moral issues aside, it is bad business.

CASE STUDY #3

The Artistic Tenant: Laura's Lesson's Learned

When Luke and Linda gave notice that they were moving out, Laura was in the middle of an office crisis and could not take the time to lease her unit again. She called her old friend Annie Agent and asked her to list the property for her. Luke and Linda were less than enthusiastic about allowing Annie to show the unit to prospective tenants but complied with the terms of the lease, which indicated that 24 hours' notice was required and the unit could be shown Monday to Friday from 9:00 a.m. to 5:00 p.m. This made it difficult for working people to arrange to view the unit, but Luke and Linda would not give Laura any help in that regard.

Once Luke and Linda moved out, Annie was able to show the unit more freely and soon was able to find a tenant, Rodney Renter, who leased the unit for $1,000 per month. Annie got a 10 percent commission. Fortunately, the unit wasn't empty for very long, and although it cost Laura some money to find a new tenant, she considered herself fortunate that the unit rented quickly.

Rodney was an interesting fellow. Apparently, he was a well-known interior decorator, famous for designing and decorating hotel lobbies. Laura recalled seeing a picture of him in a magazine with his two dogs, Boozy and Snoozy. Laura, who was not a pet person, was not overjoyed with the idea of two dogs living in her apartment. But Annie advised her that it was not against the rules of the condominium association and that Rodney would pay a "pet deposit" of $100 for each pet to cover the cost of any additional cleaning attributable to Rodney's dogs. Annie used the standard rental lease agreement that was approved by her local realtor association. One of the clauses read:

> Tenant may not alter or improve the property without the express written consent of the landlord.

Rodney and his dogs lived in the unit for the first year and renewed for a second term. Annie negotiated a $50 per month increase. During the two years the unit was leased by Rodney, there had been little contact between him and Laura. The rent, which was automatically deposited in Laura's account, was always credited to her account by the fifth or sixth of the month, and Rodney never complained of any problems in the apartment. Laura never came to the unit or otherwise instructed Annie to inspect the unit. In fact, Annie had relocated to Florida, where she opened her own office. She and Laura had lost touch.

At the end of the second year, Rodney got a job decorating a new hotel in Bora Bora and advised Laura that he was leaving. He asked when he might receive his security and pet deposit back, as the apartment was immaculate. "In fact, Laura, your unit now has the 'Rodney Touch,' which, as you know, I am famous for, and you now have a valuable little apartment. But I won't charge you for it," he said, laughing at his own joke.

Laura wasn't sure what the famous "Rodney Touch" was, but she figured that before she returned any security, she had better check the unit personally. It had been a while since she had had a vacation, so she took a few days off and went back home to inspect her unit. It was then she discovered the Rodney Touch. Her living room was now divided in the center by a glass block wall that extended almost to the ceiling. Behind the glass block, Rodney had pulled up the carpet and placed a Mexican tile floor in the newly created area. The walls were painted deep purple, but with a type of fluorescent paint that seemed to give off an eerie yellowish glow when the lights were off.

Laura was stunned. She looked in the kitchen and was relieved to see that the Rodney Touch hadn't extended to that part of the apartment. "Well," thought Laura, "I guess I can live with the glass block. It is sort of impressive, even though it makes the room look smaller, and I can always paint the walls again. It has been two years and it was due anyway. I can always throw a rug over the tile floor."

Feeling a bit of relief, Laura next looked in the bedroom. Her relief was short-lived. Rodney had removed the wall separating the bathroom from the bedroom. The walls were painted with the same luminous paint, only dark green instead of purple. In what had been the bathroom, Rodney had removed the bathtub and created a standing shower instead. The bathroom was painted black. Thankfully, it didn't glow in the dark.

Laura called a contractor who advised her that restoring the unit to its original design was not that complicated from a technical standpoint. Rodney had not done any structural damage to the unit. It was mostly time-consuming, especially painting over the dark, luminous colors, which would require gallons of white paint. Also, Rodney had done some plumbing work that would be expensive to restore. The contractor checked with the local government and Laura's condominium association, and in fact, Rodney had received permits from the city along with permission from the association to perform the work. Laura was dumbfounded. It was her unit and nobody had even notified her. The total cost to restore the unit would be about $5,000.

"By the way, what's that smell? Is that the paint?" asked Laura.

"Oh no," replied the contractor. "Your tenant must have had some pets that he didn't take care of very well."

Laura didn't ask any further questions.

Questions and Conclusions
1. Should Laura withhold Rodney's security and pet deposit? Why or why not? Be specific.
2. What are Laura's remedies against Rodney, the condominium association, and the city?
3. What specific steps should Laura take in handling the various issues involved?

1. Obviously, Laura is well within her rights to withhold the security and pet deposits. The issue here is why. The relevant portion of the lease reads that Rodney could not alter or improve the property without Laura's written consent. While Rodney may consider his decoration a work of art, he still needed to comply with the terms of his lease agreement.

Restoration of the Walls

Rodney added walls, took out walls, and basically changed the structure of the unit. The cost of restoration to its original condition may be subtracted from the security deposit. Since Laura had a one-month security deposit, that cost would probably be subsumed in the effort. Rodney is liable for restoring the unit to its basic configuration.

Repainting the Unit

This is a closer issue. After two years, it may be hard to justify deducting for a repainting based upon the principal of "normal wear and tear." However, in this case, there is a very good argument that painting the walls in glow-in-the-dark deep colors is not in the normal course of decoration and required the express written consent of the landlord. In addition, it is not that easy to cover up. Rodney's eclectic taste in paint requires considerably more paint and labor-hours to remove or cover. Therefore, I would charge the difference between a normal paint job and the extra costs involved in covering up the dark colors.

The Pet Deposit

Although there are not enough specific facts given as to damages caused by the pets, if the pet odors were sufficient that they permeated throughout the unit or damaged the carpets, simply treat the pet deposit in the same fashion you treat the withholding of a security deposit. Be careful not to use the pet deposit to offset security deposits. Although some laws that I have seen don't specifically address pet deposits and therefore it can be argued that they are unregulated, I would recommend they be treated in the same fashion as your state requires you to treat security deposits.

In this case, Laura could advise Rodney that since he owes more than the security deposit covers, Laura is withholding the pet deposit to help offset the costs of the repairs. She should be careful to include a sentence stating that if Rodney objects to this withholding, she will forward the pet deposit back less whatever costs she incurs for deodorizing the unit, and that the additional withholding does not constitute any type of settlement of her claim.

The Tile Floor

Rodney's tile floor presents a number of issues. The facts indicate that he pulled up part of the living room carpet and replaced it with tile. In this case, does Laura get to charge only for the portion of the carpet that was taken up for the tile or for the whole carpet? The law tends to favor a concept of making the injured party "whole," i.e., in the same position he or she was in prior to the injury. Rodney would argue that he didn't ruin the whole carpet, simply one portion of it, and therefore that is all he should be liable to replace.

Laura would counter with two very strong arguments:

A. Replacing a portion of the living room carpet would not put her in the same position as she originally was because replacing only a portion would mean matching the old carpet with a new piece and would give the carpet a "patch effect" that was not present to begin with. In addition, the patch would be clearly visible, as it is in a significant portion of the center of the room. Therefore, the entire carpet is ruined.

B. Rodney's defenses should not be given great weight because he violated the terms of the lease to begin with by not getting written consent from Laura before ripping up carpeting. Rodney therefore does not have "clean hands" to assert defenses on his behalf. In my opinion, under these facts, Laura is entitled to credit for the entire living room carpet.

2. Laura's remedies are extensive.

Rodney

As discussed in answer #1, Laura can withhold the security deposit from Rodney. She can also sue him for the difference in the damages. If she withholds the $1,000, she can file suit in civil court for the remaining $4,000. The problem is that Rodney is on his way to Bora Bora. Even if Laura were to get a judgment, it might be difficult to collect. For practical purposes, Rodney is not going to help Laura with her $5,000 repair project.

The Condominium Association

We may have a more viable defendant in the association. Laura is entitled to sue all potential parties who may have contributed to her problems. In this case, the condominium association had to grant permission for the work to be done in the building prior to the city's granting a construction permit to Rodney. The association should have known that a renter might not have the authority to make structural changes in the owner's apartment. Furthermore, most condominium association documents provide that the association must deal directly with the unit owner and not the renter. It was the association's duty to contact Laura and verify that such changes were authorized prior to authorizing the work, and it breached that duty, which resulted in damages to Laura. As a result, Laura may be able to win against the association.

The City

This case is a bit tougher. The city wrongfully granted a permit to Rodney to make structural changes in the apartment. However, it may have acted in good faith based upon the application presented to it. What information was required in the permit application to the city, and what information was provided, will determine if Laura can successfully sue the city. For example, if Rodney truthfully put down that he was the tenant, the permit inspector should have questioned whether a tenant has the authority to apply for a construction permit instead of the owner. In some cases, the owner doesn't apply for the permit, but rather the contractor performing the work files the application. The city may have had no duty to investigate who the rightful owner was. A suit against the city for the wrongful issuance of the permit is going to be very fact sensitive but should nonetheless be considered. One final thought: If Rodney did employ a contractor and he signed the permit application, he too might be liable if he knew or should have known that Rodney was not the owner of the unit.

3. Laura needs to follow procedure as outlined by her state landlord-tenant laws. Usually, this means that within a specified period of time, Laura needs to either send Rodney back his deposits or send him a letter stating the reasons why those deposits will be withheld. Let's follow Laura's next steps as she tries to solve Rodney's "redecorating" of her unit.

First, Laura considered her legal options. She has been quoted $5,000 to restore the unit, and Laura has the clear right to retain one month's security (either the original $1,000, or $1,050 if she required the additional $50 for the second year). She also elected to hold the $200 unless Rodney complained, which she guessed he would not.

Laura then consulted an attorney. He agreed that Laura had a cause of action and would charge about $5,000. He felt he could get attorney's fees back for Laura, but she would still have to front the cost. Laura thanked him and said she would let him know.

Laura had learned from previous experience that getting mad was not the answer. Laura reasoned that Rodney had paid on time with no bouncing checks and no complaints for two years. She was withholding $1,200 bringing her actual damages to $3,800. She figured that with a little negotiating, she could probably bring that cost down a few hundred dollars, so she calculated that it would cost her about $3,500 to restore the unit, all of which should be tax deductible, as it is clearly a business related expense. Things were not looking so bad after all.

Laura decided what she needed to do was get the apartment repaired and rented as soon as possible. Clearly, it didn't make sense to sue because not only would it take months of litigation, even if she won the case, she would still have to collect the money, a separate legal action. The cost of pursuing a legal remedy was more than her actual damages. Laura formulated a plan. First she wrote a letter to Rodney indicating that she was keeping the security and pet deposits (a sample letter is provided in Appendix A). She then called the president of the condominium association and explained the situation to him. Although initially he denied any responsibility, she knew she had struck a nerve. She followed up her conversation with a letter to the president and the building manager. Although polite, the letter was firm in demanding that she be reimbursed for her damages or she would be forced to seek legal action.

Laura calculated that it would take about one week to get a response from the association. She was fairly certain that Rodney would not contest withholding any deposits. About four days later, Laura received a call from the condominium association manager indicating that they had several contractors working in the building and that they would restore the apartment to its original design at the association's expense. They would not, however, replace carpeting or paint because that did not require a permit and they were not involved in those activities. Laura countered by pointing out that the laying of the tile did require a permit because Rodney had to place soundproofing under the tile and that caused the carpet to be destroyed. After a brief consultation with the association board, the manager indicated that if Laura paid for the carpeting, the association would pay the labor costs of pulling up the tile and laying the new carpet. Laura agreed, reasoning that her costs were pretty much being absorbed by the association and she had already learned that sometimes you needed to compromise. The association's lawyer prepared the terms of the agreement between Laura and the association. Rodney called to complain about withholding the security and pet deposits, but Laura held firm. She figured that if Rodney took her to small claims court, the most he could get back was his pet deposit if he could prove there was no added expense directly attributable to his pets. He might also recover part of the security if he could prove that Laura's withholding the entire sum was unreasonable. As it turned out, the pet odors were so imbedded in the walls that extra fumigation of the apartment was required, which cost $205. In addition, Rodney's redesign of her apartment had been so outrageous, she doubted that he would have much sympathy from the court. Rodney was never heard from again. Shortly thereafter, Laura's unit was returned to its original state. The $1,200 covered the cost of the repainting and the new carpeting. The association did the rest.

Observations and Conclusions

Notice the differences in Laura's reactions as she progresses from case study #1 to case study #3. Although always confident and able to deal with crisis situations, with each new tenant experience, Laura's reactions are more considered and calm as she confronts new challenges. By case study #3, Laura projects an image of a person who is willing to fight for her rights, but is also willing to discuss and negotiate, and even compromise where practical to do so. Laura has learned to combine the proper attitude, use of her lease agreement, and a basic working knowledge of the legal system to solve her problems. In short, she has become a landlord.

CASE STUDY #4

The Little White Lie

Laura has rented her property once again to Lucy Lessee. Lucy is an artist and demands privacy during her work hours, which are from 9:00 a.m. to 8:00 p.m. every day except Thursday. Lucy takes a few hours off in the afternoon for a *siesta*, a custom that she learned in Europe which allows her to revitalize and work later hours. Lucy's lease with Laura was for one year and specifically stated that Laura could not disturb Lucy under any circumstances without 24 hours' notice and that Lucy has the right to refuse entrance by Laura except for emergency purposes or for "periodic inspections." Lucy was sponsored by Massive Giant Universal Corporation's young artist's training program, which paid Lucy's rent in advance for the entire year. Laura agreed to sign a lease under those conditions because she received the entire year's rent in advance. It seemed like a very good deal.

About halfway through the lease period, Laura, who had been given yet another promotion and raise, received a letter from Conversion Development Corporation. She was informed that Conversion Development Corporation was taking over the building where she rented and was converting it into a condominium. Enclosed was a price list with her unit and the price underlined. Laura was told that her lease would not be renewed, but she had the option to purchase her unit (or any other unit in the building that was available) at pre-conversion prices. Laura loved her apartment, and the price seemed very fair. She decided to make the purchase.

After consulting her banker, Laura was advised that she could obtain a loan if she lowered her "debt to equity ratio." Her banker explained that even though she had an excellent salary, she was carrying too much debt. He suggested that she sell her old condominium, thereby paying off the mortgage on it. This would bring her ratios in line, and the bank would give her a new loan. Her condominium had appreciated in value sufficiently to pay off the mortgage and leave enough over to put down a sizable deposit on the new apartment. She was all set to put an ad in the paper when she remembered one problem: her tenant, Lucy. How could Laura show the apartment with Lucy in it?

Laura considered her alternatives. Her lease allowed Laura to make "periodic inspections," but showing the unit was not an inspection. She had a key and could probably sneak in during Lucy's siestas, but that might be considered trespassing. In any event, even if it wasn't, Lucy (through her sponsor) had paid the entire year in advance, and Laura did not want to place herself in a position where she might be accused of breaching her lease.

Just as Laura was about to give up, she received a letter from Lucy. It read:

> Dear Laura:
>
> Massive Giant Universal Corporation just advised me that I won its annual art competition and will be awarded an exhibition in Paris. I will be away for one month beginning next week. As I have all my supplies and stuff lying about, I would ask that you not schedule any inspections while I am away. If there are any emergencies, please contact my mom at 555-555-5555.
>
> Lucy

Great, thought Laura, she'll be away for the month in Paris. I can place an ad in the paper. Who'll be the wiser?

Laura placed an ad in the newspaper, scheduled appointments for the weekends, and began showing the unit. All was going well, and Laura received a cash offer. Laura was careful not to touch any of Lucy's "stuff" while showing the unit, and a hefty tip to the doorman bought his silence.

All was going well until the buyer requested a second visit to "measure" the apartment for furniture. The end of the month was fast approaching, but the buyer was adamant about seeing the unit one last time. Laura scheduled an appointment but advised the buyer that they had to be quick. The buyer showed up, measurements were taken, and Laura and the buyer were about to make their escape when Lucy's mother met Laura and the buyer coming out of the apartment. Laura told Lucy's mother that the upstairs neighbor had complained about "noises" and Laura and her friend had come to investigate to make sure everything was O.K. Lucy's mother thought that was wonderful and complimented Laura on being an excellent and conscientious landlord.

Several weeks later, Lucy received a letter from the new landlord indicating that the purchase had taken place and giving a new point of contact for Lucy. Lucy had previously spoken with her mother and put two and two together. She was furious.

Questions and Analysis

Question 1: *What are the legal implications of Laura's actions? Are there any ethical implications?*

Analysis: Laura acted improperly in this case. The facts state that Laura received the entire year's rent up front on condition that Laura not disturb Lucy or enter her unit without her prior consent and 24 hours' notice. Laura could argue that when she entered the unit, Lucy was in Paris and therefore could not be disturbed, but Lucy specifically indicated that she did not want Laura to enter the unit except in an emergency situation. The intent of the parties to the lease, which as we have discussed is a two-party or *bilateral* agreement, was that Laura stay out of the unit in exchange for, or "in consideration of," her receipt of a year's rent in advance. Laura believed that she was in the wrong, as is evidenced by the fact that she lied to Lucy's mother. It is also possible that Laura was trespassing, which is a criminal offense. Even though Laura was careful not to disturb Lucy's property, what if Lucy accused Laura of stealing a painting? Laura would be in a poor position to defend herself because she was wrongfully in the unit. Therefore, Laura should not have entered the property without first contacting Lucy's mom and asking permission. Most probably, Lucy's mom would have granted the request or possibly would have agreed to be present at the showings to protect her daughter's property.

There are also certain ethical issues here. Even if Laura got away with it, what she did was still wrong. I have stressed that you should treat landlording as a profession. Laura did not act in a professional manner unless you believe that the ends always justify the means. Recent events in the business world, from the Enron scandal and the Arthur Andersen case to the New York Stock Exchange regulatory problems, suggest that ethics in business has been neglected for too long. Laura may not be the New York Stock Exchange or Enron, but the results could be just as grievous on an individual level. The teaching lesson here is, if you make a deal, stick to it and don't try to be clever.

Question 2: *What remedies, if any, does Lucy have against Laura?*

Analysis: Lucy could argue that Laura breached the lease and ask that the lease be terminated. If a judge were to grant that request, Laura would have to return the remaining rent that was paid. There could be other claims associated with Laura's trespass such as mental distress, which is beyond the scope of this example, but suffice it to say that Laura opened herself up to all sorts of potential legal problems. Fortunately, most claims are based on realistic and provable damages, and merely making naked claims is not enough to carry the day in court. The facts of this case don't indicate any damages to Lucy beyond the fact that she was angry. The lesson learned: Timing is everything, and you need to play by the rules. You are a landlord, you have a profession, and you should conduct yourself in a professional manner.

Exercise

Review the case studies again. Then compare the fact patterns to the lease agreement in Appendix B (and which was discussed in this and the preceding chapter). Try to see how the model lease deals with each of the situations presented. What modifications would you make, if any, to solve the fact patterns presented above? There is no right or wrong answer here, but you will hone your landlording skills a bit more.

CHAPTER 7

The Tenants Are Moving in Next Week

What Have I Done (and What Do I Do Now)?

Y ou have your lease. The tenants loved the house, signed up, and paid the first and last month's rent. You have also just received a check for the security deposit. The move-in date is approaching, and you have been notified that the tenants are on their way. Panic begins to set in. "Why did I do this?" you ask. "I'm going to have strangers in my house. What if they are really axe murderers that never got caught? It wouldn't show up on the credit check. They could be arsonists and be planning to burn the place down. Was this really worth it?" Sure it was, or you wouldn't have signed the lease. Calm down! Take a few deep breaths, do a little yoga. It will be all right.

Sure enough, after you compose yourself, you begin to realize that your fears were unjustified. You review the paperwork once again to see if you've missed anything. Nope, it all looks good. You have rented your house to a thirtysomething couple. The husband is an executive with a Fortune 500 company, and the wife is an elementary school teacher. Both have excellent credit and a long history as tenants, individually and as a couple. No property that either has previously occupied appears to have burned down, which pretty much eliminates the arson theory. In addition, now that you are calm, you remember that you are living in Washington, D.C., and your house is in Dayton, Ohio (which is why you rented it in the first place). So even if they were axe murderers, you and your family are probably safe from a midnight attack (at least from them). The house is being rented in "turnkey" condition, meaning it is furnished with all amenities, including but not limited to dishes and linens. All you need to do now is take care of some final matters, which is the subject of this chapter.

As in previous chapters, let us set up some working parameters. Let's stay with the example cited above, that you, landlord, now situated in Washington, D.C., have rented your house in Dayton, Ohio. During your last vacation, you traveled to Dayton for the express purpose of leasing the property and were successful in securing these tenants. You now have another week's vacation coming up. You have a choice between going to Madrid for a romantic vacation with your wife or going to Dayton for the final installation of the tenants. My advice: *Adios* Spain, go to Dayton. This is business, and you have some final matters to take care of.

Checklist

This is one of those areas of the transaction that is ripe for a checklist. I am not a big fan of checklists, which are added paperwork and usually a pain to accomplish, but they do serve several purposes. The main purpose is to act as a reminder of things to do before the tenants move in. Done properly, a checklist can serve as further evidence should a legal dispute arise later on. The proper use of a checklist can help avoid disputes, which is what you really want.

The first thing you need to do is be certain the utilities are off. By now, the tenant should have already switched the accounts to his or her name, and this generally cannot be done unless you have closed down the existing accounts. In fact, there is often a lead time involved in doing this, so give the utility companies at least two weeks to make the changes. Don't assume that the tenant has taken the time to contact the utility companies. Even though you should have already advised him or her to do so, sometimes tenants don't do it. Unless I know for sure that the tenant has specifically arranged for utilities, I generally arrange two weeks early to shut them down one day after the move-in date, just to be certain. What you don't want is for a house (especially one in extreme climates) to be without heat or air-conditioning, as the case may be. You need to contact the utility company two weeks in advance to account for the lag time. Obviously, telephone accounts should be shut down as soon as possible.

The next thing you need to do is draft an inventory of contents. Obviously, if you are leasing the property unfurnished, this is going to be a very short list. It should possibly consist of a chandelier or other lighting fixtures that you kept on the property, window treatments if applicable, and whatever appliances or other equipment, such as pool supplies, for example, that you are providing. While it is fairly certain that the tenant will not walk away with a refrigerator, a portable microwave is an appliance that you may wish to note, so put everything down to maintain an accurate record. If you are renting your property furnished or with some furniture, you will need to do a more detailed inventory. There is a sample inventory in Appendix C.

In Chapter 5, we discussed the fact that many landlords love to take photographs or movies of the property prior to the move-in. Again, while this may give you the opportunity to play with that new digital camera or further express your artistic side, it shouldn't replace a written inventory for one very important reason. The reason is simply that when you have a written inventory, it is very easy to have the tenant sign it, acknowledging its veracity. Taking pictures is fine, but where is the acknowledgment from the tenant that these pictures are a true reflection of the contents *as the tenant received the property*? Pictures are good and may be worth a thousand words, but not in this case. They are not a replacement for the written inventory.

How detailed should the inventory be? Common sense should prevail here. It should be enough to identify the item in question, for example, one six-piece set of green "x" brand dishes. If the set is not complete, or one of the dishes is missing, note that in the inventory, i.e., five dinner plates only. The same procedure should be followed for furniture and appliances. Note any scrapes and scratches or other defects. That way, you have a baseline for comparison when the tenants move out. This is where pictures may be of some assistance as an evidentiary matter. "Your honor, here's the inventory list signed by the tenant; notice that the scratch on the television is noted, and this is a photograph of the television with the scratch. The tenant also initialed this photograph. Now, judge, here is a picture of a giant gash on the other side of the set. This was not present in the original photograph. Please note the time and date, which are electronically imprinted on both photographs." This is a perfect scenario, and in nine out of ten cases, you are not going to have that degree of evidence available, nor do you really need it. In fact, in nine out of ten cases, even if you have the evidence, you probably will not get the chance to present it, but we'll talk about that later. However, what the example does illustrate is what you are trying to achieve, which is an accurate documentation of the existence and condition of the items prior to the tenant's taking possession. Of course, it is easier and more fun to take pictures, but the easy way is often the hard way in the end. Do the written inventory.

By this time, the tenants should have a complete and signed copy of the lease agreement and you should have your first and last month's rent and security deposit in the bank. If you do, you are in a very good position. The only position you want to be in. The next step is to have the final walkthrough of the property with the tenants.

The Final Walkthrough

The final walkthrough is important and should be completed, if at all possible, because it establishes with finality the condition of the property immediately prior to the tenant's move-in. However, sometimes the tenant will try to treat it as an opportunity to renegotiate the lease. This is where you need to maintain your leadership qualities. You are in charge and need to control the event. If it helps you, keep thinking that you are holding a good chunk of the tenant's money and you have a signed lease agreement. Unless you removed a bathroom from the house, or some other drastic change has occurred, you are in the driver's seat.

"You know, this room seems smaller than I remember it; doesn't it seem smaller to you, Emma?"

"Yes, Paul, it does seem much smaller."

At this point, you need to maintain your composure. Don't get excited. Simply reply that nobody's changed the dimensions of the room since you have been here. Smile a little when you say this, but maintain a degree of firmness. The subliminal message should be, "Look, you need to check the property, but I'm not going to stand for any nonsense." Then gently lead them on to the rest of the property. Look at your watch as if you have another appointment while you are moving them along. They will get the message that they need to get going.

I recall a tenant who looked at our unit several times before he decided to sign a lease. But after he signed the lease, he looked at it again. Then, prior to giving the first and last month's security, he once again checked the unit. After that, you guessed it; he checked the unit again. Each time he and his wife looked at the unit, they acted as though it was the first time they had ever seen it. Then he decided to pay the entire year in advance and checked the unit again. We knew they were after something, but we couldn't figure out what. Actually, it was very simple. Each time they saw the unit, they haggled over what items they could put in the unit prior to moving in. They wanted to use the unit to store their property for a few months prior to the lease while they were out of town. This was a furnished apartment, and there wasn't all that much extra room. As we have previously seen, there are also some legal consequences attached to this. They were also jockeying for removing a wall, something that we were not willing to do. However, since this particular tenant had paid us an entire year in advance, we tended to be a bit more liberal in allowing storage of items in the unit prior to move-in. We remained firm on the renovation, however.

The fact that the tenant paid one complete year in advance bought him some additional leeway. It need not have. Often, when you buy a car, once you make the selection, the car is taken away and driven to the back lot for "preparation." This is to keep you from remembering additional "stuff" you may want from the dealership free of charge. It should be the same with property. Once you see it, that's it until the final walkthrough. Of course, sometimes it may be necessary for the tenant to view the unit a few times, especially if he or she is furnishing it. But, basically, you should try to avoid this as much as possible.

"Hi, Mr. Landlord, my mother-in-law is in town and would like to see the unit. Is that okay?" So you drag yourself down and show it again. "This is so small, and it's far away from shopping, blah, blah, blah." We have found that when the prospect brings a second opinion, he or she is going to get it, and rarely is that opinion going to be positive. Human nature is such that when put in a position of ostensible superior knowledge, that person will want to show how expert he or she is. If the so-called expert just agrees that you have a great property, he or she hasn't really done anything. But if the expert berates the heck out of the property, pointing out all sorts of defects, then that person has shown how smart he or she is and how truly worthy they were of being called in on the consultation.

In this case, we are in the final walkthrough. It is of no consequence how many friends and relatives (a.k.a. experts) the tenant brings with him or her. You have the money (or should by this time), and you don't have to defend yourself or your property. Again, be patient and polite, but you can always remind the tenant or the "advisers" that, in fact, this is a walkthrough, the purpose of which is to make sure everything is in order in accordance with the lease agreement. You can also add that you simply cannot entertain any further conditions or changes at this time. They'll get the message.

Once the walkthrough is complete, have the tenant sign the inventory. By this time, the tenant should have a copy of the lease, the inventory, and any other relevant documents such as appliance repair contracts and building rules and regulations, as applicable. Then you should wish the tenant luck, give him or her a set of keys, and get out. As I have said earlier and will continue to stress throughout this book, resist the temptation to become "buddies" with your tenants. This is business. Keep it professional. Don't go to lunch with them and by no means accept any dinner invitations. The last thing you want to do is visit them, unless it is an "official inspection" in accordance with the terms of the lease. Obviously, if you are renting it to a relative or a friend, this may be difficult, but even under those circumstances, do your best to maintain a distance between you and your tenant. Generally speaking, it is bad practice to rent to a close friend or relative, because mixing business with personal relationships often leads to trouble. "Familiarity breeds contempt" is a good motto in these cases.

Condominium Rules and Regulations

Depending on the nature of the property, there may be a few other items that need to be addressed. If you are renting an apartment in a condominium, you need to be assured that all of the preconditions of the condominium association are fulfilled. Has all the paperwork been completed, have any and all fees to the association been paid, and, if required, has the service elevator been reserved for move-in? In most cases, you as the landlord are going to still retain responsibility for the tenant in terms of the association. In many of these cases, associations, especially those that have been operating for a long time, are very picky about rules and regulations as they relate to tenants. Avoid the temptation to circumvent those rules. If the board needs to interview the tenant, arrange for it. In most cases the law prevents a board from actually vetoing your lease. Boards generally welcome the tenants and give them the rules and regulations of the building, and that is it.

As in most cases, Nora and I learned our lesson the hard way. The building we lived in had a rule that all tenants had to be approved by the board of directors prior to move-in. While Florida law has diminished the powers of the board of directors in this respect to a welcoming committee, they were nevertheless very strict in not allowing the tenant to move in prior to the so-called "welcoming interview." The tenant was in a hurry to move in, as he was situated in an expensive hotel, and the vice president of the board of directors, who conducted the interviews, was not available until the second week of the month. The move-in date on the lease was for the first of the month, which fell on a weekend. Our unit was to be rented furnished and the tenant, a single fellow, only had a suitcase full of clothes, so that there was no real issue of move-in. The building manager did not work on weekends, and the front desk person was prepared to turn a blind eye to any shenanigans that we were plotting. And plotting we were. After all, the tenant was thoroughly checked and could not be turned down for any reason. This interview was a stupid technicality and threatened the entire transaction. The tenant was getting petulant. He had a lease and insisted on taking occupancy. So what was the harm? The oversight with regard to the "interview" had been ours in the first place, and so we succumbed to temptation. This was a definite failure in our leadership abilities.

We allowed the tenant to take possession but reminded him of his appointment with the vice president of the association the following week and pleaded with him to keep a low profile. "Don't worry," he assured us, "I leave early in the morning for work and come home late at night. Nobody will even know I'm here. I just can't pay that hotel anymore, and I do have a lease. You won't get in any trouble." Famous last words!

The tenant moved in, or rather walked in, on Saturday afternoon. That evening, he threw a party for his friends. He did have the presence of mind to tell his friends to use our name at the front desk, and, fortunately, the evening guard was new and didn't suspect anything other than that we, the actual owners of the unit, were having a party. But on Monday, several of the residents complained to the manager of loud music and conversations well into early Sunday morning. Worse, one particular nosy neighbor mentioned to the association president's wife that she thought my wife was having an affair because she had seen a young man coming in and out of our unit, and she had heard that I was out of town. To make matters still worse, on Sunday, the new tenant went to the swimming pool and introduced himself to several of the young ladies of legal age, including the granddaughter of the treasurer of the association, a particularly mean old biddy who didn't like us in the first place! The charade was over. We got a call from the president of the association, who was outraged that we had flagrantly violated the rules of the association. He stated that due to this violation, he was not going to approve the tenant and we were to be fined $100 per day for each day that the tenant occupied the unit. He was so angry that nothing we could say would appease him.

Fortunately, the lawyer who represented the association was an acquaintance of mine and owed me a favor. Even more fortunately, I managed to reach him before the president of the association did and quickly briefed him on the problem. I suggested that if the association were actually going to try to evict the tenant, it would be a pretty tough case, since the cure was pretty easy—just conduct the interview. I also suggested that we would defend on the basis of the fact that it was unreasonable for the association, which had seven members, not to conduct an interview with someone other than the vice president, and therefore, it was culpable in causing the problem. Finally, I argued that all of this litigation would cost the association thousands of dollars in legal fees, which I doubted the tight-budgeted association would be willing to spend or even be able to justify, given the circumstances. Shortly thereafter, the president spoke with the association's attorney, who presented these arguments, and we settled for an interview with the secretary of the association, a written apology to the association from Nora and me, and a $100 penalty, which went to catering the forthcoming annual board meeting. It could have been worse. The moral of the story is, play by the rules.

That is pretty much it. The tenant moves in, and you have become a landlord. You look to the heavens and hope that you have done the right thing. Don't worry, you have. Property needs to be occupied. Economics aside, a vacant property tends to run to decay. The appliances need to be used. It's like a car. When you purchase a used car, the seller often likes to note that it has hardly been driven, as if that is a big asset. In actuality, if the car has not been driven very much, that may be a bad thing. Cars need to be driven. The engine needs to be used. So from a practical as well as an economic standpoint, your rental of the property is very positive. Don't look back—you're a landlord.

CHAPTER 8

"Honey, the Rent Check Didn't Arrive"

Problems with Tenants

In the previous chapters, while looking at other aspects of the landlord-tenant relationship, we have already discussed, in some measure of detail, the various problems that can arise during the tenancy. In our exploration of the lease agreement, we reviewed a good portion of the components of the transactions that can cause unwanted aggravation to the life of the landlord. In this chapter, we proceed to a more in-depth study, using the information you have already learned, to see how we can avoid problems with the collection of rents.

The Scenario

As in previous chapters, let us set up our scenario. This time, let us suppose that you have purchased a condominium in Miami. The building is fairly liberal in terms of rental policy, and you lease your unit for two years. You have elected to lease the unit furnished. You run the credit check, draw the lease, fly down to meet the tenants, and complete the inventory. For the first year, the tenants pay pretty much on time, although the checks tend to arrive around the fourteenth or fifteenth of each month, rather than within the first ten days, as stipulated in the lease. However, you have never applied any penalties, and no check has ever bounced. During the second year, things begin to get worse. The tenant skips payments and does not respond to phone calls or certified mail. This is not good.

Politics and the Law

Before we go further, we need to take a small digression to help you fully understand what is about to happen. We have previously discussed, albeit very briefly, the history of landlords. We also took a very compact look into how laws are made and interpreted. What we haven't looked at is the political aspect of the legal system. In Chapter 6 we touched on the fact that in a case in dispute, the judge will look at your lease and the relevant law that he or she will then apply. To be sure, if you appear before a judge and act like an idiot, the judge will most probably go out of his or her way to interpret the law in favor of your opponent, if at all possible. However, all things being equal, a judge will do his or her best to interpret the law fairly and dispense justice. However, although the judge may be impartial, sometimes the law isn't.

We have already seen that in terms of landlords and tenants, Europe had a number of landed gentry, usually the nobility, and the remainder of the populace were tenants on the land. As a result, historically, to this day, Europeans are used to leasing property.

Historically speaking, home ownership among the general populace is a relatively new concept. The same applies in many countries in South America. In most South American countries, the vast majority of the population is poor, and there is only a small middle class, if any. The dichotomy between the rich and the poor is much greater than that found in the United States. As a consequence, home ownership was and still is something reserved for the rich and upper middle class, while the remaining population pays rent.

Now, remember that in our discussion of how laws come into effect, we talked about the legislature passing statutes. In a country with legislatures, the members of the legislature are presumably elected. Therefore, in countries where the voting population is by and large renting its homes, it stands to reason that those legislators elected by this type of population are going to pass laws that favor the group who put them in power, in this case, the tenants.

For example, if you owned a home in Scotland and you rented it, the law was so greatly in favor of the tenant that it was virtually impossible for the land-lord to ever get a tenant evicted. The same holds true in many countries in South America to this day. In Scotland, the law has just recently begun to change because property owners, disgusted with the system, simply refused to lease their property, and rentals became scarce. At that point the legisla-tures were forced to pass laws that made it more palatable for a property owner to lease his or her property. In other words, the laws were changed so that the landlord was given real remedies at law if the tenant did not pay the rent. Therefore, a judge's hands are often tied by the politics behind the laws.

This applies in the United States as well. If you want to know if your state favors the landlord or the tenant, listening to gossip about judicial preferences is not going to give you an accurate reading of the outcome of a case. Instead, study the political history of the area as it involves tenancies.

New York City provides an excellent example. I remember growing up in the borough of Queens in the 1960s and 1970s. Queens was (and still is) a middle-class borough that contained mostly rental apartments. The concept of the condominium had not yet taken hold, and apartment ownership, if it existed at all, was limited to a concept known as "the cooperative." In a condo-minium, you own your unit in what is known as *fee simple*. Fee simple is an old English legal term that means you have a deed to your home. With this deed, you can transfer your property by sale or gift to others. With a con-dominium, you get a deed to your apartment, just as you would with a house. But in a cooperative, you own shares in the building itself and the board of directors grants you the right to live in your unit. You do not own your unit outright. Everyone we knew rented. Of course, there was always someone who owned a cooperative, but he or she was an odd person talked about in hushed tones and whispers. "There's where your Uncle Moe and Aunt Esther live," my mother would say when we walked by this six-story brick building. Some friend who was with us would always chime in with "that's a co-op," as if it were a house of ill repute. Both women would sagely nod in agreement, as if poor Uncle Moe were some sort of pitiful creature. Renting in those days was the established norm in Queens, and New York City in general.

As renting was the status quo, you would expect that legislation favored the tenant as opposed to the landlord, and you'd be right. Actually, New York had established regulations called *rent control* and *rent stabilization*. Basically, they were laws designed to protect the poor that actually wound up having the opposite effect. Buildings that qualified under rent control essentially prohibited the landlords from raising a tenant's rent during the time the tenant occupied the apartment. Under rent stabilization, the landlord could raise the rent periodically, but only in limited amounts. What generally occurred was that middle-class people in good neighborhoods who could afford to pay increases had the same rent payment for as long as they lived in the building, and they never moved out! Although the cost of living increased over the years, the landlords' incomes did not, and so both the middle-class and poorer buildings tended to fall into disrepair, with the poor being hit the hardest. In fact, the only way a landlord could get a tenant out and then be permitted to increase the rent for the new tenant was if the current tenant failed to pay the rent or died (and the landlord found out). Landlords tended to be merciless when a tenant was late in paying the rent, because this was the way to evict the current tenant and raise the rent. Whom did this affect? Certainly not the middle-class families, who paid their rent like clockwork year after rent-controlled year, but the poor, who often ran into trouble. Unfortunately, they were the ones the law was designed to protect, an example of the best of intentions sometimes yielding some very bad results.

The point of this little digression is to illustrate that, as a landlord, you should understand the political background of the community in which you will be leasing your property. Let me give you an example. Miami is known as the gateway to Latin America, and a great many of the local property owners have their primary residence in such nations as Colombia, Venezuela, and Brazil. In many of these nations the landlord-tenant law totally favors the tenant.

As we have discussed above, it is possible that once you put tenants into your property under these circumstances, it is virtually impossible to get them out, even if they don't pay their rent. Therefore, many Latin American investors are initially very reluctant to lease their homes in Miami, even though they only use them a few weeks out of the year. They are afraid that, as in their native countries, once tenants move in, the landlords could never get them out, even if they don't pay the rent. This is simply because their frame of reference is different based on the laws and experiences where they live. In addition, many foreign investors rely on the rent to pay for the mortgages, and if the tenants don't pay, they could have serious problems with the banks that financed the purchases.

Remember that at the outset of the book I told you the landlord-tenant relationship was inherently an adversarial one. That was a general theoretical observation of the inherent relationship between the two parties to a lease transaction. However, when you decide to take legal action against a tenant, this is no longer theory—this is reality. It is a battle of two opposing sides, and barring some sort of settlement agreement prior to the conclusion of the case, there will be a winner and a loser. One of the reasons you are reading this book is because you want to be the winner. So treat it as though you are going into battle, because you are. Therefore, it is not enough merely to know the mechanics of the courtroom, such as when to get up and how to speak to the judge, but you need to understand the battleground as well. That is why I have spent time on the politics of the law. It will help you to understand the conditions you are operating in.

Late Payments

If your tenant is late with the rent, you need to send a letter, usually at the point the late payment penalty kicks in but certainly not later. In Appendix C (Late Notice), I have provided a sample. Some statutes require that before any legal action may be taken, a formal warning letter must be sent to the tenant by certified mail indicating the failure to pay the rent, the amount of the payment due, and that the tenant has a certain amount of days to make payment. Regardless of whether the law requires it or not, you should always send a letter to the tenant first to give him or her the opportunity to pay the rent before you go to court. If the tenant sent the check and it got lost in the mail, notifying the tenant would solve the problem and avoid the time, effort, and cost of a lawsuit along with a fight with your tenant. However, if the tenant fails to pay the rent within the time stipulated in the letter, it will be necessary to go to court.

It is a relatively easy matter to find out what the rules of procedure are for your state by going to the local courthouse and checking with the Clerk of the Court. There will be a pamphlet that explains what the procedures are in a landlord-tenant action. In many jurisdictions, there will also be preprinted forms available for you to simply fill in the salient facts and file the papers with the court. These papers are known as the "summons and complaint."

Summons and Complaint

The summons announces the lawsuit or in effect "summons" the defendant to court. The summons gives various instructions to the defendant concerning the action, such as the name and location of the court where the action is to take place, and the amount of time he or she has to answer the attached complaint.

The complaint consists of the forms you filled out at the courthouse and, where necessary, any ancillary documents, such as a copy of the lease and the formal letter notifying the defendant that he or she failed to pay the rent, along with the required proof of mailing. The complaint "complains" to the court of the fact that the tenant failed to pay his or her rent and requests that damages be awarded to you as a consequence; we examine the issue of damages at the end of this chapter. There will, of course, be a filing fee, which varies from state to state, that you will pay when you file your complaint. This is the easy part. The next step is called *service of process* and is a bit more complicated.

Service of Process

Service of Process is an integral part of the legal action, and you have to get it right. Once you file your action with the Clerk of the Court, you become known as the "plaintiff," and the tenant becomes the "defendant" in the legal action. Service of Process is the formal notification to the defendant that he or she is being sued. The defendant is given a copy of the summons and complaint, and, in a perfect world, he or she signs a receipt indicating that he or she has been served, and the case continues.

But obviously, we don't live in a perfect world, or there would be no need for legal actions, so this is where it gets tricky. The rules of procedure for the landlord-tenant court in your jurisdiction will detail how and when Service of Process may be made. You need to comply with these procedures, or the case cannot go forward. Now, if the defendant is purposely avoiding the payment of rent, this person is probably not going to sit around waiting for you to hand him or her a summons and complaint. Besides, in some cases, the defendant may have become desperate and possibly belligerent, and you don't really want to confront the tenant. There are several ways to handle this matter.

Some states allow for what is called "nail, mail, and file." This means that if the defendant does not answer the door, you can post the paperwork on the door and file proof of such notification with the court. This is called an *affidavit of service*. If the defendant does not respond within the legal amount of time, the sheriff will forcibly evict the tenant and take possession of the property for you. The problem with this method is that in most cases, it is a limited service, with the only remedy being eviction.

By serving the tenant "*in personam*" (in person), you get a whole range of available remedies. The best way to accomplish service in person is to pay an additional sum of money and let the Sheriff's Department handle it. Sometimes the court has its own "process servers." They will serve the defendant for you and file the "affidavit of service" with the court, showing proof that the servicing of the summons and complaint was accomplished. However, it is still your responsibility to make sure that the documents are in order. The process server does not check your paperwork. In some states, you can hire your own process server, usually a detective agency that specializes in this type of work. It is more expensive, but as it is more personal, it often gets the job done faster.

So far things are going on schedule. You have your summons and complaint, and the sheriff's deputy was lucky enough to catch the tenant on his or her way out the door and served the paperwork. Both you and the court will receive a copy of the affidavit, and you are ready to proceed, sort of. The whole purpose of this procedure is to make sure that the defendant understands why he or she is being sued and is given adequate opportunity to respond. In most cases, the defendant will have twenty to thirty days, depending on the method of service, to respond to your allegations. So, that is one more month you have to wait. If the tenant does not respond or "answer" the complaint but "defaults" by not responding within the allocated time, you then file additional papers with the court indicating such a default, and you win. In other words, you pretty much get whatever you asked for, including eviction, costs of the litigation, and damages. Sometimes you actually can collect them.

Getting the Tenant to Pay

I recall early in my career as an attorney I represented a client who had purchased some furniture for his apartment. The client lived out of the country and was foolish enough to pay a rather large sum of money to the dealer in advance. The dealer never delivered the furniture. Several months later, the client retained me to collect the funds.

Oddly enough, the dealer was still in business, and it was relatively easy to serve him. Thirty days came and went, and he never responded to the complaint, so I filed a default with the court, which was granted. The "judgment" that the court issued commanded the defendant to return the money that my client had paid for the furniture. This too was served on the defendant, and he again failed to respond. I then filed and received a contempt of court order against the defendant based on the fact that he had disobeyed an order of the court. (Some judges will not grant such an order without the plaintiff first taking a "deposition" of the defendant to ascertain his or her ability to pay a claim, but this judge granted the motion without the deposition.) However, by this time the defendant had disappeared. That was it. My client was furious that I had failed to recover the money. My only response was, next time don't pay in full in advance. I forgot about the incident.

Several years later, I received a phone call in the middle of the night from an officer at a Miami jail. Apparently, the defendant had returned to Miami and was stopped for a traffic violation. On a routine check of his license, the contempt order showed up, and he was arrested. The following day, the defendant (in handcuffs) was brought before the judge in my presence, and we discussed the original case. In return for being released and "vacating the contempt order," the defendant agreed to make monthly payments for the furniture that he had failed to deliver. The defendant made several payments but then disappeared again. I contacted the client and sent him the money I had collected for him. The odd thing is, rather than being happy at having finally collected what had surely been found money, the client was furious that it had taken this long. When the defendant disappeared again, the client practically accused me of stealing the remainder of the money. Well, sometimes you just can't please a person. The point of this story is that, depending on the circumstances, it sometimes pays to pursue the action. Other times, it may be better to get the eviction and write it off. Hopefully, by the time you file the action, a defaulting tenant will be gone, and that will be the end. But as we shall see, it usually doesn't work that way.

In many cases, the failure to pay rent stems from some ongoing dispute between the landlord and the tenant. In other cases, it is purely because the tenant has undergone some economic difficulty that, unfortunately for you as the landlord, occurred during the tenancy of your property. It happens. In those cases, however, the tenant will generally not disappear into the night, but rather will remain in the property, hoping things will get better. If the tenant is forthright about this, you may wish to work out some arrangement in order to help him or her out. Perhaps lower the rent temporarily or proclaim a "rent holiday" for a month or two to try and help the tenant out. Aside from the fact that it is a charitable thing to do, often the tenant truly is experiencing a temporary setback, and if that is the case, your kindness will pay dividends in unexpected ways later on. If you do agree to help the tenant, whatever arrangement you make should be considered a modification of the lease and put into writing as an addendum to the lease agreement.

You may think this contradicts my earlier message that kindness is mistaken for weakness, and that "business is business." Remember that I also taught you about attitude and strategy. Early on in our discussion of real estate, we discussed the fact that a person's home is his or her castle. While the tenant is occupying your property, it is his or her castle we are talking about. Understandably, judges are reluctant to toss people out of their castles unless there is sufficient cause.

In our scenario, the defendant did not pay the rent and did not respond to any calls from the landlord. In such a case, all bets are off, and you do what you have to do. But what happens if the tenant tells you that he is going through a divorce or has just lost his job or whatever and needs a bit more time? You are within your rights to say no, and you can pretty much insist on prompt payment of the rent. But what does it hurt if you reduce the tenant's rent for one month without dismissing the claim? All you have to do is postpone the action for one month and see what happens. Courts like that, because it is an attempt to resolve the issue without adding to an already overburdened system. Then, if the tenant gets back on his feet, you earned good will and the tenant presumably will pay not only his rent but his arrearages as well. Arrearages are monies that are past due. In this case, the back rent and penalties would be examples of arrearages.

But what happens if the tenant still doesn't pay? In that case, you prepare the case for trial, and when the judge asks you if there has been any attempt to settle the matter, you can take the high moral ground by stating that you did try to work it out, but to no avail. You've made a good faith effort to keep the tenant in his or her castle, and you don't come off as a bully. Also, you have shown the court due deference by trying to settle the matter with the tenant. At this point, the judge will pretty much be able to give you what you want. I can also tell you that unless you are totally merciless, you are going to feel a lot better as well.

The Tenant's Point of View

Another variation on the scenario occurs when the tenant files an answer to your complaint. Now, all of a sudden, you discover that the tenant is living in a virtual hellhole. None of the appliances work, there is no heat in the winter, no air-conditioning in the summer, and no hot water any time. It turns out that the poor tenant has been bathing in cold water for a year and a half. In addition, you find that the tenant is alleging that you were informed of all of this and, brute that you are, refused to make the necessary repairs.

There is no evidence to indicate that any of this is true—no letters sent to the landlord in accordance with the lease, no action filed by the tenant with funds placed with the court registry while the issue is being investigated. You can make all of these arguments, but you are now on the defensive. In most cases, the judge will see through this litany of baloney, but it is really aggravating. Most landlords will think, "What a dirty liar my tenant is." Remember that you are suing the tenant and he or she is defending against your lawsuit. If the tenant fights back, he or she will do so with as strong an argument as possible. Lawyers are famous for exaggerating the response. There may also be some legitimate arguments in all of those allegations. Always keep in mind that the tenant has a point of view as well, even if you don't agree with it.

That is why you should be organized. Document everything—phone calls, messages left on answering machines, and correspondence sent and received from the tenant. An experienced judge will get the picture very fast. The more documentary evidence you have, the better off you will be.

Mediation

In some jurisdictions, there is something called *mediation.* What happens is that you appear before the judge fully prepared to state your case, but instead, the judge simply asks if there has been any attempt to mediate the action. You're not sure what he means, but since you haven't done anything except show up at his courtroom, you figure it's a safe bet the answer is "no." All of a sudden, you and a very angry tenant are in a small room, and in comes a person who introduces himself or herself as the mediator.

The job of the mediator is to get the parties to settle their dispute without seeing the judge. This helps clear the calendar and reduces the burden on the court system. The key word here is "settle." That means there won't be a winner or a loser. You and the tenant get to tell your stories, and the mediator takes notes (which may or may not go to the judge). He or she will try to get you to compromise. In some jurisdictions, the mediators will try really hard, because they get paid on the basis of the cases that are settled. Some mediators play it straight and make a good faith attempt to resolve the issues, while others use less than savory tactics, such as suggesting that if you don't settle the case, the judge will be angry and rule against you. This is nonsense. If you can't settle it, you can't settle it.

Another problem is that mediators, while often well trained, are not necessarily attorneys and often don't know the law of each case they are trying to mediate. The problem is, as an attorney who has had to appear before mediators, I do know the difference and can tell when they are trying to bluff you into a settlement. The fact of the matter is that if you've given your tenant every opportunity to pay, which I have suggested that you do, no amount of mediation is going to help. Tell the mediator your story, listen politely as the tenant tells his or her version, and at the end, simply inform the mediator that this dispute cannot be resolved and that you wish to see the judge. The mediator will frown, but don't worry. Just stay the course.

If you should decide to settle, the mediator will write a settlement agreement that you both will sign. The case will not be dismissed until the terms of the settlement are met. For the most part, I prefer to take my chances with the judge, especially in landlord-tenant actions, where I know that I have followed the steps as outlined above, and as a matter of law, the outcome should not be in doubt.

Bad Risks

Let me give you a story that illustrates just how these cases can play out. Early in our careers, Nora and I had been working for a broker in Miami who was also a friend of ours. As a favor, she asked me to handle an eviction case for her. The tenants were a couple who owned a manufacturing business and lived in a luxury condominium. Apparently, they had paid first month, last month, and a security payment and not another dime. The couple were apparently both social and business partners. He was from Sweden and had no credit in the United States, but her credit was very good. The landlord complained that they were now several months late in their rent and wanted them evicted.

I filed the papers and received an answer from their lawyer. He alleged that the landlord had breached the contract by not effectuating repairs to the walls and the water heating system. Apparently, the water heater installed in the unit was incapable of sufficiently filling the extra-large Jacuzzi bathtub with sufficiently hot water for "milady's" bath. The tenants also complained that the walls were cracked due to a construction defect in the building, and aside from being aesthetically unpleasing, it ruined a delicate sponge paint job that must have been done by a descendant of Leonardo da Vinci, based on the tenants' pleadings. But most importantly, the lawyer stated that he had deposited the past due rent in the court registry, along with the following month's rent, and was prepared to fully litigate the case on behalf of his clients to fight the eviction.

The landlord was notified and was adamant that he would not sink a dime into fixing that unit. He argued that the water heater in his unit was the same as in every other unit, and nobody else was complaining. In addition, the wall was not his problem and the developer would eventually fix it. In any event, the landlord indicated that the tenants knew about the cracks when they moved in. The broker, our boss, agreed with him.

I disagreed, which, as you can imagine, didn't go over well. But here was my logic. If the water heater was indeed broken, the terms of the lease called for the landlord to repair or replace it, so he was stuck either way. If the water heater was working but unsuitable for the purposes it was designed for, I figured there was a fifty-fifty chance I could win the argument based on the fact that it was the standard water heater for the building. After all, is the tenant liable to accept the developer defects? The same logic applied to the issue of the wall. Sure I could argue that they knew about it when they rented the unit, but there was nothing in writing on this issue, so it was the word of the landlord and his broker against that of the tenants.

Additionally, the tenants claimed that the defect in the wall manifested itself after the tenants had moved in. They stated that when they moved in, there were no cracks in the wall. "Why would we do an expensive paint job on a cracked wall?" they argued. To cover up the cracks was one obvious answer, but you can see their point.

The other persuasive issue was the fact that a bird in the hand is worth two in the court registry. The landlord's money was deposited in the court registry. Remember the present value of money? Plus, if we settled the case, there was no award of attorney's fees, which meant that the tenants had to pay their own lawyer (who was considerably more expensive than I was). This would discourage the tenants from fooling around with late payments in the future. To my way of thinking, I got the landlord his money, so let's all go home.

Reluctantly, the landlord agreed, and the case was settled. The landlord got his money, and the case was over. The landlord also fixed the wall, which didn't cost all that much, and I suggested to the tenant that if she turned on the cold water first to fill the tub and then blasted it with hot water, the tub would be hot enough. That worked and saved the landlord a new water heater. Actually, when I met the tenants at the settlement conference, I knew I was probably right. The man looked like a fashion model. He was tall and muscular with blond curly hair and dressed to kill. The female was middle-aged but clearly took great pains to preserve a youthful image. She too was dressed to the nines. In short, they presented a very good image and would have been extremely credible witnesses. My landlord client, on the other hand, was somewhere in Europe and couldn't be bothered returning to Miami, even though he traveled throughout the world. So the only person representing him was his broker, a paid representative. I knew I had made the right choice.

Several months later I got another call from our broker. The rent was late again, and the couple apparently was splitting up. This time there would be no mercy. My instructions were clear—evict at all costs. After going through the procedural matters of sending the required notification letters, I filed the lawsuit once again. This time there was no fancy lawyer and no money deposited in the court registry, and the tenants were eventually evicted.

There are several aspects to this story that bear some examination. The broker conducted a background check of the tenants. Neither had bad credit. However, a closer examination of the credit report revealed that the woman's credit history was based entirely on her credit cards (which were extensive) and utility bill payments. Apparently, prior to meeting her partner, she had owned a home that she had sold, ostensibly to finance their new business venture. Nevertheless, she had a rather extensive credit history that was not adverse, and she paid her bills on time. Also, the business appeared to be doing well. In fact, Nora and I had passed the showroom several times, and it was impressive. In short, the couple projected an image of being well-to-do, albeit a couple with a somewhat exaggerated taste. However, that image fit in with the general populace of the South Beach portion of Miami, a community of high-profile people. In addition, the condominium association approved them, and in fact they had a friend on the board of directors of the building who knew them and vouched for them. Thus, there was no foreseeable reason not to rent to this couple.

Of course, hindsight being 20/20, there were perhaps clues that this tenancy may have been suspect. The credit and background report showed that this was an unmarried couple whose relationship was less than two years old. Nothing conclusive in and of itself, but add a relatively new business, no credit history on one subject, and no tenant history on the other, and the perfect picture begins to blur. As it turned out, the board member didn't know them all that well, and it was actually a friend of hers who knew them through business (now she tells us).

The real problem in this case was that everyone judged the book by its cover. They were a dazzling couple who projected a jet-set lifestyle. What could have been done differently in this case, in terms of a background check? The landlord knew their business was only two years old. This is relatively new, as businesses go. The landlord should have run a check on the business. Companies such as Dun & Bradstreet and other firms often maintain data on various businesses, both big and small. If a check of their business revealed that they weren't paying their bills, that would have told the landlord what he needed to know in terms of renting his unit to them. The landlord would have been well within his rights to do so because the couple was in fact self-employed. Nora and I, being self-employed, are often more closely scrutinized than when we were salaried employees. On the other hand, our income increased in our own business, so being self-employed is not in and of itself an acid test of one's ability to pay rent. However, it should serve to caution the landlord to check more into the background of the tenants.

The next aspect of this transaction that we need to look at is the diligence of the landlord. The facts indicate that the tenants paid the first and last month's rent and security, and that was it. How soon thereafter did the representative send the late notice? The fact is that until I took on the case, the required notices were not sent. There was a delay of several months. What had happened was that the representative had called the tenants, and they gave her a song and dance about money being wired from Europe. Forget it. Follow procedure. A polite phone call is fine, but follow it up with a letter. In Appendix C, you will find samples of suggested correspondence. Maintain your files and proceed step by step until the rent check arrives.

In this case, and in most cases, the issues are not clear. Here, the tenants argued that there were problems with the walls and the water heater. Since there was no walkthrough documentation, there was no evidence of what transpired prior to the tenants' moving in. To be sure, a tenant is not responsible for construction defects of the landlord, so it really didn't matter when the wall cracked. It was the landlord's duty to get it fixed. What happens if the landlord cannot fix it? I will address that issue shortly.

First, there was the matter of the water heater. The tenant complained of an inadequate supply of hot water. The usual argument is that "I'm paying good rent" (in other words top dollar) "for a luxury unit, and I demand adequate hot water." Legally, there is no such thing as "good rent" or "top dollar" for luxury when it comes to basic utilities such as hot water. The landlord has to provide an adequate supply of hot water for any rental property, regardless of its status in the marketplace.

The question in this case, which I fortunately did not have to address, is what constitutes "an adequate supply"? If the landlord provides a bathtub the size of a swimming pool, does he or she necessarily have to provide a water heater that fills it to capacity with hot water? I think the answer is yes, if the tenant relied on this feature as part of a luxury package and is paying a premium for such amenities. After all, if this were a normal bathtub, you would expect that there would be suitable hot water to take a bath. It wouldn't be an issue. In this case, you have a large bathtub featured as a luxury item. Why should the expectation be any different? The tenant could make a strong case that he or she was wrongfully induced to lease an apartment with luxury amenities that did not exist. Now, what is the remedy for this? Here is where we return to the discussion of the cracked walls as well. There are two possible remedies. The first is that you can argue with the landlord for a rent reduction and modify the lease based on the problems in the unit, or you can demand that the landlord rectify the problems. Those are the only two demands that the tenant can make of the landlord. There is no third alternative, of free rent.

Let us say that the landlord won't renegotiate the lease and refuses to rectify the problem. The tenant still has to pay the rent or move out. But if the tenant elects to move out, the theory of law, which he or she must argue, is known as the *theory of constructive eviction*. Constructive eviction means that because of defects in the unit, it has become impossible for the tenant to remain in the unit. And even though the landlord had not actually evicted the tenant, the landlord's refusal to fix the problems was the same as the landlord's evicting the tenant. There are several basic problems with this remedy. The first problem is that in order to allege constructive eviction, the tenant actually has to move out. The second problem is that the constructive eviction is a question of fact, which the tenant has the burden of proving. So the tenant cannot first allege a constructive eviction and, if he or she wins the argument, then move out. The tenant must move out first and then take his or her chances that the court will support his or her actions when the landlord sues the tenant for breach of the lease. Based on the above facts, I don't think the tenant had a constructive eviction for lack of sufficient hot water to fill the bathtub and a cracked wall. To meet the standard of a constructive eviction, the nature of the problem must be such that it is impossible for a reasonable tenant to live on the property.

The next issue was the documentation and procedure. There really wasn't any. The tenants viewed the property, signed a lease, and paid the advance deposits. Nobody bothered with the details, but those details are important. So, at the first sign of trouble, the landlord takes the hard-nosed position that he is not going to fix anything; the apartment is perfect, and the tenant had better pay the rent. That position is basically a fight looking for an opponent. This is exactly what you want to avoid. Going to court should be the last thing you, as a landlord, should do.

We know that going to court involves filing papers and serving the tenants, who are now defendants. You then wait twenty or thirty days for an answer to the complaint. You then need to set the matter down for a trial date. Depending on how crowded the court calendar is, this could take upward of a month. Then there is the stress of going to court. Here, it varies with location. For example, in highly populated urban centers, landlord-tenant courts are not exactly a trip to Disney World. The system is overcrowded, and the judges need to move their calendars along. Many people who are in court are not exactly like the jet-set couple I used in this example, but poor and unfortunate souls who are facing homelessness. It can be a tense and depressing situation.

In addition, you may not have a private courtroom, but rather, as in traffic court, you may be one of literally dozens of plaintiffs, defendants, lawyers, and property managers who are crammed into the courtroom. Your case will be heard in front of what will seem to be half of the world. In addition, the judge will not be in the mood to hear a long-drawn-out argument from either party. It is not the time for you to show what a great television attorney you might have been. The judge will hear the facts, interrupt your soliloquy to ask a few questions, render an opinion, and then go on to the next case.

In other, less populated jurisdictions, the situation may differ radically. Recently, I found myself in county court helping a neighbor of mine who was the plaintiff in a small claims action. We were seated in a private conference room with the judge, my friend, and the defendants, and we had a hearing on the case. The judge was relaxed, listened politely to everyone, and ultimately ruled in my friend's favor. I actually got a thank-you out of it. Nobody was being evicted, so the case had much less of an emotional impact.

Rules of Engagement

Regardless of what the conditions of the courtroom are, if you find yourself having to go to court, there are some general rules of engagement that we need to discuss to help you win. The first rule is to dress for the occasion. A day in court is not the time to show your sartorial individuality. If you are a man, wear a suit and tie. If you are a woman, wear a suit as well or a conservative dress.

Also, be brief. Follow Shakespeare's line that said, "Brevity is the soul of wit." This is not a television drama. As in all situations, when the judge calls your case, head up to the bench and greet the judge with a "good morning, your honor" and introduce yourself.

The ability to be a leader resides in every aspect of the landlord-tenant relationship, even in court. Let the judge know that you are the dominant party in the dispute. Set the stage on your terms. "Your honor, this case involves the fact that the tenant failed to pay rent for the last three months. I sent all the required notices, and I ask the court to evict him (or her) and award damages in 'x' amount of dollars." If you can get this all in, you did great.

The judge will then turn to the defendant and ask him or her for his or her side of the story. Now comes the litany of woes that you read about in the tenant's response, which we discussed earlier in this chapter. Keep your temper and avoid the temptation of chiming in. Let the defendant-tenant finish. You'll get your chance. When the defendant has finished his or her character assassination of you and your property, the judge will ask you what you have to say in response. This is where you get to shine, if you are organized. "Judge," you *calmly* respond, "you will note that the lease calls for repairs under $100 to be paid by the tenant; it's in paragraph 5, judge, on page 3." Give the judge a second to look it up in his or her file, then continue. "When the tenant called me to complain on March 31, and here is the memo I made of that phone call, I told the defendant that he is responsible for these items. I then followed up with a letter to that effect and sent it by certified mail. Here is a copy of the letter and the receipt by the defendant. Besides, judge, what right has he got not to pay the rent? He should have sued and placed the money in the court registry. Anyway, your honor, if his life is so miserable, why didn't he move out and allege a constructive eviction? The fact is, your honor, these are all excuses, and the tenant just won't pay the rent."

The judge may ask you or the tenant some more questions and may determine that there is truth to both sides, and the judge's opinion may reflect that. If the judge rules that the rent must be paid but that you must make some repairs that the tenant has complained of, and does not evict the tenant, that is the judge's opinion; accept it gracefully. Not all tenants are cheats and liars, nor is it my intention to portray them as such. They have legitimate complaints as well. Maybe you, as the landlord, weren't as responsive or sympathetic as you should have been. But at the end of the day, the rent still must be paid, and that is what you are after.

Remedies

What you win if the judge rules in your favor is known as "remedies" and is an important, albeit often overlooked, portion of the law. The glitzy part that everyone cares about is the win. But trust me when I tell you that, if you have won the case, nothing will annoy a judge more than if you ask for something stupid in terms of remedies. Winning the case is winning the battle; getting the remedies you desire is winning the war. So what are we asking the judge to do for us?

In each of the cases we have discussed thus far, the tenant hasn't paid his or her rent but has remained in the property, so you probably want the tenant evicted. That is really the essence of the action. You want a tenant in your property who will pay rent. Also, you may wish to ask the judge for the past due rent or whatever else your local statute allows, as well as costs for the action, such as your filing fees and fees associated with service of process. If you hired an attorney, you would be awarded those fees as well.

You will need to do a little research into your landlord-tenant statute to find out exactly what remedies are available to you. Sometimes, the information pamphlet you received at the outset of the case will list the available remedies. If not, ask the Clerk of the Court for more information on what remedies to ask for or where to find the statutes.

Let's change the scenario somewhat. To this point, we have been discussing cases where the main "cause of action," the essential element of your complaint, is the eviction. You get the tenant out of your property; that is going to be pretty much it, because at the point of the eviction, the lease is terminated. Everyone moves on.

But what happens if the tenant leaves on his or her own and stops paying you rent? In this case, there is no eviction, because the tenant has already vacated the unit. You find out where he or she is now living and file suit and serve the person with a summons and complaint. The case comes before the judge, and the tenant's defense is that the rent was too high, so the tenant found a cheaper property, or the tenant got a better job in a different city and left. Unfortunately for the tenant, those are not defenses. The tenant has signed a lease, which is a contract, and that contract has not been terminated. You win. But what do you ask for now?

In this case, there is no eviction, but the lease has not been terminated. In this case, many statutes offer a variety of remedies. You have to refer to your local statute for guidance. Some states will give you a choice of remedies. For example, you may be offered the choice of accelerating the rent due and owing by the tenant for the entire term of the lease. Sounds good; you get a year or two in advance, but assuming you can collect it, which is another issue we will discuss at the close of our exploration of remedies, this remedy generally comes with a catch.

The catch is that you can't rent your unit until the natural expiration of the lease. "But why?" you ask. The reason is simple: Under this remedy, you have received the rent under the terms of the lease. It doesn't matter whether the tenant actually occupies the unit. In some states, you are required to let the unit stay empty during the term of the lease and then go into court and ask for the full amount. The point is that you can be awarded the entire amount of the lease, but if you choose that remedy, you can't re-rent the property at the same time because the tenant has paid (or will pay, as the case may be). You can't "stack" remedies. It would be considered "unjust enrichment" if you were allowed to take the money under the lease and rent the property again at the same time.

The second remedy, which some states offer as an alternative, is to attempt to lease the property. If it takes two months, once that is determined, you would ask for two months of lost rent as your remedy. If it takes six months, that's what you ask the court for. The idea with this remedy is that you are making a good faith effort to "mitigate" your damages by trying to lease the property once again. As soon as you do so, the tenant is discharged from his or her further liability, but not from previous responsibility under the lease. Notice the consistency of the remedies. In neither case is the landlord allowed to "stack" the rental income by collecting from two different parties, that is, a new tenant as well as the previous one.

Sometimes, you will get an experienced tenant who will deposit the rent in the court registry. Then you cannot evict and must litigate the case. If you have your records in order and have followed the precepts outlined in this book, while you will be inconvenienced, you should prevail. However, it shouldn't get to this point. Let's review the different scenarios we presented and the various problems that can occur:

1. In the first case, we encountered the situation where the tenant failed to pay the rent and occupied the unit.

2. In a variation of that scenario, we examined a case where the tenant initially failed to pay the rent but, through a lawyer, paid the money into the court's registry and attempted to litigate the case.

3. In a third variation, the tenant voluntarily vacated the unit.

Regardless of the differences in the facts, your actions as the landlord should be consistent. From the outset, you should have a documented file on the tenant. You will have his or her credit history, the lease, any addenda or amendments, an inventory, and final walkthrough by the tenant. In addition, any oral communications with the tenant should be documented by a memorandum for the record and followed up with a letter confirming the contents of the conversation. Be responsive; in the long run, it costs more in time, money, and aggravation to go to court than to try to resolve a problem. Of course, sometimes, problems can't be resolved, but it behooves you, for every reason, to give it your best shot.

Sometimes, this can be extremely aggravating. For example, you place a tenant in the unit. He has excellent credit and pays his rent on time, but he calls you every other day with a different problem. We have already seen some examples of the type of harassment a tenant can heap on a landlord. In such situations, don't let it get to you. Deal with it calmly, firmly, and responsively. After a while, the tenant will either get the message and calm down or go to court. If the tenant elects to sue, you will be ready. Most problems can be resolved without going to court if emotions are taken out of the equation. Sure, the tenant turned out to be a jerk, but if the jerk is still paying you rent every month, you deal with it. There is no job, no profession that doesn't come with its own set of problems. Every professional, every blue-collar worker, every self-employed entrepreneur has problems on the job. Being a landlord is a job and eventually will have problems. As in every other profession, what separates the winners from the losers, the successful people from those who fail, is how they cope when the going gets tough.

The Profession of Landlording

Being a landlord is a job, a profession, a function of property management. Treat it as such and do it by the numbers, and it will be a rewarding profession. When you think about it, it really is a great profession. You are the property owner who is deriving income from your property. In addition, you are the boss. This is your operation, and you get to make the executive decisions. It's fun and exciting.

While the materials in this chapter may leave the impression that being a landlord is a constant battle, nothing can be further from the truth. You need to be prepared if things go wrong, and so we have to discuss it, but litigation is going to be the exception. Each month when the rent check comes, and it will come, you pay your bills more easily, have some extra spending cash, or start that savings plan you were putting off. More than likely, you will begin to think about acquiring more property to rent. My wife and I have been leasing our property as well as representing clients for more than twenty years, and with rare exceptions, some of which we have already told you about in this book, it remains fun and exciting. When the tenant's lease is over, you will hope that he or she plans to renew, because in all likelihood, it will have been a positive experience.

In the next chapter, we talk about what happens when the tenancy does end. Legal obligations aside, attitude plays an important role in the overall transaction as well. To this point, I have portrayed the tenant as the focal point of problems but cautioned that sometimes you as the landlord can be at fault as well. Before you get angry and start cursing the tenant, try to look at a particular problem from his or her standpoint. Maybe there is something to the complaint. Sure, if the tenant turns out to be a nut who calls you at 2 a.m. to tell you that the lawnmower isn't working, it's going to be hard to contain yourself, and you may have some other problems as well. But if you get a reasonable call describing a reasonable problem, address it calmly, referring whenever possible to the clause in the lease associated with that problem. Whatever happens during the tenancy, you should be consistent. Take it step by step, and it should work out in your favor.

We have covered a lot of material in this chapter. Don't panic; we will discuss many of these issues again. So hang in there as we explore the termination of the lease and revisit issues involving the security deposit.

CHAPTER 9

End of the Tenancy

"Do I Have to Return the Security?"

In Chapter 5, we explored in detail the legal issues involved in returning the security deposit. If you do not recall that discussion, you may wish to review the section on advance deposits. In the current chapter, we describe the step-by step procedures so you know what to expect when your tenant moves out.

My Tenant Wrote Me a Letter

You have held the money in a separate account for two years, as required by your state's law. Now the tenant is getting ready to move out. You get a nice letter from the tenant advising you that at the termination of the lease, he will be relocating, and, not to worry, the unit will be in better shape than when he moved into it. That phrase tends to make me nervous, because I believe that we always give a unit that is in excellent shape. What did the tenant do to "improve" it? Actually, if you conducted a periodic inspection of the unit per your lease agreement, there should be few surprises, but for purposes of this chapter, let us suppose that the tenant has been paying his rent on schedule. Additionally, he never bothered you with problems, and as a consequence, you didn't conduct any inspections. Don't worry; in a few weeks the moment of truth will come. The letter ends with a reminder that you are holding one month's security deposit, and the tenant politely reminds you to mail it to his new address. This is hardly a concealed message indicating that the tenant expects you to return his full deposit without delay.

You are just a little irritated when you get this response. After all, the contract clearly states the parameters for the return of this money. Remember, few people think they are less than perfect. For example, there is an experiment I have seen performed with large audiences in which the speaker will ask audience members to raise their hands if they think they are ugly. Nobody does. Then the speaker will ask the audience to raise their hands if they think someone else in the audience is ugly. Invariably, lots of hands will go up.

It's the same psychology with tenants. Tenants rarely think they are sloppy and believe that any changes they make to the property are just wonderful. No tenant thinks that he or she is not deserving of receiving a full return of the security deposit. In fact, on the whole, although it is an accepted custom, tenants very much resent having to leave a security deposit at all. That is why you insisted on taking the last month's rent up front. If you hadn't, the tenant most likely would have just "lived through" his or her security without any hesitation or guilt. It is not that tenants are "bad people." It is purely a matter of human nature.

The Final Inspection

It is now time for you to conduct your final inspection. The inspection should be conducted *after* the tenant moves out. This sounds obvious, but there is a great temptation to inspect by convenience rather than by common sense and rules. For one thing, you want to inspect without the presence of the tenant. The tenant does not have the right to be present during the inspection. For what should be obvious reasons, you are much better off without the tenant there at that time. This is a very good example of the landlord-tenant relationship being inherently adversarial. Your basic instinct is going to be to withhold the security deposit, while the tenant's is just the opposite. If the tenant is standing next to you, it is going to be an uncomfortable and potentially contentious situation. When it comes to returning the security deposit, both parties should be objective, but they rarely are. This is where leadership comes into play once again. You as the landlord are going to have to be the more objective of the two and rise to the occasion. In a close case, you are going to have to make the command decision of whether to fight or just return the security deposit and move on. We have already learned that when you make this decision, the law offers you guidance. That guidance is the standard of "normal wear and tear."

Normal Wear and Tear

This is a very subjective concept. When you have subjective standards, you have to try to take the emotional aspect out of the equation. I repeat again and again that this is a business proposition. After your inspection, you have to apply the "normal wear and tear" standard and decide if you will hold back some or all of the tenant's security deposit. If you do, you usually have to say in writing that you are planning to withhold the tenant's money.

One yardstick for withholding those funds is your ability to describe the nature of the withholding in writing. Does your letter pass the "straight face test?" Be objective. The biggest complaint that I hear from landlords is that the unit was filthy and required a professional cleaning service to be brought in. The landlord wants to deduct the cost of the cleaning service from the security. "Nonsense," replies the tenant. "I brought in a cleaning person before I left, and the place is spotless, cleaner than when I received it. Don't you dare take a dime from my security!" In this case, I agree with the tenant.

Forget about cleaning fees, which are part of the cost of doing business and are speculative at best. If the U.S. Environmental Protection Agency can't figure out how "clean is clean" in terms of pollution abatement in our rivers, ground, and air, there is certainly no empiric formula with regard to how clean your kitchen should be when the tenant moves out. It is not worth fighting about. We knew a landlord who lived in New York but owned a condominium in Miami Beach. She used the unit a few weeks out of the year in the summer and then leased it, furnished, and at top dollar, for six months during the winter season. One year she rented the unit to an elderly lady from Canada who could not take the harsh Canadian winters. The woman, who was quite well-to-do, paid the entire season, plus one month's security, in advance. She also had a live-in companion. The companion's principal occupation was to clean and launder for the tenant and take care of the household duties. The companion was not young either. At the end of the season, the tenant moved out. The place was a mess. There were literally food particles and residues of undetermined age and identity on every cabinet in the kitchen. We won't even discuss the refrigerator. However, the bathrooms were almost spotless because both women used the poolside bathrooms for most of their related ablution activities, and the bedroom, while not pristine, was acceptable.

In addition, complicating this scenario was the fact that the tenant took a couple of towels and a bed sheet. On receiving this report, the landlord went berserk. "She took my towels and my percale sheet. That old biddy (I'm paraphrasing here), how dare she, those were matching towels, and I've had them for years. The sheets were matching as well, and I'll need to get a new set. Keep her security. I'll show her." Was the landlord within her rights? Let's try a multiple-choice question: Choose the correct answer:

   a. Food residue and a few stolen towels are normal wear and tear; therefore, the landlord may not retain a portion of the security deposit.

   b. The landlord should retain the security in full.

   c. The landlord is within her rights to withhold the security but probably should not do so in this case.

   d. There was no actual physical damage to the property, so the landlord may not withhold the security.

What do you think? Remember that we are looking for the correct answer. If you chose *c*, that would be the correct answer. This was a hard question, so let's analyze the choices.

Choice *a* is not correct. Food residue on the walls is clearly beyond what is reasonably considered normal wear and tear, and removing property of the unit without the consent of the landlord is technically petty theft. Whether it's worth withholding security or not, the landlord is within his or her technical legal rights to withhold a reasonable cleaning cost and the cost of some replacement sheets. Since the sum is negligible, we won't deal with depreciation here.

Choice *b* is clearly not correct. There is no evidence that the damages caused were equal to the total amount of the security deposit. The basic purpose of a security deposit is to compensate the landlord for damages to the property. It is not meant to be punitive in nature. Punitive remedies are remedies designed to punish a person for a wrongdoing. Sometimes, the landlord would like nothing better than to punish the tenant, but that is not how it works legally.

Choice *d* is also incorrect. Since food residue is not normal wear and tear, and neither are stolen items, these constitute damage to the property.

Choice *c* is the correct answer. Rather than rehash what I have already stated about business judgment, let's see how this played out in real life. What actually occurred was that the landlord was so outraged over the loss of her towels and sheet that she wanted (in addition to sending the statutory security withholding letter) to telephone the woman in Canada and demand the return of the missing items. The woman apologized for the items, indicating that her companion didn't see that well and probably took the towels and sheet by mistake. Also, the tenant indicated that if she had the missing articles, she would gladly return them, but she wasn't sure she could locate them. The items never showed up, and the landlord retained the security deposit.

The tenant didn't complain, but the following year, she rented the unit next door to my client, which was virtually identical. She paid more money, in advance, while my landlord had difficulty leasing the unit. She finally rented the unit to a retired couple who had children and grandchildren living in the local area and who visited every weekend. Talk about wear and tear. Oh, yes, they did not pay in advance, and the rent was less than what the elderly lady and her companion were paying next door. Was it worth withholding the security over a few towels and a dirty kitchen? You tell me.

Remain Objective

The problem in dealing with one's own property is the loss of objectivity. That is what you have to fight. Try to place yourself in the third person. Would you give your friend the same advice as you are considering for yourself? Probably not!

People tend to see things much more clearly when they are not emotionally involved. These were not just towels and a sheet. These were items that the landlord had probably had since her wedding and had some emotional attachment to.

If you, the reader, take away anything at all from this book, it should be that if you are going to be a landlord, you are going to be in business, and you should treat it like a business. Not every decision is black and white. Most decisions have shades of gray, hence the phrase "gray areas." You have to weigh the pros and cons of withholding the security deposit. Just because you have the right to do it doesn't always mean you should. The next question, then, is when, as the landlord, should you withhold the security deposit and how much of it should you withhold.

The standard that we have been discussing is "normal wear and tear." In other words, property, by virtue of its use, depreciates normally over the course of time. You wear shoes, and after a while, the shoes wear out. Of course, there are people who purchase shoe trees to maintain the shape of the shoes when they are not being used, or who tape the soles of the shoes to extend their life, but the average person doesn't normally do this. The average person buys a pair of shoes, wears them till they wear out, and then buys a new pair.

Now, let's stay with the shoe example a bit longer and be a bit more specific. Let us suppose that you and your neighbor both purchase identical pairs of running shoes designed for marathon runners. Your neighbor trains for the Boston Marathon each year, while you run around the block a few times on weekends. Obviously, his shoes will get more wear and tear and will not last as yours, which receive only occasional and very limited use. What is normal wear and tear for running shoes? It depends. If they are shoes specifically designed for professional runners, it may be six months or so, although yours might last two years or more, and it is likely you will replace them for stylistic reasons rather than because they actually wore out. So if the shoes were to wear out in one year, the professional runner could not complain based on the fact that yours lasted for two years.

Before going back from shoes to real estate, I want to discuss one other concept. That concept is the "reasonable person" standard. When we talk about normal wear and tear, it is based on use by a reasonable person in similar circumstances. I've already indicated that I don't like loose terminology such as "reasonable," but in this situation, that is what we have to deal with, so there is no choice. Substitute "average" for reasonable and it may be of some help.

So in the case of our running shoe example, our baseline for measuring normal wear and tear of that particular item is the "average" person who is training for the Boston Marathon, not the average weekend warrior who runs around the block and buys an expensive pair of shoes. In this case, we would look to the average training program for the average marathon runner to provide some quantifiable baseline for defining the "average" use of a running shoe by a marathon trainee.

Okay, we are talking about renting real estate, not running, so let's return to our landlord-tenant situation. In this book, we are discussing normal wear and tear by an average person or persons living in a property. But what kind of property are we talking about? Is the standard the same for a house in the country as it is for an apartment in the city? Is it the same for one person as for a couple? What about a couple and three teenagers? What is normal wear and tear in that situation? These are very difficult to quantify.

If you rolled your eyes or otherwise reacted when I added the example of three teenagers, that is really a tacit admission that most people believe that a household with three teenage children will receive more wear and tear than one with a single person. So what should your benchmark be when inspecting a reasonable household with three teenage children? For one thing, the carpeting will probably be more worn out, the appliances will be getting more use, and I'm sure you can think of many other examples. But that's different from damages, isn't it? Exactly! Now we get to the heart of the matter of withholding security. It doesn't matter how many people were living in the property. If the oven was damaged due to negligence or willful misuse of the item (and, presumably, insurance won't cover such a case), then you can withhold the cost of the repair of the item from the security deposit.

Let's say there was a wild party in the unit the night before the tenant moved out and a window was broken. Broken windows are not normal wear and tear, and, in the absence of negligence, willful misconduct, or (remember the other example?) *force majeure,* an act of God or war, windows don't break. So you can withhold the repair costs of the window from the security. The problem is that nobody contests items that are clearly broken. Now, let's look at the measure of damages for a moment.

Measure of Damages

As we indicated earlier, the measure of damages is part of a concept of law known as remedies. Remedies are designed to make the injured party whole, to put him or her in the same position as before the damage occurred. Unfortunately, depending on the case, what makes you whole in the eyes of the law doesn't always make you whole in real life.

Remedies and Depreciation

For example, you are in a car accident and your car is completely destroyed, which in the car insurance industry is affectionately known as "totaled." Let us further suppose that your car is a 1999 Chevrolet Camaro with 68,000 miles on the odometer. You live in a no-fault state, so the insurance company is going to replace the car irrespective of who caused the accident. The question is, how much will you get? "Well," you say, "I had a Camaro before; the insurance company should pay me for a new Camaro." Of course, if you have ever had to deal with an insurance company on this issue, you know that is not the case. You don't get funds to buy a new Camaro, you get the value of a 1999 Camaro after depreciation. That is the value of what you had before the accident, and that is the value of what you have now. You are in the same position as you were before the accident. Theoretically, you should be able to use the insurance money to buy the same Camaro you had before, to wit, a 1999 model with 68,000 miles on the odometer. That's fair, isn't it? You had it before, and you have it now.

Depreciation

Now, let's apply this to a security deposit example. Although somewhat more complex, the way the insurance companies, and ultimately, the way you as a landlord must, consider depreciation is by subtracting the actual life of the product from the estimated useful life of the product to give you the depreciated value. Depreciation is really nothing more than an accounting function, and each industry has information regarding the useful life of a product.

The Basic Principles of Returning Security Deposits

Let's state some general principles or guidelines to be followed regarding the withholding of security deposits:

1. A security deposit is not a tool for making a little extra money from your lease.

2. The purpose of a security deposit is to cover damages to an item that is outside the realm of normal wear and tear.

3. Normal wear and tear refers to the reasonable depreciation of an item by virtue of the use of that property for the purpose intended.

4. The remedy for damages to an item may be the repair cost or the replacement cost, depending on the item and the nature of the damages. Where replacement is the only option, you may have to consider the characteristics (such as the useful life, the age, and the model) of the item being replaced as a factor in the amount of damages that you are seeking.

5. Think before you withhold. Remember that this is a business, and there are costs associated with any business enterprise. This is probably the most important rule. Let me give you an example to put it in perspective. Let us suppose that you buy two pieces of furniture, one from store "A" and a second from store "B." Both pieces of furniture are delivered with defects. You return the first item to store "A," and it gives you a hard time, refusing to replace or refund the item. Store "B" has a "no quibble" policy and sends a truck within the next three days for the damaged item, no questions asked, and gives you the choice of a store credit or full refund. Obviously, you will continue to do business with store "B." It is the same with being a landlord.

6. Human nature is fairly predictable. As a general rule, people tend to treat their own possessions better than the possessions of others. Don't expect that tenants will treat your possessions as if they were their own. If they do, consider yourself fortunate and try to keep those tenants, because they are a rare find.

Security deposits serve a number of excellent purposes. (1) The tenant is aware that you are holding his or her money and will make a natural effort to be more careful because he or she does want that money back. So it serves as a deterrent, albeit a minor one, to the tenant's having a free-for-all with your property. (2) There are times when it is very suitable to withhold a security deposit.

Landlords must understand the law and be fair with their tenants, even when it appears that the tenants themselves are unfair. One object of this book, as I've stated repeatedly, is to *keep you out of court.* Once you are in court, you become part of the system. You give up a certain degree of control. Your advantage as the landlord is diminished. What you want to do as a landlord is maximize your profit, keep that property rented, and not waste time being penny-wise and pound foolish. Court should be a last resort and only for serious issues, not because you want to keep an extra few dollars or have the tenant pony up for a new paint job or a cleaning that the property needed in any event. I don't want to make you tough landlords—I want to make you good landlords. Sure, you may take a hit now and then, but in the long run, you will come out ahead, and with a lot less stress. With that in mind, let's now move on to taxes and insurance.

PART THREE

CHAPTER 10

"Honey, It's the Accountant"

Taxes and Other Legal Considerations

The tenant is fine and is paying his rent. You deposit the rent in your checking account each month and pay the mortgage, on time. Life is beautiful, until the phone rings. "Honey, it's the accountant, he wants to talk to you, he says he needs some more information on our rental." You feel a cold sensation in the pit of your stomach. "I told him what the rent was; what other information does he need?" Actually, you need to provide a whole lot more information, unless you want to pay considerably more in taxes than you need to. In this chapter, we take a look at the tax consequences of renting a property.

Taxes are generally viewed as one of the most complex, mystifying, and often terrifying aspects of our lives. The basic tax code, recently revised, is still a multivolume highly complex piece of work. Yet conceptually, taxes are extremely simple. If you don't get caught in the web of accounting minutiae, you should not encounter any problems. First let's take a look at the fundamental principals of taxation.

Principles of Taxation

The basic rule of taxation is that all income is taxable unless there is an exception or deduction. That's it! That is really all you need to understand. If you made income, it is subject to taxation unless it falls under an exemption or deduction. For example, if you bought tax-free bonds, by definition those are exempt from taxation, even though you may derive income from them in the form of dividend-type payments. So, here is an example of where you earned income, but because the income was exempt, you don't pay taxes on it. No problem so far, right? But what if the income is not exempt, but you had certain expenses that offset the income amount you earned? Do you still pay taxes on the gross amount of the income? The answer is no, if the expenses are part of doing the business that earned the income. These expenses are considered as costs of doing business and are deductible. Again, conceptually not difficult to understand. You have income, exemptions, and deductions. If the income is not exempt, then you take the allowable deductions, and the difference, if any, is the taxable amount. This is the same concept whether you are talking about federal taxation or individual state taxation. Everything else is just rules and regulations. Let's apply these concepts to rental property.

Taxation and Rental Property

You have moved to a new house and rented your old property. You are receiving $1,000 per month, which is $12,000 per year. Thus far, there should be no difficulties with the math. Is this income? You rented your property, and you are receiving money in return. That's income. The next question you ask is whether this $12,000 is exempt from taxation. Assuming that you are not some sort of charitable or not-for-profit institution with tax-exempt status, the answer is probably no; the money is not exempt from taxation. The only question left to ask is whether or not you have any deductions that will reduce the income figure from $12,000.

Legitimate Deductions

"Well, when I moved out, I had to prepare the house for rent. I spent $200 to repaint the walls. I also bought a new refrigerator and a microwave, which the tenants demanded. That cost $750. The tenants demanded a new carpet (even though the old carpet was still in very good condition). The new carpet cost $2,000. I placed an ad in the newspaper, which cost $300 for three Sundays in the real estate classified section of the local newspaper. A local real estate broker saw the ad and brought the tenant over, for which we paid a 10 percent commission (that is, 10 percent of $12,000), or $1,200. I also paid for a Renter's Insurance Policy, which cost $300. We also bought an Appliance Repair Policy, which cost $200."

Thus far, it appears that you have had a number of legitimate expenses with regard to this rental property. You haven't made $12,000, because you had expenses that offset the income. Of course, you paid everything by check or credit card and kept the canceled checks, credit card receipts, and bills from the purchases to prove that the expenses you made were for the rental property. In our example, you spent $4,950 on the rental; deducting that from the $12,000, your taxable income has dropped to $7,050.

"Wow, this is great, you can deduct everything. We shouldn't have to pay any income tax at all; we'll just apply more stuff to the deductions." This is where you get into trouble. Tax-deductible items are not a free-for-all. If questions about the legitimacy of a deduction arise (the word "audit" comes to mind), it is up to you to defend your tax return. Here is a questionable example.

Rather than hire a professional painter, you paint the interior of the house yourself. You know that a painter costs $700 to do the job, so you deduct $700 as your own labor cost. The problem is, you are a computer programmer and not a professional painter, so you don't get to apply someone else's professional fees as your own, if it isn't your profession. But what if you are a painter or a "general contractor?" Could you now deduct the labor costs? Maybe, if you painted the house during normal work hours. Presumably, you could have been painting someone else's house at the time, and so you should be able to charge for the work. But what if you did the work on Sunday? Now it is less clear. Do you normally work on Sundays? If not, you may not be able to claim your work hours. What is the question you should be asking at this point? If you are wondering where the $700 factors into the picture, you are sharp indeed. As we have indicated, you have to have an actual expense. Did you pay your company (or yourself) $700, which you or your company will declare as work-related income someplace else on a tax return? In taxation and accounting, everything has to balance in the end. You cannot merely take an expense as a deduction because you performed a task and that is what the task cost. If you deduct $700 as an expense, that means you spent $700, and whoever received that $700 has income subject to deductions, just as you did. When you get too clever is when you get caught and find yourself in trouble.

It works something like this. The Internal Revenue Service (IRS) receives hundreds of thousands of tax returns. From those hundreds of thousands of returns, they select a percentage for review. Some pass review and nothing more is mentioned, or you may get a letter from the IRS indicating that you either overpaid or underpaid some amount. Usually it is not very dramatic. Other tax returns become subject to a full audit. Since most of this is now computerized, one of the items that might trigger a closer inspection of a tax return other than random selection would be a dramatic change in income. If every year, your deductions on your taxes come in at about $5,000 and then suddenly they jump to $75,000, this could "red flag" your return.

One rule of thumb that I learned as a young lawyer was "never dip into the client's escrow account and never mess with the IRS." Taxation is an area where you want to have excellent records, and the rewards of being too clever are dubious at best. In the case of taxes, proof is the best defense. If you can show that a deduction was legitimate, it will generally be allowed, unless there is some specific paragraph of the tax code that forbids it. For example, let us suppose that you drive from your new home to your old home to show the property to a prospective tenant. What, if anything, can you deduct? Good multiple-choice question:

a. You can't deduct anything.

b. The car has become part of the expense of doing landlord business, and therefore you can deduct any reasonable expense associated with the use of the car.

c. You can deduct the cost of the percentage of gas used to drive to and from the showing as an expense of trying to lease the property.

d. None of the above.

What do you think? If you said *c,* you are correct. Choice *a* is technically not correct because you do have expenses related to the leasing of your unit. Choice *b* is too broad. Just because you used a vehicle once or twice to travel to the rental property doesn't make every nonrelated use a tax deduction.

Choice *c* is the correct answer, provided that you can prove what percentage of gas you used in traveling to the leased property. Choice *d* is wrong since there is a correct answer, choice *c*. Is it really worth figuring out what the percentage of gas is? That is up to you, but I would suggest that it is not worth it to do so. My advice is to take the normal expenses associated with renting property and forget the clever stuff. Taxation is an area where it pays to be conservative.

If you understood the concepts above, you understand basic tax law. The rest is strictly the application of those concepts. When tax time rolls around, if you are organized, you should not have any trouble with taxes as they relate to rental income.

The Federal Taxpayer Relief Act

However, there are other aspects of tax law that you need to be aware of besides income, exemptions, and deductions. On May 6, 1977, the Federal Taxpayer Relief Act became law. This act significantly changed the tax benefits a homeowner receives under the law.

Primary Residence and Capital Gain

The problem is that in order to take advantage of these tax benefits, the property must be your *primary* residence. A primary residence is any property that has a kitchen, a bathroom, and a place to sleep that is *occupied* by the owner of that property. But you get only one primary residence, which must have been occupied by you, the owner, for at least two of the last five years to derive the capital gains benefits. Why is that important? It's important because, presumably, property increases in value, and when you sell a property, you make a profit. That profit is known as a *capital gain* and is taxable.

Under the old rules, you got a one-time exemption from capital gains taxes if you were over 55 years of age and did not have to reinvest the profit from the sale within a certain period of time. Under the new rules, sellers of any age may claim an exemption no more than once every two years. Each person who files a return gets up to $250,000 worth of exemption on a capital gain, so a husband and wife filing jointly would get $500,000 in a capital gain, tax free, on the sale of a property.

If you rent your property, the property may no longer qualify as your primary residence, and these tax advantages may also no longer apply. However, if you rented the upstairs portion of the house, or the garage or the basement, the property should still be considered your primary residence for capital gains tax purposes. The portion of the property that is rented may have to be considered separately. I would recommend consulting an accountant at that point.

The real problem is that taxes are not figured out in a vacuum. They are interrelated. Thus, you and your spouse or significant other, as applicable, will probably have other sources of income. Let us suppose that you earn $50,000 each per year. You have some stocks and bonds, which give you a few extra dollars in dividend income. Then, there is the rent from the tenant. Your taxes are calculated based on what income bracket you fall into. Other related areas such as capital gains from sales of nonprimary residential property have rates that are in part based on what tax bracket you are in.

For example, the 1977 Taxpayer Relief Act reduced the capital gains tax rate from 28 percent to 20 percent for those taxpayers who were in a tax bracket above 15 percent. For those within the 15 percent tax bracket, the capital gains tax rate was reduced to 10 percent. Sounding more complicated? It can get worse. But here is what you really need to understand. Tax liability is based on your tax bracket—which is determined by your total income minus your applicable deductions, which is your total net income. In 2006 taxes will range from 10 percent to 35 percent—as opposed to 15 percent to 39 percent today. So is this good news for landlords? Sure it is, because it makes it more attractive to invest in property for income-producing purposes, and that will be more advantageous taxwise when the property is ready for sale or when you may need to sell. Let's look at some examples.

Selling

The need to sell is self-explanatory. People sell assets when they need to raise capital. While real estate is generally not considered a liquid asset that can be converted into cash quickly, it is nevertheless something that can be converted into cash sooner or later, depending on how urgently you need the funds. Sometimes, you may want to sell the property simply because you feel it has reached its highest value in the real estate market and you want to take your profit. After all, this is an investment property. You may have even received an offer from the tenant.

But there is a third alternative that applies to condominiums and other types of planned urban developments (PUDs) that have homeowners' associations. Recent case law suggests that the associations' articles of incorporation may be amended to abolish the right of an owner to lease his or her unit or house. If such a case were to arise with regard to your association, you as a landlord might seek to sell the property and invest elsewhere. As a result, the tax consequences of a sale are important to consider.

As you can see, the myriad rules and regulations regarding tax liability as a whole can be very complex, but the theory is quite simple. As we have already noted, it is more important to understand the underlying theory, because once you understand that, the rest is application of the theory. You can research the answers to specific issues or consult with an accountant. However, unfortunately, it doesn't stop there. The taxable income that you derive from a tenant is only one piece of your income puzzle. As stated above, your total income picture determines your tax bracket. So you also need to consider such items as other income from work and any deductions that may apply, as well as other investments such as stocks or bonds. Also, something we haven't spoken about with regard to your properties is the mortgage. If you don't own property free and clear, your interest on the mortgage may be deductible. This all factors into your income picture. But are there other alternatives to individual property ownership? The answer is yes.

Incorporation and Taxes

Thus far in our analysis, we have presumed that you own the property in your name, and any income is declared on your personal tax return. There are alternatives to this set-up, which have different legal and tax consequences. For example, many people question whether it pays to incorporate. This is a very interesting issue.

A corporation sounds grand. Names such as Exxon and General Motors conjure up visions of corporate enterprise. But for a few hundred dollars, anyone can form a corporation. But should they? There are really two main reasons for doing this; the first is liability, and second is taxation. Let's look at the issue of liability first.

Liability

Conceptually, a corporation is an artificial entity. It is a separate being, but with certain qualities that we humans don't possess. The first is an unlimited life span. Death of directors and shareholders does not affect the life of a corporation. A corporation remains in existence until it is legally dissolved. Thus, if you, John Smith, were to die, your real estate would pass to your beneficiaries in accordance with the terms of your last will and testament, if you had one. If you did not have a will, state law would determine who got the property and, tangentially, where the tenant of your property would pay the rent. In a corporation, your death does not affect the existence of the corporation. It goes on with a new director and, perhaps, shareholders. The tenants still pay their rent to the corporation. The property remains with the corporation and is not part of your individual estate. So we know that a corporation is a separate entity with a life of its own, legally speaking. How does that relate to liability?

Let us suppose that you have rented your property to a tenant. The tenant slips and falls on your property and alleges negligence on your part. Whom does he sue? He sues the owner of the property. If the property were in your name, that would be you, the owner of the property. But what if the property is in a corporation? Then the owner of the property is no longer you, but the corporation. We have defined a corporation as an artificial being and that being is the one party that is liable, not you. So personal protection from liability is one reason to incorporate. "But I'm only renting my upstairs bedroom. Do I really need to be a corporation for that?" The answer is no. In the next chapter, we see how insurance should protect you from a lawsuit by a tenant or his guests for acts of negligence. A single property landlord probably has no need to incorporate solely on the basis of asset protection.

Taxation

However, as always, there is another category to consider. That is the area of taxation. As we have seen, taxation is a very personal matter, and each person must assess his or her own tax situation. There are several key points to note here. The first is that there are several types of corporations, and these various types carry with them different taxation advantages and disadvantages. Remember that our core principle of taxation applies to corporations as well. We have stated that the basic principle of taxation for individuals is income less exemptions and deductions. This applies to corporations as well. The only difference is that the rates at which corporations are taxed differ from those of individuals. Thus, the corporation, as an artificial being, files its own set of tax returns. Generally speaking, it doesn't make sense to incorporate if you are renting your upstairs bedroom, either for liability or for tax purposes.

However, if you do wish to incorporate, you may wish to consider what is known as the *Subchapter S* corporation. This is a type of corporation that operates legally like a regular corporation but is designed to accommodate the small business owner. As such, with a "Sub S" corporation, the income of the corporation may be taxed to the shareholders of the corporation as opposed to the corporation itself. This can be a valuable tool if you as a shareholder of the corporation have more deductions or exemptions than the corporation, or are taxed at a better rate than the corporate rate in terms of income. It allows both you and the corporation more flexibility in the preparation of your taxes.

Generally speaking, a small business corporation may have no more than seventy-five shareholders, and a husband and wife are considered as one shareholder. If you and your significant other decide to form a corporation, Subchapter S is generally a good way to go.

Preparing Your Tax Returns

Taxation can be a daunting proposition. Many people take up the challenge and prepare their own returns, while others go to tax clinics or have personal accountants. Whatever works is fine, so long as you don't try to be too clever. It is not my intention to impart moral imperatives in this book. I have argued throughout that as a landlord, you are engaged in a business. You want that business to run with as few complications as possible, because in the long run, you lose more in time and often money by fighting. On the other hand, people are always tempted to save as much money as possible and are further tempted to take risks to do it. To some, tax returns are viewed as almost a challenge to see how much one can get away with. I'm suggesting that you avoid the temptation to take an extra deduction if it is not legitimate. If you somehow manage to get the attention of the IRS, I assure you it is not worth the few pennies you saved here and there by cheating.

The other advice I always give, and hope that people listen to, is to rely on research and advice from experts. Avoid listening to your friends and relatives or, worse, total strangers. Let me give you a quick related story. Human nature is such that a person will often pay more attention to a stranger than to someone close and trusted. Did your spouse or significant other ever tell you something, or give you some information or suggestion, and you ignored it? But then some total stranger tells you the same thing, and all of a sudden it's pure genius.

There's a variation on this phenomenon that happens very often in real estate. My wife and I will sit down with a client who wants to rent his condominium in South Florida. We show him the comparable prices for his property and for other similar properties in the area. No comparable property has rented for more than $1,500 per month, and the average rental amount was about $1,100 per month. The client examines the figures, nods a few times, and seems to understand the research we showed him. "So, Mr. Client, shall we list your property for $1,500 per month?" There is a pause and then comes the reply, "My friend Herb said that I should be able to get at least $2,500 per month rental because the apartment is near the ocean." My initial instinct is to toss the client out the door with a gruff, "Let your friend Herb rent the apartment and leave us alone," but you can't do that. The conversation usually goes something like this:

"Tell me, Mr. Client, your friend Herb, is he in real estate?"

"Herb, heck no, he owns a grocery store in Duluth, Georgia, but he knows a lot about real estate."

"I see, so he owns property in Florida?"

"Florida, heck no, he hates Florida, won't go into the state, he has an ice fishing cabin somewhere in Minnesota."

Get the picture? The point is that people believe what they want to believe in spite of the facts presented to them. They'll go along with anyone if what that person says sounds more lucrative to them than what the facts actually are. If the person is a stranger, or totally inexpert, what he or she says seems to carry all the more validity. Don't fall into that trap, especially when it comes to taxes.

"Oh yeah, I deducted my whole vacation as an expense. Never got caught. Just do it, everyone does." Well, not everyone does it, and maybe this person didn't get caught this time, and maybe you will get caught. It isn't worth trying. The same rules apply to tax matters that apply to all other aspects of the landlord-tenant transaction that we have discussed. Do the research, be professional, and be honest. In the long run, it pays, if only to avoid aggravation.

In the next chapter, we discuss the issue of insurance. This is one of the most overlooked, but important, aspects of the landlord business, and, as we shall see, it is tax deductible.

CHAPTER 11

The Importance of Insurance

"My Neighbor's Daughter Tripped on My Carpet (and She's a Ballerina)"

In our previous discussion of corporations, we explored the issue of liability protection. However, this book essentially deals with the landlord who has one piece of property or perhaps part of his or her home as the subject of the rental. There is hardly a need for incorporation under these circumstances. Yet the problem of liability is real and must not be ignored. The United States is an extremely litigious nation, and a home or apartment is a fertile ground for lawsuits. What kinds of dangers could possibly lurk in your upstairs bedroom? Let's take a look.

Slips and Falls

Picture yourself sitting back getting ready to relax. This time you turned off the phone to ensure that there are no interruptions. The bills have been paid, the tenant is quiet, and all is right with the world. Suddenly those ominous words waft through the living room in the form of: "Honey, there are these guys at the front door with papers, and they want to see you." You guessed it, process servers. You accept the papers and sign their document. Your stomach is churning as you look at the heading of the summons. It reads "Joan Smith, plaintiff vs. You, the Landlord, defendant." "But the tenants' names are Sam and Bertha Johnson. Who is Joan Smith?" You read on to discover that Joan Smith is Bertha's grown daughter (and Sam's stepdaughter) and was visiting several weeks ago when she tripped in the backyard of the house Sam and Bertha are renting from you. Apparently, there was a hidden rock in the backyard, and Joan tripped and broke her foot. As it turns out, Joan is a ballerina and has to cancel her entire season of performances while her foot heals. The doctors seem to feel that the break is so serious that it may actually affect her career. She is suing you for 15 million dollars. You call the tenant while trying to remain calm, which isn't easy considering that you are somewhere between total panic and a nervous breakdown.

"Yeah," replies Sam, the tenant. "I heard about the lawsuit, what a shame, but Joan's a real problem, and she hates me; you know how it is; gee, I hope this won't affect our landlord-tenant relationship?" Yeah, right.

That is one scenario, a worst-case scenario, to be sure, but slips and falls are one of the most common causes of lawsuits. When you hear "code blue, aisle D" or words to that effect announced over the supermarket loudspeaker, it is not because someone has stolen merchandise from aisle D, but, more than likely, because there was a spill and it needs to be cleaned up before somebody slips and files suit. It is the same theory in your home. If the resident, his guests, or invitees (which could be a salesperson or any other individual who is on the premises with the resident's permission) are injured, you could be liable for damages. The plaintiff, the injured party who files suit, must prove that the injuries sustained were proximately (directly) caused by your negligence. "But I didn't put the rock there, I didn't even know it was there." Actual knowledge is not an issue here. The question is, should you have known of the hidden danger, and were you negligent in not removing it? If the proximate cause of the injuries sustained were due to that negligence, you have problems. So how do you deal with these problems? The answer is by purchasing insurance.

Insurance

Most people have homeowner's insurance, so why not have renter's insurance as well? Oddly enough, this is very often overlooked. "You mean that I can have a landlord policy?" That is correct. It is very much the same as homeowner's insurance, except that you as the landlord are the beneficiary. First, let's talk about the standard homeowner's policy and then compare it with a renter's policy.

Homeowner's Insurance

The standard homeowner's policy covers liability and medical payments (the injured ballerina) as well as losses caused by theft, fire, personal property damage, flood, and windstorm. Some policies pay for living expenses if your home is rendered uninhabitable. What items would you want your renter's insurance policy to cover as the landlord? Well, you don't really care about the personal property of the tenant. That is his or her business. We will discuss that shortly. Would you want flood and windstorm coverage? You might, depending on where the property is located. If you own a condominium, then you would check the building's policy to see what is covered with regard to the structure. Obviously, you would also want the liability coverage.

If someone visits you and slips in your home, the person can sue you just as if the visitor slipped and fell in your rental property. Does that mean you'll never have guests or invite anyone to visit you? Of course not, although it is an intriguing idea. So if you have homeowner's insurance, why can't you have renter's insurance? Absolutely no reason whatsoever. All you need is a landlord's policy. Let's see how this plays out in the real world.

Renter's Insurance and Condominiums

Here is an excellent example if you own a condominium unit. The example is a bit complex, so follow along, and you will see all of the different insurance issues that can arise. You are the landlord of unit 701, which is rented. Unit 801 directly above is owner occupied. In terms of insurance, you have a landlord renter's policy, and your tenant has renter's insurance as a tenant on the personal contents. Unit 801 has a homeowner's policy, and the building has a condominium insurance policy as well.

During the past year, there was a series of storms. One particularly violent storm caused a pipe to burst, which resulted in damage to the interior walls of unit 701 (your unit). In addition, unit 801 left the bathtub running, and it overflowed, causing major flooding in your unit. The water damaged most of the tenant's furniture, and while the tenant was trying to rescue her stuff, she slipped and injured her back. As she was a professional golfer, you anticipate the worst. You are about to sit down and watch television when you get the call. Besides cry, what do you do?

The first step is to report the incident to your insurance company. When you call, be prepared with as much information as you can ascertain. You will need your policy number and any information you have regarding the insurance policies of the other parties. Contact the owner of 801 and simply ask for the name of his company. Do the same with your tenant. When obtaining the information, don't get into the specifics of the claims or indulge in accusations. That is the job of the insurance companies, and they do it very well. Also, try to get a rough idea of the amount of damages you foresee. Unfortunately, as much as I advocate obtaining insurance, you need to know how to deal with insurance companies.

The basic problem with insurance companies is that their first loyalty is to themselves and not to you. The automatic reaction of any insurance adjuster is, how can I either deny this claim or pass it on to someone else? That may or may not be made apparent to you, depending on the personality of the adjuster. Some of the less forthright companies will begin by telling you that they are not responsible for this claim and that you should look to the policy of the building or the other unit owner—to anyone but them. "I don't think so," is the reply they get from me. "You are my insurance company, and I am reporting the claim to you." If that doesn't work, I ask, trying to sound as naïve as possible, "Do you think I need to call my attorney on this claim?" Insurance adjusters tend to dislike lawyers, and they will do anything to keep you from bringing them in on the case. "No, we'll send an adjuster to the property, no need to go to any extra expense," is the general response. The translation is, "Okay, you win this round; we'll play by the rules." They will then take your information, and shortly thereafter, the adjuster will call to set up an appointment.

During this initial conversation, always tell the person taking the information that you want their permission to call a plumber or any other repairperson necessary to contain the damage. They will tell you to go ahead, but be sure to keep the receipt. This is important because you want it on record that your insurance company knows you are going to begin incurring repair costs. Sometimes, the repairpeople will wait for the insurance company to pay, although many demand cash in advance. It is a good idea to have an electrician and plumber you can trust ready for action, rather than search for one at the worst possible time, which is when the problem occurs.

Back to our leaking condominium. The adjuster will come to the property and probably ask you for the same information you already reported to the insurance company. Some companies hire independent adjusters to investigate claims; others retain in-house adjusters. The adjuster will take pictures and generally try to explain why your insurance company is probably not liable on the claim. Once again I ask in my naïve voice, "I see; well, I was about to send a copy of the condominium association's documents and the building's plumbing diagrams to my lawyer. Would you like a copy for your files, too?" Usually, the reply is something like, "Uh yeah, good idea; I need to look at those." Of course the adjuster needs to look at those, because they will determine which insurance companies are going to have to pay for damages.

This is how it works. There are two ways by which liability may be determined. The first is by general negligence law, which, as already indicated, deals with proximate causation of the damages. The second is state law. In certain states, such as Florida, statutes regulate what portion of damages each insurance company is liable for. Proximate cause is no longer an issue. The key factor in both cases, though, is where the leak began. Here is the problem in condominiums.

Common Elements

Condominiums, as we noted earlier, are comprised of individually owned units and common elements such as hallways, swimming pools, elevators, and lobbies. Slabs of concrete separate each individual unit. Within those slabs are common elements such as plumbing and wiring, which connect to individual units as necessary. Generally speaking, if the particular pipe is located "outside the slab" of a unit, it is in the common elements. Conversely, if it is located "within the slab," it is your pipe, and you are responsible. The condominium documents and construction diagrams help to discern which pipes fall inside and outside the slab. In our case, let us suppose that the pipe burst within the common elements of the building. How would the insurance companies resolve the dispute?

First, let's look at the wet walls. That was proximately caused by the common element pipe's failure. In that case, the building's insurance should cover the damage to the wet wall in unit 701. However, the wet wall wasn't the only problem. We still have the issue of the flood from unit 801's bathtub to deal with. The proximate cause of that damage was clearly from the negligence of the unit owner in 801, and his insurance company would have to handle the flood damage to the unit below.

However, in states such as Florida, where state statutes govern the disposition of insurance proceeds, proximate causation is not as much a significant player in certain situations. Again, let us say that the pipe that caused the damage is a common element pipe. The damage to your unit included damage to the wallpaper you had placed on the wall, along with fixtures. Guess what? Even if the proximate cause of the damage to the wallpaper and ceiling fixtures was the common element pipe's failure, the building's policy won't pay.

Under Florida law, condominium association policies do not cover floor coverings, wall coverings, or ceiling coverings in the individual units; neither do they cover electrical fixtures, appliances, and built-in cabinets. There is one exception, which involves fixtures initially installed by the developer of the building before July 1, 1992, but the odds of that exception arising are extremely slim. So in our example, in Florida, the building's policy would pay for repairs to the wall. Your insurance company would handle any other damage that occurred to the unit caused by the common element pipe.

Tort Law

With regard to the bathtub, as that does not involve the association, the state statute would not apply and general tort law takes over. A tort is simply a civil wrongdoing. The law of torts is law relating to noncriminal acts committed against an individual or his or her property. For example, if you are not paying attention and accidentally drop an object from a terrace and it injures someone on the street, that is a tort. In the case of the flooding bathtub, the homeowner's insurance policy of unit 801, whose owners caused the flooding, would have to pay the damages.

But what happens if unit 801's owners don't have homeowner's insurance? Fortunately, you do, and whether or not your insurance company can collect from the owners of 801 is not your problem. Insurance companies always like you to pity them, "Oh poor us, always having to pay out money." Did you ever notice that the biggest buildings in any city center always belong to insurance companies? Please—they can afford to pay your claim.

Understanding Insurance Policies

The trick is to understand what protection you are purchasing. This is not easy, nor is it meant to be. Let's see if there are some common rules that may assist you.

The irony of the insurance industry is that while it dislikes attorneys, it is the "legalese" found in its policies that offers it protection. Most purchasers of insurance do not read the complex terms and conditions of the insurance policy, but rather take it on faith (or the word of the insurance broker) that the policy will provide sufficient protection. My advice is to take the time to understand what you are buying. If there is ever a claim, you will appreciate the effort you made. Let me give you an example of how to read a policy.

Coverage

The main thing you need to look at is what specific damages the policy covers. This is known as "coverage" or the *covered peril* clause. However, that is not enough. Once you know which damages or "perils" are covered, you have to look at the "definitions" clause to determine if what you think you understand is in fact correct. Here is an example of a trap that I fell into when I was the manager of a condominium.

During the hurricane season, we had several bad rainstorms. This particular building had an outdoor elevator that was flooded when the water seeped from the third floor garage deck into the elevator shaft. The second elevator, located in the interior of the building, was also flooded when the machine room that contained the elevator controls became flooded. The machine room was located on the 34th floor of the building. We had a flood rider as part of the building's insurance policy. This seemed like a no-brainer.

I notified the insurance company, and it sent an adjuster to take pictures. Several weeks later I received a letter denying the claims on both elevators. Apparently, this was not a "covered peril." Furious at the denial, I immediately telephoned the adjuster. "This is going to court" I screamed, but the adjuster was unmoved. "Look, Ken," he calmly said, "this issue is clear; check the definition of flood in you policy." Sure enough, when I looked up the term "flood," it was defined as damage resulting from groundwater buildup. Groundwater was further defined as water that, you guessed it, touched the ground. Since the damages to both elevators occurred from water that did not actually "touch the ground," the damage to the elevators did not meet the definition of "flood." Isn't that cute? Actually, after some more arguing and wrangling and a letter from the association's attorney, the insurance company did pay, based upon the Fire and Casualty portion of the policy, which included elevator damages. The lesson learned, though, is to find those pertinent portions of the policy and read them carefully. In this case, you want to see what are covered items and how those items are defined.

Types of Insurance Policies

If you are only renting a room in your house, you may think you don't need insurance. Let me give you an example closer to home (no pun intended). As I write this book, the latest homeowner threat, which received national attention, was the issue of mold. Major newspapers nationwide covered the heartbreaking stories of people who had gotten sick from mold and were forced to leave their homes. Pictures of exterminators in "moon suits" going in to try and remove the mold made for frightening journalism. No problem, though, one thinks, because these people had homeowner's insurance. Actually, there were many problems, as insurance companies took the position that mold was not in fact a covered peril. Instead, they argued that the homeowners were responsible because they failed to keep their homes dry and free from moisture and humidity over the years it took for the mold to build up. Pretty outrageous!

The fact is that you need insurance to cover yourself in case of emergencies or disasters. There is no way around it. However, that doesn't mean that you accept whatever the insurance agent sells you on faith alone. Ask specific questions about coverage; use examples if you can't remember specific terminology. Ask if your policy is based on "named peril," which means the risk covered must be specifically stated or "named" in the policy, or if you are buying "all-risk insurance," which covers everything unless it is specifically excluded in the policy from coverage.

All Risk

"All risk" is the preferred choice because in this case, you know in advance what the policy won't cover, and everything else is included. Presumably, with an "all-risk" policy, if you discovered mold, and it was not specifically excluded, the insurance company would have to pay, whereas in a "named peril" policy, if mold wasn't specifically listed, the company would simply deny coverage. However, I just received a renewal notice from my insurance company that stated that mold will be specifically excluded in all circumstances from my homeowner's policy.

Replacement Cost

Another important issue that we have already discussed is replacement cost versus actual cash value. Replacement cost coverage pays for the present cost of replacing the item without considering depreciation. Actual cash value is the cost minus the depreciation, which, as we have already seen, severely reduces the value of your recovery.

The real problem that I have with insurance is philosophical. When you purchase insurance, you are betting that something bad is going to happen to you, while the insurance company is betting that it won't. As a result, you are paying money to bet against yourself. However, philosophy aside, let me tell you a story of a family who paid health insurance for years and was never sick. Times got bad, and the family had to look to reduce costs. Since nobody ever got sick, they decided to cut out their health insurance, which was expensive and was never used. Shortly after they cancelled the policy, the wife was diagnosed with cancer and the family went into great debt to pay for treatment. Fortunately, the cancer went into remission and the family is now in good shape, financially and otherwise, but it took a long time and it serves as a valuable lesson when it comes to insurance. It is one of those things that you should always have, and even though it is costly and, hopefully, rarely needed, if you use it once, it is worth acquiring. Actually, renter's policies, both for the landlord and the tenant, are not too expensive.

Tenant's Renter's Insurance

There is one other aspect of insurance that we need to discuss. The question arises as to whether you can force your tenant to procure a renter's policy for the tenant's personal property. Thus far, we have really been exploring renter's insurance from the landlord's perspective. In fact, the landlord needs to consider the issue of a tenant's policy. What happens if your tenants are the victims of a robbery? Their furniture is ruined and personal property is stolen. Who pays? Your landlord policy probably wouldn't cover it, and the building's insurance does not cover personal property of the residents, unless it could be proven that the building had inadequate security and that, somehow, this factor was related to the proximate cause of the theft.

Apply that same scenario to water intrusion. Personal property of the resident is ruined, but who pays? Depending on the cause of the water intrusion, possibly your policy or the building's policy (if applicable) will cover structural damages, but personal property of the resident is a tricky issue and may not be covered by anyone. Now the tenant comes looking to you, the landlord, for satisfaction. There is a third twist to this situation. What about a case where the tenant causes a flood in the apartment? What damages will your policy cover? You may wish the tenant to carry additional fire insurance in case a fire causes damage to both the residence and the tenant's personal property. Landlords may place, as a condition of the lease, a clause requiring the tenants to obtain their own renter's insurance and provide proof to the landlord that such insurance was acquired. It would also name the landlord as the principal beneficiary.

If you don't want to go that far, you should still have a clause in the lease stating that while the landlord and the building (if applicable) carry insurance, these policies may not cover the personal property of the tenant. It is therefore recommended that the tenants obtain a renter's policy of their own. At least, the tenants are put on notice that the landlord is not going to assume full liability for damages that may occur to the personal property of the tenants. In addition, in states where insurance proceeds are regulated by statute, the insurance companies may not legally be able to make a payment on certain items, even if they were payable under general law. This is a situation where the insurance companies will interpret the statutes as broadly and liberally as possible. "Hey, we would love to pay for that furniture, but the law says we can't." Oh darn!

The bottom line with insurance companies is they are in business, just like you are. They try to maximize their profits, and that means paying out only when absolutely necessary. That is fair as far as it goes. But you are running a business, too, the business of being a landlord. You have an obligation to yourself and your business to do things right. One of the first things we talked about is leadership. This applies to dealing with insurance companies as much as with tenants. You need to be the leader, understand your policy, shop it around, treat it like any other part of doing business, and don't be bashful about filing a claim when appropriate. When the adjuster shows up, give him or her the facts and be firm. Let the adjuster know that you are not going to stand for any cursory denials. A good insurance agent is very valuable in these instances, because agents are in sales, and happy customers are what keep the sales rolling in. Some insurance agents will actually help you if you run into an adjuster who feels that it is his or her job to deny each and every claim, no matter what the circumstances.

By now, you must be wondering why you ever considered becoming a landlord. It really isn't all that complicated, and as I have indicated, once you go through the process, it will be less daunting, and the ease in which you handle situations will make them seem little more than routine. It is a matter of experience.

I can give you rules and guidelines and war stories, but you still need the first-hand experience. You need to take the information I have given you and go out and use it. For example, I can write a book on how to in-line roller skate. You can follow my directions to the letter about moving forward, braking, and making turns, but until you try it, until you put those skates on and go out in the street, it's all theory. Even an experienced ice skater or skier is going to be a little wobbly the first time he or she tries to skate on wheels. But sooner or later, you are going to be literally flying down the streets on those skates. The more you practice, the better you get.

I can tell you from personal experience that it is easier and far less painful to lease a property than to learn to in-line skate. Also, it is more profitable. At the end of the day, a successful lease will bring you income, and that's what it is all about. You are going to have money to cover your expenses, pay the mortgage, and, in general, make your life better. When that first rent check comes in, you are going to feel a sense of accomplishment. You've done it! You took your investment and made it pay off now, not in the future, when you sell it, but right now, every month. In the prologue to this book I described how the wealthiest people have great real estate holdings. This is your first step to building wealth.

In addition, look at the various issues you have dealt with: credit checks, leases, insurance, law, and advertising. These are things that should help you in everyday life as well as in your landlording profession. Confidence comes with experience, and in the case of landlording, so does income.

In the next chapter, we summarize the material presented thus far and offer some final observations on being a successful landlord.

CHAPTER 12

Some Final
Observations

The ad in the newspaper was crisp and clean; it read simply "one bedroom apartment, furnished or unfurnished, walk to shopping, minutes from golf and tennis, close to all public transportation. $1,200 per month, yearly leases only. Professionally decorated. For more information, call John or Mary." A phone number was provided. The ad ran on consecutive weekends.

The first week following the placement of the ad, John and Mary received a few inquiries but no requests to view the apartment. This began to worry the couple, who had invested a good chunk of their savings in the apartment.

The apartment was located in a developing residential area about a half-hour from the city center. The golf and tennis club was open to the public but was part of a major resort that had just been completed. There was also a new shopping mall minutes from the apartment, and although it was a healthy walk, it was easily accomplished by anyone in decent physical condition. It was less than five minutes by car. The downtown area was being revitalized. A new state law offering tax incentives to businesses that relocated to the state was attracting many large corporations. That area and a new commercial corridor were emerging, with factories being constructed along the expressway minutes from John and Mary's apartment. This made a purchase of a unit in the surrounding residential area a good real estate investment. Besides, John and

Mary loved the area. It was new and clean, with lovely restaurants and parks, and they were hoping to use the apartment as a vacation getaway in the future. In the meantime, they would rent it. They had hoped that the $1,200 per month rental income would defray the cost of the mortgage and pay the taxes, as well as provide a nice monthly profit.

The next weekend was basically the same as the last in terms of responses to the ad. A few people did call, and one wanted to see the apartment, but after viewing it, the prospect was noncommittal in terms of signing a lease. John was beginning to worry. "I don't understand it," he said to Mary. "Why aren't we getting any interest in this place? It can't be the price. Mr. Smith, our neighbor who owns the apartment next door to ours, said he could easily get $1,500 per month. He ought to know, because he bought his unit at the same time we did, and he lives in the building. Your aunt was a top decorator in the 1980s, and she decorated the apartment. I was a bit concerned about the Hawaiian motif, but she said it looked beautiful. What are we going to do?"

You are now all landlords. What red flags did you spot in this scenario? What did John and Mary do wrong? Let's take a closer look. In terms of a real estate investment, it appears that John and Mary did make a wise purchase. Although we are not told the geographic location of the property, the facts indicate that it is in an area that is growing commercially. There are malls, recreational facilities, and new industries coming to the area. This should create a vibrant real estate market, yet John and Mary's unit is not renting. Let's see if we can spot their mistakes, beginning with the ad in the newspaper.

Advertising Your Property

At first glance, the ad seems to tell you what you need to know, or does it? How many bathrooms does the unit have? Is there a view? Does the apartment have any extra utilities? Is it a one bedroom, one bath, or is there a second full or half bath? That is an important detail. What about the building itself? Is it new and modern or an elegant classic? The ad then advises that the unit may be rented furnished or unfurnished. That's good; it widens the scope of prospects by providing choices. Not everyone wants to furnish an apartment. But if they have their own furniture, why would they want to pay the same $1,200 as for a furnished unit? Conversely, as a landlord and business-

person, why would you rent out a furnished unit at the same price as one that
is unfurnished?

Decorating the Unit

The ad also states that the apartment was "professionally decorated." That
would appear to contradict the fact that you are willing to rent it unfurnished.
People have their own tastes, and claiming that an apartment is professionally decorated indicates that it is more expensive, perhaps more delicate,
probably won't go with your own furniture, and is generally more intimidating. So the ad itself could have used some more thought. How did you do?
Did you spot the same issues and perhaps find some others as well? Let's
move on to the price. At the core, money talks and baloney walks. The items
we have discussed thus far are important marketing principles, but at the root
of every transaction, not only in real estate, is the price. What do we know
about their price?

Valuation of the Unit

Thus far, we know that John and Mary are asking $1,200 per month. We also
know that they appear to have gotten this price from their next-door neighbor, who owns the unit he is living in. That is the biggest of mistakes. We have
seen that the rental market is governed by many factors. Let us suppose that
interest rates on mortgages are very low and the people coming into the area
are buying instead of renting to take advantage of the low rates. What about
supply and demand for rental units in the area? Do we know how many units
are available for rent in the building or in the neighborhood? The first thing
real estate appraisers learn is never ask neighbors about the value of property.
John and Mary made a common mistake. The fact is that we don't know if
$1,200 per month is correct in terms of a rental price. We haven't got any facts,
other than a statement by the next-door neighbor, who is not even a tenant,
that the unit is worth $1,200 per month. We also suspect that the $1,200 per
month, based on John and Mary's stated expectation, will cover the expenses
of the apartment and generate a profit. If that is possible, that's excellent; that
is what we are after. However, if it is not possible to attain, it may be better to
lower the price than to keep the unit empty, as I have already argued. Again,

did you spot the red flags concerning the issue of valuation? With this in mind, let's go back to the placement of the ad.

Be Creative, Have Fun, But Get the Reader's Attention

Placing an ad is one of the aspects of leasing that should be fun. Here is a chance to get your name in print. You are about to enter the glorious and exciting world of advertising. Okay, so you may not be a New York City ad executive about to have cocktails in midtown Manhattan, but you can still have fun with your ad. It is a chance to exercise your creative juices. Be proud of your property. You can exaggerate or "puff" a little bit, so long as you don't lie. If you face a park, rather than simply state, "view of park," you can write, "lovely view of park, see the beautiful trees." Or, if it's in a family neighborhood, try "lovely view of park, see the children play." You are creating beautiful and serene images in the mind of the reader. By now, your prospect should be experiencing images of beautiful forests or laughing children happily jumping rope. It seems like a great place to live. It may also sound a bit hokey, and people may not take it too literally, but if it gets the attention of the reader and he or she calls to see your property, that is what you are after. You got the best of their curiosity. I once put an ad in a newspaper advertising our apartment for rent. It was a unit in a building with very good security, including some fancy cameras, which I wanted to play up. Instead of merely writing "excellent security," I wrote, "state-of-the art super spy security." You'd be surprised how many people who responded either asked to see or at least commented on the "super spy security" portion of the ad.

Create a Sense of Urgency

The other thing you wish to accomplish in your ad is to create a sense of urgency. Phrases such as "call now" or "won't last" are always good because they tell the prospects that you have a good property and they need to jump on it now. It is also giving them a subliminal command. You are literally telling them to "call you now!" Also, you may wish to let them know that it is "easy to show." Tell the readers that you are available to show them the unit at their convenience. Sometimes, you may wish to pay a little extra and have a border or highlight placed around your ad to make it stand out more. I always do it and find it is worth the added cost. Check the professional ads, especially the automobile ads, in the newspapers; you will get the idea.

I always enjoy the advertising portion of the process. Just remember that a little "puffing" is okay, but don't say "lovely view of park, watch the children play" if your apartment has a view of your parking lot. In that case, stress the proximity and convenience of the apartment. You might try, "don't shlep groceries, super close to parking." The word "shlep" will stand out, and most people will know what it means even if they are not specifically familiar with the term. Let them ask you. If they do, it means they have responded to your ad. Be creative, be flexible, and have a good time. Let's now look at the issue of leadership.

Reviewing Leadership

One of the first concepts presented in this book was that landlords should exhibit leadership qualities. Clearly, it is not necessary for a successful landlord to possess the leadership qualities of Napoleon. Studies are constantly conducted in attempts to define the perfect leader. However, at its core, leadership is merely being more assertive than the next person or group of people. Every time you enter into the public domain, you have to assert yourself at some time. Whether it's battling your way from a busy entrance ramp onto the freeway, asking your boss for a raise, or selling an idea or product, it's your force of personality that usually wins or loses the day. All I am positing is that in the business of being a landlord, you need to apply your leadership skills as you would in other areas where you may normally assert yourself without thinking about it. Going back to the example of John and Mary, we'll review this concept.

At this point, John and Mary researched the rental market more carefully and discovered that their unit in fact will rent for only $850 per month unfurnished or $1,000 per month furnished. They painted the apartment white and took out the Hawaiian motif. They also replaced the carpet with a standard beige color rather than the ornate designer carpeting that basically matched only the Hawaiian motif. Because of low interest rates, the rental market is at a weak point, and fewer people are still renting. At these prices, John and Mary will not receive any profit, but the monthly income will cover the mortgage, as well as the monthly maintenance payment and a portion of the real property tax, depending on whether the unit is rented furnished or unfurnished. Thus, John and Mary can keep the unit empty until the rental market improves or sell the unit at a profit in the new and robust market.

At the moment, John and Mary feel that it is better to rent the unit than to keep it empty until they find someone willing to pay their price. They place a new ad in the paper and receive some serious interest in the apartment. Sid and Martha, executives with a newly relocated company, accept the $850 per month rent. Sid, who is very assertive, insists that while he will sign a lease, he will not provide his Social Security number or any other personal information. "Look, you can check with my employer, but that is it. Also, anywhere I have ever rented, the landlord was responsible for everything. If a light bulb goes out, the landlord replaces it. And this stuff about penalties for late payments, forget it. I never agree to pay those either, just on principle alone. Also, I don't like the carpeting. I'll replace it and charge you for it. Now, give me the lease and I'll show it to my lawyer; if he approves, I'll sign it."

John and Mary are stunned. The unit has been empty for quite some time, and these people appear to be quite prominent. John noticed that they drove up in a Mercedes, and Mary observed that the couple, although dressed casually, wore expensive clothes. John could check with Sid's employer; surely that was enough, and he would agree to replace the carpet. That couldn't cost too much. At least the apartment would be rented. Hopefully, the tenant's lawyer would not object too much to the lease. John and Mary agree to all of the tenants' terms.

What do you think? Who is running the show here? Is it John and Mary or Sid and Martha? Obviously, it is Sid and Martha. They are calling the shots. Notice that Sid intimidates John and Mary by speaking in "absolutes." I never pay, I never agree, I'll replace and you will pay. Just to throw in a little more intimidation, he ends with the fact that he has a "lawyer" who will have to review the lease. John and Mary are totally overpowered by these people.

There is an old saying among pilots that "any landing you walk away from is a good landing." In terms of real estate transactions and in business transactions in general, I would alter that saying to "any bad deal you walk away from is a good deal." John and Mary should clearly walk away from these people.

What are the red flags in this scenario?

The most obvious red flag is the fact that Sid and Martha were not willing to submit to a credit search. This is standard practice, and if they refuse, there is probably a good reason, such as bad credit. The fact that they wore good clothes and drove an expensive car is indicative of nothing. Maybe the nice clothes were their only good outfits worn to impress, and anyone can lease an expensive car. Again, it means nothing.

The demand for new carpeting, even though the carpet was in fact new, was unreasonable. It is an indication of a demanding tenant whose demands would probably continue throughout the terms of the lease. Then, to nail the position, Sid brings up the fact that he has a lawyer. Lawyers are supposed to be scary people who can cause you problems. But in this case, it is an empty threat. You are offering to rent an apartment.

The tenant can take it or leave it. There is no actual legal issue here, and even if the tenant wants to show the lease to his or her lawyer, if you don't like what the lawyer has to say, there is simply no deal. In short, there is no reason to be intimidated. Besides, lawyers are expensive, and few people keep them on retainer, and certainly not for lease reviews. Also, even if the tenant has a friend or relative who is a lawyer, you don't even know in which state or what field of law he or she is practicing. Criminal attorneys don't generally know all that much about real estate law. At this point, talk of a lawyer is usually bluff.

Of course this is all supposition. In fact, Sid and Martha may be very good tenants but even better negotiators. There are people who can sense inexperience or desperation in a person and try to take advantage of it. While this is not exactly the finest example of human nature, it is how some people function. In this case, John and Mary had to assert themselves. There were two opportunities to do this. The first was when Sid and Martha began their litany of demands. At that point, John and Mary could have halted the conversation. "Sid, please stop. Mary and I would love to have you as tenants, but if you refuse a credit check, we cannot rent the apartment to you." You can even add, "Our lawyer told us that under no circumstances should we forgo a credit check." Note that you are now using the " my lawyer said" gambit first.

The second tactic is to let Sid finish his demands, and then for John and Mary to simply state that they are not willing to lease the property under those terms and conditions. If Sid and Martha walk, so be it. No bad tenant ever results in a good deal. You cannot let the tenant be the boss. In my opinion, it is better to keep the property empty than to lease to a bad tenant. On the other hand, if Sid and Martha are legitimate, and they want to lease, they may decide to proceed under your terms, which are the industry standard and without which they probably couldn't lease anywhere else. You have also established yourself as a landlord who cannot be toyed with. If the prospects are not legitimate, then you have lost nothing if they don't rent. It's your property, your rules.

Law, Taxes, and Insurance

With regard to the law, taxes, and insurance, we have argued that a successful landlord must understand the general concepts of these disciplines. In addition, as a landlord, you must understand and apply the specific rules of law. It is true that the law is complex. We have seen that there are federal laws and state laws, with variations in each of the fifty states of the union as well as Puerto Rico. However, as you already know the fundamental principles of landlord-tenant law, the rest is just a few specific procedural details, such as how long you can hold a security deposit before returning it to the tenant.

Doing Research

In the old days, it merited a quick trip to the library to research local laws. However, in today's Internet-driven society, there are numerous Web sites with excellent charts and information. Just type "landlord & tenant" into your search engine, and you will have more than enough sites to explore. There are numerous legal Web sites that offer plain language information on landlord-tenant law. Many of these sites also contain multistate charts, which will give you the specific data for your state.

It's basic research, the same type of research you do every day in other areas of your life. If you are going to place a bet, you will look up the statistics of the team or contestants in the event you are betting on. If you are going to purchase an automobile, you will research the cost, reliability, and resale value of the vehicle you are planning to purchase. In this case, you are going to start a business, the business of being a landlord, and that will require some research as well. Remember, as long as you know the basic theories, the rest, as I have previously indicated, is merely application. You also know the basic legal principles as well as the insurance and taxation issues. To be a successful landlord, you need to apply those principles. Therein lies the challenge.

Landlord-Tenant Transactions

My wife and I have been in the real estate business for more than twenty years. In our opinion, the most difficult of the various real estate disciplines involves landlord-tenant transactions. The reason for this is simple. When you sell a piece of property, barring any unforeseen complications, the deal is over until the new owner decides to sell his or her property. However, when you are in the position of being a landlord, during the term of the lease, you are part of an ongoing transaction where anything can happen.

The transaction doesn't end at the closing table. In fact, when the tenant signs the lease, that is when the transaction truly begins. But that is what often makes it exciting. First, the money starts coming in after the tenant signs the lease. If nothing else happens and the tenant pays each month, great. In most instances, that is what will happen. The best of all possible worlds is that you will have an uneventful experience. But let's face it. Life is really a series of experiences, and the odds that every tenant is going to be perfect are pretty slim. So if something does go wrong, look at it as a challenge. You are prepared, and you will rise to the occasion.

In the final analysis, being a successful landlord is being a good businessperson coupled with some people skills and a working knowledge of the rules and regulations of leasing a property in your state. It means putting your prejudices (if you have any) aside and running your business in a professional manner. If you are fair but objective, you should do fine. As I said in the beginning of the book, the leasing of property is a time-honored tradition often reflecting the highest and best use of a property. So good luck and enjoy being a landlord.

Test Your Skills

Before being accepted in law school, each student has to take what is known as the LSAT (Law School Aptitude Test). For our purposes, I have devised what I will describe as the SLAT, the Successful Landlord Aptitude Test. There is no passing grade. It is merely designed to see if you grasped the principles that we have been discussing throughout this book. I will give you the answers at the end with explanations, but no peeking. Let's begin:

1. As a landlord, which laws do you need to consider in renting your property?

   a. Federal law
   b. State law
   c. Local ordinances, homeowners' association rules and regulations, or condominium documents, as applicable
   d. All of the above

2. You demand a security deposit from the tenant. This money may be held:

   a. In a segregated bank account located within the state where the rental property is located
   b. In your personal savings account

    c. In your personal checking account, provided it is noninterest bearing

    d. In accordance with state law

3. In considering a tenant for your property, you may refuse to lease the unit to that tenant:

    a. If you don't agree with his or her religious beliefs

    b. If he or she looks dirty

    c. If he or she refuses to submit to a credit check

    d. Both *b* and *c* but not *a*

4. A lease agreement may not contain the following clause:

    a. Restriction as to pets

    b. Restriction as to number of guests sleeping over

    c. Who pays for repairs to the property

    d. Restriction as to the national origin of a guest

5. For a lease to be valid, it must contain the following information:

    a. Date of commencement, date of termination, and parties to the agreement

    b. The names of the landlord and tenant, the dates of commencement and termination, and the amount of the rent

    c. The names of the landlord and tenant, the amount of security, and the date of commencement

    d. The dates of commencement and termination, the amount of security, and the amount of the lease

6. A lease may be best described as:

    a. A unilateral contract

    b. A bilateral contract

    c. A friendly agreement between the landlord and the tenant

    d. A personal services contract

7. If the tenant fails to pay the rent, the best course of action for the landlord to take first is:

    a. Call the police

    b. Send the tenant a notice demanding the rent

    c. File suit in landlord-tenant court

    d. Hire a group of thugs to beat the tenant until he or she pays

8. You have rented your property furnished and ready for the tenant to move in. As well as a good lease agreement, what additional documents should you have?

    a. An insurance policy for the appliances

    b. An inventory of all personal property, such as furniture, linens, and dishes

    c. A landlord's renter's insurance policy

    d. All of the above

9. The tenant is demanding items that are not in the lease agreement. The landlord should:

    a. Ignore the tenant.

    b. Respond in writing that the tenant's demands are outside of the lease agreement and are denied.

    c. Call the tenant on the telephone and curse him or her out.

    d. Hire an attorney and commence eviction proceedings.

10. Which of the following items is not tax deductible as related to the rental of property?

    a. Cost of hiring painters to repaint the apartment

    b. Buying a microwave for the kitchen

    c. Advertising costs for renting the property

    d. A vacation to the Bahamas after you rent the property as a reward for a job well done, and to rest from the effort of finding a tenant

11. The lease is over, and the tenant elects not to renew the lease. What should the landlord do?

    a. Check the lease agreement to see when he or she can begin to advertise for a new tenant.

    b. When the tenant moves out, inspect the property and determine if any security will be withheld.

    c. Start showing the apartment immediately, irrespective of the tenant's wishes.

    d. Answers *a* and *b* only.

12. You have elected to withhold security because of damages to the property. What steps do you take?

    a. Within the time stipulated in the lease, send the tenant a letter indicating that you intend to withhold security.
    b. If you have determined that the damages are either willful or negligently caused by the tenant, you may withhold the security without any further notification to the tenant.
    c. If the tenant contests your withholding of the security, you must return it to the tenant within 10 days of receipt of the tenant's demand.
    d. None of the above.

13. The tenant has damaged a five-year-old carpet beyond what is considered normal wear and tear. It costs $2,000 to replace the carpet. You are holding $3,000 in security. You may withhold:

    a. $3,000
    b. $2,000
    c. The depreciated cost of the carpet
    d. The original cost of the carpet five years ago

14. Which of the following is not considered normal wear and tear?

    a. Holes in the wall where the tenant hung pictures
    b. A high-traffic area of the carpet that is worn beyond the rest of the carpet
    c. A broken window
    d. Fingerprints and dirt on the walls that will require repainting of the guest bedroom

15. The tenant has a party on your property. Drinks are served, and one of the guests drives home inebriated. He crashes and is killed. His estate sues you because you are the owner of the property. Which of the following statements is true?

    a. The estate will prevail because you are the owner of the property.
    b. The estate will prevail, but your insurance policy will cover the damages.

    c. The estate will not prevail because you did not serve the drinks.

    d. The estate will prevail, but the damages will be split between you and the tenant.

16. Your tenant has a party. During the party, which takes place on the backyard patio, one of the tiles on the roof falls and hits a guest, causing the guest a concussion and memory loss. When the guest recovers, he sues you. Which of the following is the *best* answer?

    a. The guest will prevail because you are the owner of the property.

    b. The guest will not prevail because you were not at the party.

    c. The guest will prevail because you are the owner of the property, but your landlord's renter's policy should protect you.

    d. The guest will not prevail because the property was leased, and so the tenant is liable.

17. You decide that you want to form a corporation and place your rental property in the corporate name. Depending on your tax situation, you may well be advised to consider which of the following types of corporations?

    a. The Chapter 7 corporation

    b. The Subchapter 11 corporation

    c. The Chapter C corporation

    d. The Subchapter S corporation

18. The best way to decorate a property that you wish to rent is to:

    a. Hire a professional decorator to create the popular look of the moment.

    b. Keep it simple with beige and whites and let the tenant do the rest.

    c. Use lots of colors.

    d. Decorate it in your own taste. If it's good enough for you, it will be good enough for the tenant.

19. When determining what rental price you desire from the tenant, you should always:

    a. Ask the neighbors what they think.

    b. Check the prices other similar properties are commanding in the neighborhood.

    c. Price it at the value it is worth to you.

    d. Demand enough rental income to cover expenses, plus a 10 percent profit.

20. The tenant wants to bring a pet to the apartment and is willing to pay a pet deposit. You have no objection, and a lease is signed that includes the pet. After the tenant moves in, the president of the condominium association sees the pet and informs you that pets are not allowed in the building. Which is the best answer?

    a. The lease prevails, and the tenant may have a pet in the unit.

    b. The rules of the association prevail, and the tenant may not have a pet.

    c. The tenant must obey the rules of the condominium association and may not have a pet, but may declare the lease null and void.

    d. The landlord should report the condominium association to the Humane Society.

How did you do? Let's go over the answers.

1. *d.* Federal, state, and local laws as well as any rules of the condominium association or homeowners' association, as applicable, must be considered when leasing a property.

2. *d.* At first glance, answer *a* seems appropriate and is probably a safe way to hold the money, but it may not be necessary. As a landlord, you need to know your state's specific rules regarding the holding of security deposits, and therefore *d* is the best answer.

3. *d* is the correct answer. You should never discriminate based on race, color, religion, or national origin. You should also add to that basic list sex, sexual preference, and age. The only exception is if your condominium association is organized as a senior citizen community under the laws of the state where the property is located. In such a case, you may not lease to people under the age classified as "senior citizen."

Cleanliness is not a protected class of individuals, and you have every right to request that your prospective tenant submit to a credit check. Refusal to do so is grounds for not renting the unit. However, if you only demand credit checks from a certain class of people and that class is protected, you may be in violation of antidiscrimination laws. Therefore, you should be uniform in your rental policies.

4. *d* is the correct answer. The analysis is the same as in question 3.

5. *b* is the correct answer. This question is a bit tricky. To create a contract, there must be an offer, an acceptance, and a consideration. Those are the basic elements. The landlord offers the property, the tenant accepts, and the rental amount is the consideration. However, in order for the lease agreement to be valid, those elements must be communicated in the contract. Thus, the contract requires the names of the parties to the agreement and the rental amount.

Security is irrelevant, because that is just a term of the agreement; it is not the primary consideration. In addition, in order for a contract to be valid, it must have a specific date of commencement and a specific date of termination.

Contracts may be drawn in such a way that the contract renews automatically after a specific time unless one or both of the parties object, but those contracts are still considered as having a termination date.

6. *b*. A lease is a bilateral contract between the landlord and the tenant.

7. *b*. While beating up the tenant may be tempting, the lawful method is to first send a notice to the tenant, by certified mail, that he or she is late in the rent and a demand for the rent within a stipulated time, usually three calendar days. However, state law may lengthen that period. Most states require the proof of notice as a condition before going forward with an eviction proceeding.

8. *d*. As a landlord, you should carry as much insurance as possible. Appliance insurance, a renter's policy, and an inventory of the items left in the apartment or house should always be in the landlord's file.

9. *b*. While some of the other choices may be tempting, choice *b* is the best answer because it both is impersonal and creates a record of the issue involved, especially when you are going to deny the demand. Send the response by certified mail so that there will be no issue of whether the tenant received your response.

10. You can deduct only items directly involved in the business of renting or maintaining the property. A trip to the Bahamas to recuperate from the ordeal of leasing the unit is clever but not legitimate.

11. *d* is the correct answer. Once the tenant elects not to renew the lease, you may begin showing the apartment in accordance with the terms of the lease agreement. After the tenant moves out, you should inspect the property to determine if the security deposit needs to be withheld. While the lease is in effect, the rights of the tenant must be respected, irrespective of the fact that he or she will not renew; therefore choice *c* is incorrect.

12. *a* is the correct answer. Almost all states require a written notification to the tenant from the landlord that he or she intends to withhold the security. Each state has its own rules regarding how soon the landlord must accomplish this.

13. *c* is the correct answer. The Law of Remedies is a difficult subject and creates many problems with regard to the landlord's withholding of security deposits. In most cases, the courts will not award the actual cash value or replacement cost but will depreciate the item.

14. *c* is the correct answer. A broken window is not considered normal wear and tear. When tenants lease a property, they are expected to use and enjoy the property, which creates wear and tear. Thus, walking on carpets or putting pictures on a wall is part of normal use of the property. The cost of cleaning may be tax deductible as well.

15. *c* is the correct answer. This is a harder question. The landlord is not responsible for every injury that occurs on his or her property, only those injuries that result from a defect in the property that the landlord knew or should have known about and failed to correct. If that defect was the immediate cause of injury to the tenant or the tenant's guests while on the property, the landlord may be held liable. But if the proximate cause of the injury to a guest was not a defect on or about the property, but some independent action of the tenant, the landlord is not liable. In this case, the tenant held a party and after serving alcohol to a guest, allowed him to drive drunk.

Various states have Dram Shop (Barroom) Acts that hold the host liable if he or she allows a guest to drive drunk. These acts used to apply only to commercial establishments, including bars and restaurants; however, many states have extended the acts to private gatherings. In this case, the tenant held a party, served the drinks, and allowed his guest to drive drunk. The immediate cause of the tenant's injuries had absolutely nothing to do with any defect in the property, and thus the landlord is not liable.

16. *c* is the correct answer. In this case, the defect that directly caused the injury to the guest was a roof tile, part of the landlord's property. The law charges the landlord with responsibility for the defect, whether or not the landlord had actual knowledge. If the law imposes knowledge to the landlord where the landlord was not aware of the defect, it is referred to as "constructive knowledge." However, the landlord's insurance policy should cover the loss up to the limit of the policy.

17. *d* is the correct answer.

18. *b* is the correct answer. Taste is subjective. In this case, beauty is truly in the eyes of the beholder. Therefore, it is best to keep the property as neutral as possible and let the imagination of the prospect take over.

19. *b* is the correct answer. In order to value a property, you need to know what other comparable properties in the area are commanding. While launching your investigation, you should consider such factors as location, views, building amenities, and whether the comparable units are furnished or not.

20. *c* is the correct answer. The rules of a condominium association may restrict pets in the building. In that case, the tenant may not have a pet. However, the facts presented in the question suggest that the landlord and tenant had agreed on the pet as a condition of the lease. Since it is the landlord who is the owner, he or she is presumed to know the rules of his or her condominium association. The tenant may successfully argue that the pet is part of his family and the landlord knew or should have known that pets weren't allowed. As a consequence, the agreement should be voided because the tenant was wrongfully induced to sign a lease. An alternative legal argument is simply that there was "no meeting of the minds" as to an essential element of the lease, that is, whether or not pets were to be permitted.

So, how did you do? If you got 100 percent, you understand the essential elements of becoming a successful landlord. If you made a few mistakes, don't worry. It just means you didn't quite grasp a particular concept. Reviewing the applicable chapters should solve the problem.

Residential Lease Agreement

1. DATE OF AGREEMENT

(Month) _____ (Day) _____ (Year) _____

2. PARTIES TO AGREEMENT

A. LANDLORD

(Name)

_____

(Address)

_____

(City) _____ (State) _____ (Zip Code) _____

B. TENANT(S)

(Name)

_____

(Name)

_____

( ) ( ) ( ) ( ) Parties place initials here.

255

C. ADDRESS OF RENTAL PROPERTY

(Address)

_____

(City) _____ (State) _____ (Zip Code) _____

3. TERM OF RENTAL

Date Lease Commences

(Month) _____ (Day) _____ (Year) _____

Date Lease Terminates

(Month) _____ (Day) _____ (Year)_____

4. AMOUNT OF RENT _____ ($) per month

A. Address Rent Is to Be Paid:

(Address)   (Unit # if applicable)

_____

(City) _____ (State) _____ (Zip Code) _____

B. Due Date of Rent

Rent payment is due on the _____ day of each month commencing on _____.

Last Rent Payment is due on the _____.

C. LATE PAYMENTS: Payments received by the landlord five (5) days after the due date stipulated above shall carry a penalty of one hundred dollars **($100.00)** as a late fee. Any dishonored check fees are the responsibility of the tenant and shall be a charge to the tenant along with late fee charges. **If a check is dishonored for any reason, the landlord may require all future rent payments to be made by certified check only.**

Under no circumstances is tenant permitted to live through security deposit. Security deposit will be returned in accordance with state law.

OR

( ) Check here if rent is to be paid in partial or full sum in advance

( ) ( ) ( ) ( ) Parties place initials here.

Tenant will pay the sum of _____ ($)
not including security, on the _____day of _____,_____ in advance,
which covers _____ term of the lease.
(enter amount of the term that rent covers, e.g., full term, 6 months, etc.)

(If payment is less than full term, describe additional payment details below.)

Remainder of rental payment is to be made in the following manner:
(Describe below)

_____

_____

_____

5. **SECURITY AND ADVANCE DEPOSITS:** On or before the 10th day of
   _____ 2004, tenant will deposit with AQUAVISTA INTERNATIONAL
   INC. ESCROW ACCOUNT, the sum of twelve hundred dollars ($1,200) as
   a security deposit, and the sum of twelve hundred dollars ($1,200) as last
   month's rental payment. The landlord, in accordance with state law and
   without interest, if allowable, shall hold security deposit under such state
   law. The security deposit shall be returned to the tenant in accordance with
   state law provided, however, that the leased property and its contents and
   fixtures are returned to the landlord in the same condition as received by the
   tenant, normal wear and tear excluded. Normal wear and tear is defined as
   use of the property by a reasonable tenant living in the property and using
   it, its contents, and fixtures in a reasonable manner as they were designed to
   be used.

6. **OCCUPANCY AND USE OF THE LEASED PROPERTY**

   A. **Number of People Allowed to Occupy Property:** The tenant agrees that
      the property shall be occupied by no more than _____ (   ) per-
      sons, to wit: the undersigned signatories to the lease and the following
      other individuals:

      _____ age: _____

      _____ age: _____

(   )(   )(   )(   ) Parties place initials here.

B. **GUESTS:** The tenant must notify the landlord in writing of any other party who resides in the property more than two weeks. The tenant shall not have more than four guests staying overnight in the unit at any given time.

C. **USES OF PROPERTY:** This property shall be used for residential purposes only by the parties described in paragraph 6A herein. No business of any kind including but not limited to professional practices shall be allowed in the leased property without the express written consent of the landlord. A business or professional practice is defined as any entrepreneurial endeavor which requires a third-party consumer of the business product to enter into the property for the purpose of obtaining or being solicited to obtain the end product or services of the business or professional practice. In no event may the tenant use the subject property as a "corporate property" for employees of the tenant or other transients. The tenant understands, agrees, and acknowledges that he/she must obey all federal, state, city, and local laws, rules, and regulations as applicable, including but not limited to any and all rules and regulations of any homeowners' association or condominium association. It is the tenant's responsibility to obtain copies of said rules and regulations from the association management office.

D. **SUBLETTING AND/OR ASSIGNMENT:** This lease is not subject to subletting or assignment without the express written consent of the landlord. Any sublet or assignment by the tenant without the express written consent of the landlord is considered void *ab initio* and the tenant understands and agrees that this lease shall be terminated as of the date of the sublet or assignment.

7. **UTILITIES:** The tenant shall be responsible for obtaining, paying, and disconnecting all utilities including but not limited to electricity, water (if applicable), and telephone. Any outstanding payment of a utility bill which accrues to the landlord due to failure of payment by the tenant is subject to the landlord's withholding of the security deposit to cover such expenses.

8. **CONDITION AND MAINTENANCE OF THE PROPERTY:**

A. The tenant acknowledges that inspection was made of the subject property prior to the signing of this lease and agrees that the property is habitable and that all appliances and any other fixtures or items of the property are in working condition and functioning properly.

(   ) (   ) (   ) (   ) Parties place initials here.

B. The tenant agrees to be responsible for maintaining the property in sanitary conditions.

C. Repairs shall be treated in the following manner:

1. Major repairs: Major repairs shall be the responsibility of the landlord. Major repairs are repairs that are defined as costing more than $100 to repair, as estimated by a qualified professional in the designated area of repair. Minor repairs, those repairs that are deemed by a qualified professional in the area of repair to be less than $100, shall be the responsibility of the tenant. Landlord and tenant acknowledge that there (is) (is not) (_____) an appliance contract in effect and tenant acknowledges that he/she (has) (has not) (_____) been given a copy of such an appliance contract. In the event that an appliance contract covers the needed repair, it shall be the tenant's responsibility to contact the carrier and arrange for an appointment to repair the item. However, the issuance of appliance contract in no way abrogates either the landlord or the tenant's responsibility to repair the appliance or item in question in timely fashion in accordance with the terms of this paragraph.

2. The tenant shall be solely responsible for any and all repairs resulting from willful misuse or negligence, which proximately causes any damages to the property or its contents. The tenant shall not be permitted to engage in hazardous activities on or about the property nor keep any inherently dangerous articles on or about the property, including but not limited to weapons, explosives, or other flammable objects which could reasonably be expected to increase the risk of fire.

3. In no event may the tenant take it upon himself or herself to effectuate a "major repair" without the express written consent of the landlord. If an emergency situation exists and, after reasonable attempts under the existing circumstances are made to reach the landlord, the landlord cannot be contacted, the tenant may take such steps *as are reasonable and prudent to terminate the emergency* situation while continuing to attempt to contact the landlord. In such a case the landlord will reimburse the tenant any out-of-pocket expenses necessary only to terminate the emergency. Under no circumstances shall the tenant withhold rent as a method of reimbursement unless expressly consented to in writ-

(   ) (   ) (   ) (   ) Parties place initials here.

ing by the landlord. In a case where water leak (plumbing) or electricity or emergencies of such nature are involved, and where termination of the emergency only would not result in the return of the essential service, and the landlord could still not be reached, the tenant may authorize the "major repair."

4. If the property is damaged by fire, flood, or other categories constituting a "*force majeure*," and as a consequence, the property is rendered uninhabitable, the lease shall be terminated and the rent shall be prorated as of the time the property became uninhabitable. If the property is damaged by fire, flood, or other categories not constituting a "*force majeure*" but proximately caused by the willful or negligent acts of the tenant, the tenant shall be fully liable for all repairs and rents on the property. THE LANDLORD AND THE TENANT ARE THEREFORE ADVISED TO OBTAIN APPLICABLE RENTER'S INSURANCE DURING THE TERM OF THE LEASE.

5. The tenant may not make any alterations or improvements to the property without the express written consent of the landlord. Alterations or improvements are defined as any structural alteration in the property or removal or alteration of a fixture or appliance including but not limited to plumbing and electricity, with or without damage to the property or irrespective of any financial improvement to the property.

9. **PETS:** Tenant (may) (may not) keep domestic pets or other animals on premises. Domestic pets are pets commonly found in a household such as dogs and cats.

There shall be a nonrefundable pet deposit of $100.

10. **DEFAULT:**

A. **BY TENANT:** Where a default in the payment of rent, or any other terms or conditions of the lease exist, the landlord shall advise the tenant in writing by certified U.S. mail or other form of mail which contains a proof of mailing and receipt by tenant, that he/she is in breach of the lease, and the notification shall contain a short description of the breach. The tenant shall have three regular days (not business days) to

( ) ( ) ( ) ( ) Parties place initials here.

cure the breach. If the breach is not cured, the landlord may terminate the lease and the landlord shall be afforded all remedies under state law with regard to entering the premises, eviction of the tenant, and allocation of damages. Subject to state law, the landlord's remedies shall include but not be limited to entering and retaking the property, and upon termination of the lease, all unpaid rents on the remainder of the term shall be accelerated and become due and owing along with any other damages accrued to the landlord.

B. **BY LANDLORD:** Where the landlord fails to adhere to any duty conferred upon him or her by this lease or any federal, state, or local law, rule, or regulation, the tenant shall notify the landlord in writing of the default by certified U.S. mail or other form of mail that contains a proof of mailing and receipt by the landlord, and such notification shall contain a short description of the breach. If the breach is not cured within a time reasonably necessary or likely to cure such a breach under the given circumstances, the tenant shall be afforded all remedies under state law with regard to payment of rents or placement of rent in court registries or any other remedies available. If the tenant considers the breach to be of such a nature as to render the property uninhabitable, this shall be considered as a constructive eviction and the tenant shall vacate the premises immediately.

C. This lease shall be governed by the laws of the State of _____ (fill in state as applicable). The venue shall be _____ (fill in as appropriate) County. Prevailing party costs and attorney's fees shall apply.

11. TERMINATION OF LEASE:

A. **SURRENDER OF PROPERTY:** At the expiration of the lease, the tenant shall return the property to the landlord in the same condition as received, normal wear and tear excluded.

B. **HOLDOVER:** Subject to state law, a holdover by the tenant after the expiration of the lease shall create a month-to-month tenancy which shall be subject to all terms and conditions of this lease and shall be terminated upon fifteen (15) days written notice to the tenant by the landlord by certified U.S. mail or any other form of mail wherein a proof of mailing and receipt by the tenant can be confirmed.

( ) ( ) ( ) ( ) Parties place initials here.

C. **ABANDONMENT OF THE PROPERTY:** In the event the tenant abandons the property, the landlord, subject to state law, may enter the property by any means necessary and without liability either criminal or civil, and reclaim and re-let said property. The tenant shall be liable for unpaid rent in accordance with state law and paragraph 10A of this lease. Any personal property of the tenant, left on or about the leased property, shall become the possession of the landlord and may be kept or disposed of in accordance with state law.

D. **ADVERTISING BY LANDLORD OR AGENT:** Ninety (90) days prior to the expiration of the lease the landlord or his/her duly authorized agent may advertise or post signs on or about the property indicating the landlord's desire to procure a new tenant. The undersigned tenant shall allow and grant access to the landlord or his or her duly authorized agent to show the property with twenty-four (24) hours' notice, and between the hours of 9:00 a.m. and 5:00 p.m., Monday–Friday, unless otherwise agreed upon by the parties.

E. **RESALE OF PROPERTY BY LANDLORD:** It is understood by and between the parties that any resale of the property during the time of the leasehold shall have no effect upon this lease agreement and it shall remain in full force and effect as to the new owner. If during the term of the leasehold, the landlord desires to sell the property, he/she shall notify the tenant in writing by regular U.S. mail of his or her intent to market and sell the property. The tenant shall allow, with twenty-four (24) hours' notice, and between the hours of 9:00 a.m. and 5:00 p.m., Monday–Friday, unless otherwise agreed upon by the parties, the landlord, or his or her duly authorized agent, access to the property for the purposes of showing and selling said property. If the tenant, for reasonable cause, such as illness or other reasonable inconvenience, cannot allow the landlord or the authorized agent access to the property at the time requested, the tenant shall allow such access at the first available mutually convenient opportunity thereafter.

F. **SUBORDINATION:** The lease and any leasehold interest are subordinate to any liens and encumbrances in effect or to be placed upon the property in the future by the landlord.

12. **INTERPRETATION AND EFFECT:** This lease shall apply to the heirs, assigns, and any and all lawful representatives of the parties herein. Any

( ) ( ) ( ) ( ) Parties place initials here.

words or phrases shall be interpreted as being singular or plural, male or female as terms and conditions dictate. Should any clause be rendered invalid, such rendering shall not void the remainder of the lease. Where appropriate, the term *tenant* shall also apply to any guests, invitees, family, agents or employees, or other visitors of the tenant.

13. **LANDLORD'S INSPECTION OF THE PROPERTY:** Subject to state law, the landlord shall have the right to inspect the property from time to time and during reasonable hours to determine if the terms of the lease are being upheld by the tenant in terms of care of the property and other applicable clauses of the lease. Inspection of the property shall be conducted in accordance with applicable state law. Where state law is silent, the landlord shall contact the tenant 24 hours in advance by any communicative means available to both parties, and advise the tenant of the intent to inspect the property. The tenant shall not withhold access to the landlord for inspection purposes without reasonable cause such as illness. If reasonable cause exists, the tenant shall grant access to the landlord or his/her duly authorized agent at the first available opportunity thereafter. If a bona fide emergency exists, the landlord may enter the property for the purposes of investigating and ameliorating the situation. The landlord shall first attempt to contact the tenant prior to entering the property. If the tenant is not current in the payment of rent, the landlord or his or her duly authorized agent may enter the property for inspection purposes without the notification or consent of the tenant.

14. **DISCLOSURES:**

    A. **QUIET ENJOYMENT OF PROPERTY:** The landlord covenants that timely payment of rent and adherence to the terms and conditions of this lease shall entitle the tenant to peacefully enjoy the property for the agreed upon term of the lease.

    B. **RADON GAS DISCLOSURE:** Radon is a radioactive gas formed in the ground and may naturally accumulate in buildings over a period of time. If it accumulates in a building in sufficient quantities, it may present a health risk to persons who are exposed to it over a period of time. Levels of radon that exceed federal and state guidelines have been discovered in buildings within the State of Florida (greater than 4 pi-

( )( )( )( ) Parties place initials here.

cocuries per liter of air). For further information regarding radon and radon testing, please contact your county public health unit (Section 404.056(8) Florida Statutes). Currently, Florida law does not require inspection for radon.

C. **MEGAN'S LAW DISCLOSURE:** The purpose of Megan's Law is to inform and protect the public by notifying communities when a convicted sex offender moves into an area. Information including photographs, identities, and addresses is available from the Florida Department of Law Enforcement (FDLE) at 850-410-7000 or on the Internet at www.fdle.state.fl.us/sexual-predators/

D. **LEAD-BASED PAINT:** (For pre-1978 properties where the landlord owns four or more units.) Housing built prior to 1978 may contain lead-based paint. Lead from paint, paint chips, and dust can be a health hazard if not managed properly. Lead exposure is most harmful to young children and pregnant women. The landlord has no knowledge of any lead-based paint in the housing and no available records. There is no requirement for lead-based paint abatement by the landlord, and tenant specifically waives a risk assessment or inspection for the presence of lead-based paint.

E. **SECURITY DEPOSIT NOTIFICATION:** The landlord hereby notifies the tenant that the security deposit shall be held in a separate noninterest bearing account in a _____ (insert state) banking institution to wit: _____ (insert name of banking institution) and shall not be commingled with any other funds held by the landlord. _____ law requires that the landlord shall return the security deposit within _____ (??) days of the date the tenant vacates the unit or in the alternative, notify the tenant within _____ (??) days by sending a notice in writing by certified mail to the tenant's last known address indicating the reasons for withholding return of the security deposit. If the tenant fails to object to the landlord's claim within _____ (??) days of receipt of the landlord's notice, the landlord may deduct the amount of the claim and return the difference of the security deposit to the tenant within _____ (??) days of the notice of the claim.

F. **MISCELLANEOUS DISCLOSURES:** The landlord knows of no other factors or conditions in the property that would negatively impact the tenant's quiet enjoyment of the property including any latent defects.

(   ) (   ) (   ) (   ) Parties place initials here.

G. OTHER TERMS AND CONDITIONS:

_____

_____

_____

_____   _____
Landlord   Tenant

_____   _____
Landlord   Date: Tenant   Date:

(   )(   )(   )(   ) Parties place initials here.

Model Letters and Forms

Action of Lease Application Based on Credit and Background Check

Dear Applicant:

Thank you for your recent application to lease (insert address of property). Unfortunately, we are unable to approve your application due to a concern with your credit or background investigation. If credit information was a consideration in the denial, the name and address of the reporting agency employed is stated below. The reporting agency does not decide and had no part in the decision to deny your application.

In accordance with the Fair Credit Reporting Act, you have the right to know the information that is contained in your credit report and you further have the right to a free copy of your report from the reporting agency if you request it no later than sixty (60) days after you receive this notice. You also have the right to dispute any information contained therein.

(Insert credit reporting agency used: e.g.,)
Equifax, Inc., P.O. Box 740123, Atlanta, GA, 30374-0123
Experian, 701 Experian Parkway, Allen, TX 75013
Trans Union, P.O. Box 97328, Jackson, MS 39288-7328

App ID # _____

If you have any further questions, you may contact me at (insert phone number).

Signed: _____

Date: _____

Lease Cover Letter

AQUAVISTA INTERNATIONAL INC.

Licensed Real Estate Broker
9260 Sunset Drive, Suite 219
Miami, FL 33317
305-940-7441 (Tel)
786-299-1594 (Cell)
305-944-8343 (Fax)

R

Mailing Address:
16850-112 Collins Ave #300
Sunny Isles Beach, FL 33160

(Date)

TO: Lessor/Lessee

FROM: Kenneth Roth

SUBJECT: Lease

Recipient's Fax Number:

Dear Mr. _____ :

Following is your lease. Please read it carefully and fill in the blanks as necessary. If you have any questions, call us at 305-940-7441 (tel) or 786-299-1594 (cell).

Thanks,

Kenneth Roth

Authorization to Release Records

TO: (insert name of institution where records information is requested)

I THE UNDERSIGNED, in an effort to secure a lease agreement, authorize

_____

(insert name of party or firm who will perform the search)

to obtain all credit, banking, police, employment, prior residence information, and background information in conjunction with my lease application, and authorize you to release said records to the above described party or designated agents or attorneys of said party. Photocopies of said information are acceptable if legible, and I hereby waive any privileges I may have with respect to release of said information to the above described party or agents thereof.

_____

Applicant

_____

Date

_____

Initial Notification Letter
(Security Deposit)

Dear _____ :

In accordance with section _____ of the _____ (insert state statute), you are hereby notified that I am holding your security deposit for the rental of (insert address of property) in the amount of $ _____, in _____ Bank located at _____ (insert address). This is a noninterest bearing account.

_____

Landlord

_____

Date

Late Notice

Dear _____ :

This is to advise you that as of this date, your rent for _____ (insert property address) has not been received in accordance with the terms of our lease agreement entered into on the _____ (insert date of lease).

In accordance with the terms of the lease entered into on the _____ (insert date of lease), if (I) (we) have not received you check within _____ (insert number of days), we will be forced to take any and all legal remedies in accordance with your lease agreement and state law. These actions may include but are not necessarily limited to termination of the lease, eviction, and any resultant damages thereto including costs, disbursements, and attorney's fees associated with any related action in this regard.

_____
Landlord

_____
Date

Lease Application Form

Dear Applicant:

Please print or type the following information:

Address of property to be leased:

_____

_____

Name of Applicant:

_____

Applicant

_____

Spouse

Date of Birth of Applicant: ___ / ___ / ___ Social Security # _____

Date of Birth of Spouse: ___ / ___ / ___ Social Security # _____

Number of Occupants Who Will Occupy the Property _____

Names of Occupants Who Will Occupy the Property:

_____

_____

Number and Description of Pets:

_____

Emergency Contact Information:

_____

Applicant History

1. Present Address and Phone Number

_____

_____

2. Previous Address and Phone Number

_____

_____

3. Previous Address and Phone Number

_____

_____

4. Previous Address and Phone Number

_____

_____

Bank References

Branch Address _____

Phone Number _____

Name of Contact Person (if known) _____

How Long with This Institution _____

Account Number _____

Branch Address _____

Phone Number _____

Name of Contact Person (if known) _____

How Long with This Institution _____

Account Number _____

Employment History

Name of Employer _____

Position with Employer _____

Address and Phone Number _____

Contact Person _____

How Many Years with Firm? _____

Name of Employer _____

Position with Employer _____

Address and Phone Number _____

Contact Person _____

How Many Years with Firm? _____

References

Name _____

Address _____

Phone Number _____

Name _____

Address _____

Phone Number _____

Name _____

Address _____

Phone Number _____

Please note that any misrepresentation may be cause to deny the application. Only applicants may sign below.

I acknowledge that the above information is true and correct to the best of my knowledge and recollection.

_____

Applicant

_____

Applicant

Notice of Inspection

Dear _____ :

Please be advised that in accordance with our lease agreement, (I) (we) will be inspecting the property on (insert date and time in accordance with the lease agreement). If this is not convenient for you, please contact (me) (us) no later than (insert date) to arrange a more convenient time.

Very truly yours,

_____
Landlord

_____
Date

Notice of Previous Entry

Dear _____ :

On the _____ day of _____, 200 __, and in accordance with state law and our lease agreement, it was necessary to enter your unit to (insert reason). Prior to entering the property, we tried to contact you but were unable to do so.

If you have any further questions, you may contact me at (insert phone number).

_____
Landlord

_____
Date

Returned Check

Dear _____ :

Please be advised that your check # _____, in the amount of $ _____, has been returned for (insert reason, e.g., insufficient funds, etc.). In accordance with the lease agreement entered into on _____ (insert date), you have _____ calendar days to tender payment in cash or certified check plus a penalty fee of $25, which has been charged to my account by my bank. In addition, please include any and all other late fees and penalties as stipulated in the lease agreement.

Failure to comply will result in the undersigned taking any and all appropriate legal action in this matter in accordance with _____ law (insert name of state) and the terms of the lease agreement.

_____
Landlord

_____
Date

Security Deposit Letter

Dear _____ :

This will advise you that in accordance with section _____ of the _____ (insert state) statutes, as further stipulated in our lease agreement, I intend to withhold the amount of $ _____ from your security deposit due to the following damages incurred upon the rental property:

1. _____

2. _____

3. _____

You are hereby further notified that in accordance with the above stated statute, you must respond within _____ days if you choose to contest this claim.

Please mail your objection to:

_____
(insert your address)

_____
Landlord

_____
Date

Sample Inventory
(insert description of property)

Living Room

One Glass Coffee Table

_____

_____

_____

Dining Room

Microwave

Refrigerator

Oven

_____

_____

_____

(etc.—then insert at the bottom)

Acknowledged:

_____

Landlord   Date

_____

Tenant   Date

Tenant Warning Notice

Dear Tenant:

I have been advised that between, on or about _____ (insert date of the action you are about to complain of), _____ (insert party who performed the offending action), a (insert status of offending party, namely, a signatory to the lease, an authorized family member of the household, a guest, an invitee), without consent of the landlord and in contravention of the lease agreement (or in violation of _____) did (insert offending action) _____.

You must immediately cease and desist any and all such actions or the undersigned will have no choice but to consider that you are in breach of the lease agreement. Any further such action on your part will be considered a breach of the lease, and (I) (we) will be forced to take any and all necessary legal action with regard to this matter.

_____
Landlord

_____
Date

EXAMPLE

Dear Tenant:

I have been advised that on or about 16 January 2003, a guest of your household was observed running naked through the lobby of the condominium screaming, "Hi ho Silver, away." Obviously, this manner of conduct is a violation of state law and the rules and regulations of the condominium association.

In accordance with our lease agreement and rules and regulations of the association, you are responsible for the conduct of any and all of your guests, and you are expected to control any such aberrant behavior.

You must immediately have ***your guests*** cease and desist any and all such actions, or the undersigned will have no choice but to consider that you are in breach of the lease agreement. Any further such action on the part of your guests will be considered a breach of the lease, and I will be forced to take any and all necessary legal action with regard to this matter.

_____
Landlord

_____
Date

Welcome Letter

Dear _____ :

Thank you for leasing _____ (insert description of property leased). (I) (We) hope you enjoy our property. In that regard, enclosed please find the following:

1. Copy of Lease
2. Copy of Inventory (as applicable)
3. Rules and Regulations (as applicable)
4. Appliance Insurance Contract
5. _____

If you have any further questions, you may contact me at (insert phone number).

Very truly yours,

_____
Landlord

_____
Date

Index

abandonment, 110, 180, 186
Action of Lease Application, 62, 77, 267
acts of God, 105
acts of war, 105
addendum to lease
    rent holidays and, 175
    substitution of parties, 49
adhesionary contracts, 124
advance payments, 94–95, *see also* prepayments;
        security deposits
advertising
    creativity in, 238–239
    of property before lease termination, 110
    sense of urgency and, 238–239
    tips for, 236–239
affidavit of service, 173
all risk insurance, 228–229
alterations, 39–40, 105–106
Americans with Disabilities Act, 48
animals, domestic, 36–37, 106
antidiscrimination laws, 46–48
appliance repair contracts, 40–41, 103–104,
        160
arrearages, 175–176
"as is" condition, 71–72
assignment, 101–102
attitude, of landlords, 5, 6–9, 74–76, 160,
        184–185, 188–189, 231, 239–242
attorney's fees, 108–109, 179
audits, 210
Authorization to Release Records, 63, 269
automatic payment, 93
automobiles, 64, 73, 124

background checks, *see* tenant investigation
bad risks, 178–185
bank checks, 91–92, 94
bank references, 73
bankruptcy, 66–67
bouncing checks, 93, 275
breach of agreement, 107, 122–123
British common law, xiv
bulk sums, 53–54, 91–92, 159
business use of property, 35–36

capital gains taxes, 211–212
carpet
    normal wear and tear on, 96–98
    selecting, 18
car registrations, 61
case studies, 126–152
    The Artistic Tenant, 142–149
    The Good Tenant, 136–142
    The Little White Lie, 149–152
    The Stubborn Landlady, 126–135
cashier's checks, 91–92, 94
certified checks, 94
certified mail, 108, 171, 172
checklists, prior to move-in, 156–158
checks
    bank, 91–92, 94
    bouncing, 93, 275
    cashier's, 91–92, 94
    certified, 94
    Returned Check Notice, 275
Civil Rights Act of 1968, 47
cleaning fees, 195

279

clutter, avoiding, 16, 17, 23, 24
Code Napoleon, xiv
common elements, of condominiums, 225–226
comparables
    condominium, 19–21
    house, 31
    in rent determination, 19–21, 31
complaints, 172–173, 183
condition of property, 71–72, 103
condominiums
    background checks by, 61, 65
    common elements of, 225–226
    comparables, 19–21
    fee simple ownership and, 169
    maintenance fees and, 13–14
    move-in fees, 94–95
    as rental properties, 69
    rent determination for, 13–25
    renter's insurance and, 223–226
    rules and regulations of, 43, 45, 160–163, 213
    special assessments and, 13–14
    welcoming interviews of, 161–162
confidentiality, 73–77
consent forms, for tenant investigation, 61, 62, 63
consideration
    for lease option/option to purchase, 52–53, 122
    for opt out clause, 122–123
    for right of first refusal, 52
construction defects, 179, 181
constructive eviction, 41, 108, 182–184
contempt of court order, 174
contracts of adhesion, 124
cooperatives, 169
corporate identity
    corporation, defined, 214
    lease agreements and, 53, 55–56
    liability issues and, 55, 214
    taxes and, 214–215
    types of corporations, 215
cost-of-living increases, 33–34, 94
court registry, 178, 179, 180, 185, 187
covered peril clause, 227–228
credit checks
    components of, 62–63, 66–67
    importance of conducting, 63–67, 79–81
    lack of credit history and, 72–73, 80–81
    on landlords, 111–112
    on tenants, 61, 62–67, 72–73, 79–81
criminal records
    "Megan's Law" disclosures, 67–68, 119
    in tenant investigation, 61, 67–68
cure of default, 107–108

damages
    depreciation and, 200
    measure of, 200

day-care providers, 36
"deadbeats," 76–77
decoration
    flooring, 18–19
    furniture, 16, 17–18
    paint color, 15–16
    in rent determination, 15–19, 237
deductions, tax, 208–210
defamation, 76–77
default, 80, 107–109, 112
    jurisdiction for, 108–109
    by landlord, 108, 112
    by tenant, 107–108, 112, *see also* nonpayment
    venue for, 108–109
defendant, 172
deposition, 174
deposits
    pet, 37
    security, *see* security deposits
depreciation
    normal wear and tear and, 96–99, 109, 195–199
    remedies and, 200
    replacement cost insurance and, 229
developer defects, 179, 181
disclosures, 117–121
    lead-based paint, 119
    Megan's Law, 67–68, 119
    miscellaneous, 120–121
    quiet enjoyment, 118
    radon gas, 118–119
    security deposit notification, 96, 120
discrimination
    antidiscrimination laws and, 46–48
    unmarried couples and, 49–51
domestic animals, 36–37, 106
due date, for rental payments, 91
Dun & Bradstreet, 181

electronic funds transfer (EFT), 93
emergencies, repairs and, 104
encumbrances, 111–112
Equifax, 62
eviction
    proceedings for, 109–110, 178–185
    theory of constructive, 41, 108, 182–184
Experian, 62

Fair, Isaac & Company Score (FICO), 63
Fair Credit Reporting Act (FCRA), 63
Fair Housing Act, 47
Federal Express (FedEx), 107–108
Federal Taxpayer Relief Act (1977), 211–213
fee simple ownership, 169
filing fees, 108–109
final walkthrough, 158–160, 181
flood riders, 227–228
flooring, 18–19

force majeure, 105
foreclosures, 111–112
four Ps, 23–25
fraud, 73–74
furniture, 16, 17–18

general negligence law, 225
Grosvenor, Gerald (Duke of Westminster), x
guarantors, 51, 55, 67
guests, 35, 101

Hammurabi, code of, xv
"handyman's special," 16–17
harassment
    by landlords, 116–117
    by tenants, 188
heirs and assigns, 46
holdover tenants, 109–110
homeowner's insurance, 223
house pets, 36–37, 106
houses, amount of rent, 30–31

identity theft, 73
incorporation, *see* corporate identity
in personam service, 173
inspections, 43–46, 116–117
    checklists for, 156–158
    notice requirements for, 43–46, 115–117, 274
    photography and, 100, 157
    pre-occupancy walkthrough, 158–160, 181
    "reasonable hours" for, 43, 88, 115–116
    after tenant leaves, 194–200
insurance, 105, 200, 221–232
    common elements of condominiums and,
        225–226
    coverage, 227–228
    homeowner's, 223
    insurance adjusters, 224–225
    mold and, 228–229
    renter's, 223–226, 229–232
    slips and falls and, 221–222, 223
    tenant's renter's insurance, 229–232
    tort law and, 226
    types of policies, 228–229
    understanding insurance policies, 227–228
    water intrusion and, 223–225, 227–228, 230
interest rates, 69, 239
inventory of contents, 78, 157–158, 160, 276

joint and several liability, 48–51, 67
judgment, 174
jurisdiction, 108–109

Kanka, Megan, 67–68

land grants, x–xi
landlords and landlording
    attitude of landlords, 5, 6–9, 74–76, 160,
        184–185, 188–189, 231, 239–242

case studies of, 126–152
default by landlord, 108, 112
disclosures, 67–68, 117–121
history of, x–xi, 168
landlord investigations, 111–112
in other countries, 168–169, 170–171
politics and the law of nonpayment, 168–171
professionalism of, 9, 74–76, 160, 184–185,
    188–189, 231, 239–242
landscaping, 39–40, 106
Late Notice, 80, 107–108, 171, 270
late payments, 171–178
    getting tenant to pay, 174–176
    mediation and, 177–178
    service of process, 172–173
    summons and complaint, 172
    tenant point of view and, 176–177
lead-based paint disclosures, 119
leadership, 6–9, 239–242
    killing with kindness and, 7–9
    nature of leasehold interest and, 6–7
    professionalism in, 9, 74–76, 160, 184–185,
        231, 239–242
lease agreements, 29–56, 87–112, 115–124
    advance payments, 94–95
    alterations, 39–40, 105–106
    ambiguous language in, 123
    amount of rent, 30–31, 90–91
    bulk sums, 53–54, 91–92, 159
    condition and maintenance of property,
        71–72, 102–106
    as contracts of adhesion, 124
    corporate identity, 53, 55–56
    default on, 80, 107–109, 112
    disclosures, 67–68, 96, 117–121
    discrimination, 46–51
    guests, 35, 101
    history of, 88–89
    importance of, 25
    initial page, 90
    inspections, 43–46, 115–117, 194–200
    interpretation and effect in, 115–116
    joint and several liability, 48–51, 67
    lease option, 52–53
    lease terms, 33–34
    military personnel and, 117
    model lease, 89–90, 255–265
    nature of, 29
    number of tenants, 34–35, 55
    occupancy and use, 34–36, 100–102
    option to purchase, 52–53, 122
    opt out clauses, 33, 117, 122–123
    payment methods for, 91–92, 93–94
    penalties, 92–94
    pets, 36–37, 106
    prepayments, 53–54, 91–92, 159
    renegotiating, 182
    rent increases, 33–34, 94

lease agreements (*continued*)
  repairs, 40–41, 103–105
  right of first refusal, 52, 122
  security deposits, 31–32, 94–100, 193–202
  selling the property, 41–42, 111
  special requests, 44, 52–53, 122–123
  strict enforcement of, 71–72
  subletting, 35, 48–49, 101–102
  termination of, 46, 109–112, 186
  term of rental, 90
  use of property, 35–36, 101
  utilities, 37–39, 102
  see also nonpayment
Lease Application Form, 271–273
Lease Cover Letter, 268
leasehold interest
  adversarial nature of, 6–7, 74–75, 79–81,
    171, 194
  described, 6
  sale of property and, 41–42, 111
lease option, 52–53
legal actions
  attorney's fees, 108–109, 179
  eviction proceedings, 109–110, 178–185
  landlord-tenant transactions, 243
  for late payments, 171–178
  mediation and, 177–178
  rules of engagement, 184–185
  settlement agreements, 177–178
  state and local laws and, 45, 115–116, 225,
    226, 242–243
liability
  business use of property and, 36
  of corporate identity, 55, 214
  joint and several, 48–51, 67
  waiver of, 78
  see also insurance
libel, 76–77
liens, 111–112

maintenance, 13–14
marble flooring, 18
married couples, joint and several liability,
    48–51
mediation, 177–178
"Megan's Law" disclosures, 67–68, 119
military personnel, 117
model lease, 89–90, 255–265
mold, 228–229
month-to-month tenancy, 109–110
mortgage liens, 111–112
move-in, 155–163
  condominium rules and regulations and,
    160–163
  date of, 32, 78, 91
  fees for, 94–95
  final walkthrough and, 158–160, 181
  landlord checklist, 156–159

named peril policies, 229
neatness, 16, 17, 23, 24
New York City, 169–170
noise, 42–43, 44–45, 121
nonpayment, 32, 167–189
  bad risks and, 178–185
  due to dispute between landlord and tenant,
    175–177, 178–185
  eviction proceedings for, 109–110, 178–185
  late payments, 171–178
  occupant failure to pay, 171–178
  occupant failure to pay with legal assistance,
    178–185
  occupant vacating apartment, 110, 180, 186
  politics and the law of, 168–171
  remedies for, 185–188
normal wear and tear, 96–99, 109, 195–199
Notice of Inspection, 274
Notice of Previous Entry, 274
notice requirements
  for evictions, 180
  for inspections, 43–46, 115–117, 274
  for nonpayment, 181
  to show property for sale, 41–42
number of tenants, 34–35, 55

objectivity
  in assessing wear and tear, 197–199
  in rent determination, 15–19
occupancy and use, 34–36, 100–102
  assignment, 101–102
  guests, 35, 101
  subletting, 35, 48–49, 101–102
  use of property, 35–36, 101
option to purchase, 52–53, 122
opt out clause, 33, 117, 122–123
outstanding debt, 62–63

packaging, in rent determination, 24
paint color, 15–16
payee, 91
payment history, 62–63
payments, *see* rental payments
payments in advance, 53–54, 91–92, 159
payor, 91
penalties, 92–94
pets, 36–37, 106
petty theft, 196
photographs, 100, 157
plaintiff, 172
position, in rent determination, 24
precedents, 88
prepayments, 53–54, 91–92, 159
present value of money, 22, 34, 53
prevailing party fees, 108–109
price
  in lease agreement, 30–31
  in rent determination, 24

primary residence, capital gains taxes and, 211–212
privacy, 63, 73–77
process service, 172–173
professionalism, 9, 74–76, 160, 184–185, 188–189, 231, 239–242
promotion, in rent determination, 24–25
proof of mailing/receipt, 107–108, 171, 172
property use, 35–36, 101
protected classes, 46–48
provisional funds, 93
proximate cause, 225–226

questionnaires, tenant, 60–61
quiet enjoyment
    disclosures regarding, 118
    inspections and, 43–46, 116–117
    nature of, 42–43
    showing property and, 42, 110

racial discrimination, 47
radon gas disclosures, 118–119
real estate agents, antidiscrimination laws and, 47
"reasonable hours," 43, 52, 88, 110, 115–116
"reasonable person" standard, 198–199
references, 70–72
reimbursement, for repairs, 105
"relo" (relocation) offices, 56
remedies, 185–188
    acceleration of rent due for term of lease, 186–187
    attempting to lease property, 187
    for damage by tenant, 200, 201
    for nonpayment, 185–188
    occupant vacating apartment, 180, 186
rental payments, 90–94
    amount of, 30–31, 90–91
    bouncing checks, 93, 275
    certified checks, 94
    to court registry, 178, 179, 180, 185, 187
    due date for, 91
    electronic funds transfer (EFT) and, 93
    increases in, 33–34, 94
    late payments, 171–178
    payment methods, 91–92
    penalties, 92–94
    prepayments, 53–54, 91–92, 159
    where to send, 90–91
    see also nonpayment
rent control, 170
rent determination, 237–238
    commitment and, 15
    comparables in, 19–21, 31
    for condominiums, 13–25
    decoration and, 15–19, 237
    flooring and, 18–19
    four Ps of, 23–25

furniture and, 16, 17–18
    methodology for, 14, 19–23
    neatness and, 16, 17, 23, 24
    objectivity in, 15–19
    paint color and, 15–16
    research in, 19–23
renter's insurance, 223–226, 229–232
rent holiday, 175
rent stabilization, 170
repairs, 40–41, 103–105
    emergency situations, 104
    force majeure and, 105
    insurance companies and, 224
    landlord default and, 108
    nonpayment and, 179
    reimbursement for, 105
    willful misuse, 104
replacement cost, 98
replacement cost insurance, 229
Returned Check Notice, 275
right of first refusal, 52, 122
roommates
    joint and several liability, 48–51
    subletting and assignment to, 101–102
    unmarried couples, 48–51, 180

sale of property, 41–42
    leasehold interest and, 41–42, 111
    notice requirements for showing, 41–42
    option to purchase and, 52–53, 122
    right of first refusal and, 52, 122
    taxation and, 211–213
salesmanship, 75–76
Scotland, 169
seasonal rentals, 21–22, 54
Security Deposit Letter, 100, 275
security deposits, 94–100, 193–202
    as advance payments, 94–95
    amount of, 31–32
    basic principles of returning, 201–202
    depreciation and, 202
    disclosures regarding, 96, 120
    final inspection and, 194–200
    measure of damages, 200
    normal wear and tear and, 96–99, 109, 195–199
    prepayments and, 54
    purposes of, 201–202
    remedies and, 202
    returning, 38, 193–194
    tenant letter requesting return of, 193–194
    unusual wear and tear and, 99–100
self-employed people, 62, 181
service of process, 172–173
settlement agreements, 177–178
settlement conferences, 179
sex offenders, 67–68, 119
Sheriff's Department, 173

slander, 76–77
slips and falls, 221–222, 223
small claims actions, 97, 183–184
Social Security number
    identity theft and, 73
    in tenant investigation, 61, 62, 73–74
South America, 168–169
special assessments, 13–14
stare decises, 88
state and local laws, 45, 115–116, 225, 226,
    242–243
Subchapter S corporations, 215
subletting, 35, 48–49, 101–102
subordination, 111–112
substitution of parties, 49
summons, 172–173
surrender of property, 109

taxation, 207–217
    capital gains taxes, 211–212
    corporate identity and, 214–215
    exemptions from, 207–208
    Federal Taxpayer Relief Act (1977), 211–213
    legitimate deductions, 208–210
    preparing tax returns, 215–217
    principles of, 207–208
    rental property and, 208–213
    selling and, 211–213
Tell, William, xi
tenant investigation, 59–81, 180
    agencies for, 61
    arcane wisdom and, 79–81
    business of renting and, 68–69
    confidentiality and, 73–77
    credit checks in, 61, 62–67, 72–73, 79–81
    criminal records in, 61, 67–68
    libel and, 76–77
    Megan's law and, 67–68
    questionnaires in, 60–61
    references in, 70–72
    signs of good applicants, 61–62
    slander and, 76–77
    surprise questions and, 77–79
tenants
    "bad tenants," xi
    default by, 107–108, 112
    harassment by, 188
    in history of landlording, x–xi
    letter requesting return of security deposit,
        193–194
    move-in date, 32, 78, 91
    nonpayment by, 32

    number of, 34–35, 55
    politics and the law of nonpayment,
        168–171
    renter's insurance and, 223–236, 229–232
Tenant Warning Notice, 277
termination of lease agreement, 46, 109–112
    abandonment, 110, 180, 186
    advertising property prior to, 110
    default by landlord and, 108, 112
    holdover tenants, 109–110
    for military personnel, 117
    selling property prior to, 41–42, 111
    surrender of property, 109
term of rental, 90
theory of constructive eviction, 41, 108,
    182–184
tile flooring, 18
tort law, 226
Trans Union, 62
trees, 39–40, 106
trespassing, 43
trust, 74
TRW, 62

United Parcel Service (UPS), 107–108
U.S. Environmental Protection Agency, 195
unjust enrichment, 186–187
unmarried couples
    as bad risks, 180
    discrimination and, 49–51
    joint and several liability, 48–51
unusual wear and tear, 99–100
use of property, 35–36, 101
utilities
    in lease agreement, 37–39, 102
    shutting off, 156–157

vacating contempt order, 174
venue, 108–109

waiver of liability, 78
walkthrough documentation, 158–160, 181
water intrusion, 223–225, 227–228, 230
wear and tear
    normal, 96–99, 109, 195–199
    unusual, 99–100, 200, 201
Welcome Letter, 278
willful misuse, 104

zoning ordinances
    business use of property and, 36
    noise and, 42–43